REA ACPL ITEM
DISC

D1555129

Korea

DO NOT REMOVE
CARDS FROM POCKET

ALLEN COUNTY PUBLIC LIBRARY

FORT WAYNE, INDIANA 46802

You may return this book to any agency, branch,
or bookmobile of the Allen County Public Library.

Korea
An Introduction

James Hoare and Susan Pares

KPI

Kegan Paul International
London and New York

Allen County Public Library
Ft. Wayne, Indiana

First published in 1988 by Kegan Paul International Limited
11 New Fetter Lane, London EC4P 4EE

Distributed by
Associated Book Publishers (UK) Ltd
11 New Fetter Lane, London EC4P 4EE

Routledge, Chapman & Hall Inc.
29 West 35th Street
New York, NY 10001, USA

Produced by Worts-Power Associates

Set in Baskerville
by Papyrus Printers & Stationers Ltd.
Thetford, Norfolk
and printed in Great Britain
by Dotesios Printers Ltd.
Bradford-on-Avon, Wiltshire

© James Hoare and Susan Pares 1988

No part of this book may be reproduced in any form
without permission from the publisher, except for the
quotation of brief passages in criticism.

ISBN 0-7103-0299-1

This book is dedicated to
Dr Kim Sang Man, KBE,
and to all our other Korean friends
who made our stay in their country such
an enjoyable one

Contents

Introduction

There is one phoenix among a thousand chickens *

This book is intended to provide a general background to KPI's 'Korean Culture' series, giving an introduction to the life, history and institutions of the people of the Republic of Korea. We hope that scholars will not find too much with which to take issue, but it is not aimed primarily at those who already know about Korea. Rather, it is for the general reader, who, after the political upheavals of 1986 and 1987, when nightly on the world's television screens demonstrating students and riot police fought each other on the streets of Seoul and other cities, or after the rather different battles of Olympic Year in Seoul in 1988, wants to find out more about Korea. Perhaps also those who buy Korean goods, whether the ubiquitous training shoes or the more sophisticated products of the electronic age, will find here an explanation of how the Koreans, who 30 or 40 years ago were regarded as members of one of the world's 'basket cases' — though the term did not exist then — have come to be so successful, and why their country is today a major economic force in the world. South Korean *per capita* income and level of development are now on a par with those of a number of European countries, and continued growth is forecast.

Korea matters in other ways, too. It has a long and distinctive cultural history, which is generally little known outside East Asia. The Koreans are proud of this and of the role they have played historically as a cultural channel between the Asian mainland and

*This Korean proverb, like those that preface the other sections, is taken from Bruce Grant, *Korean Proverbs: Dragon Head, Snake Tail, and a Frog in a Well*, Seoul and Salt Lake City, 1982, which also supplies explanations.

Japan. Many things that the westerner believes to be essentially Japanese had their origins in the Korean peninsula.

Strategically, the Korean peninsula has been of major importance in East Asia, and is today the meeting place for four great powers: the People's Republic of China, the Soviet Union, the United States, and Japan. In the last hundred years, three major wars have been concerned directly with Korea: the Sino–Japanese war of 1894–1895, the Russo–Japanese war of 1904–1905, and the Korean War itself, from 1950 to 1953. The last of these is still unsettled, since the 1953 armistice agreement has not been replaced by anything more durable.

It is this strategic interest that has attracted most attention in recent years, in Britain at least. General books on Korea have been published in Britain, but they mostly date from many years ago. The most thorough in recent years, W. D. Reeve's *The Republic of Korea*, was published as long ago as 1963. A Chatham House paper by Brian Bridges in 1986, *Korea and the West*, dealt with both North and South Korea in just over 90 pages and concentrated on political and strategic issues. As the Olympic Games have drawn nearer, a number of guide books have appeared, of varying quality. The one growth area has been books about the Korean War, a subject now rescued from comparative oblivion. This new-found fascination with the Korean War has spilled over into other areas; the South Koreans regard somewhat wryly the decision by both BBC Television and Independent Television to mark the Seoul Olympics by major programmes on the Korean War. The spirit of MASH lives on.

Our aim has been to move away from this preoccupation, and to give a wider account. We have not tried to be comprehensive. This would not be possible in the space available. Neither have we attempted to produce a guidebook. At one time we had thought of doing this, and we have a large collection of material for that purpose. But it is now three years since we left Korea. In some countries that would not matter much; there are parts of the world where it is possible still to use guidebooks which are ten, 20, or even 100 years old. The traveller to the Republic of Korea is likely to find, on the contrary, that the guidebook written last year has already become outdated in this fast-developing country. (The traveller to North Korea appears to have to manage without any guidebooks at all). Rather, we have written a series of essays, some directly connected with each other, others less obviously so, dealing with major aspects of Korea. We hope at least to whet appetites, and that those who begin with this book will move on to some of the other works listed in the bibliography — where we even provide details of some of those rapidly-dating guidebooks.

When considering Korea after 1945, our prime focus has been on South Korea — the Republic of Korea. We have included a brief sketch of what has happened in North Korea — the Democratic People's Republic of Korea — since 1945, because this is helpful in understanding much about the development and the preoccupations of South Korea. The reader is warned, however, that this account is even less comprehensive than that on South Korea. In general, we have used 'Korea' to refer to the undivided peninsula before 1945, and either North or South Korea or the official titles, or the generally accepted abbreviations 'ROK' and 'DPRK', to refer to the two states that somewhat uneasily co-exist on the peninsula today. 'Koreans' in most contexts after 1945 means the people of South Korea. None of these terms is meant to imply a political judgement, but reflects the realities of the Korean peninsula today.

Many people have helped with this book. We are grateful to Peter Hopkins and his staff at KPI for their assistance and encouragement. Professor Chung Chong-wha of Korea University, the general editor of the Korean culture series, was the first to suggest that we might take on the task. We owe a debt to him for that and for many hours spent discussing Korea and things Korean with his family and friends. The Korean–British Society in Seoul also deserves a mention. Through its series of highly successful seminars to mark the centenary of the 1883 Treaty of Friendship between Britain and Korea, it gave us the chance to try out new ideas and to talk to a wide range of people all over South Korea. Many other Koreans helped too, by their hospitality and their willingness to talk openly and frankly about all sorts of issues. Not all of them will agree with every view we express, but we hope that they will understand the spirit in which we have written. Many of them will never know we have written anything, since often it was the casual conversation with a chance acquaintance, or the illumination provided by an accidental encounter, which set us thinking and awakened the wish to look more deeply at a particular subject. Thanks are also due to numerous foreign residents in Korea, who again provided hospitality and stimulating conversation. Many outside Korea have shared their

3

interests and experiences with us over the years, and to them too we are grateful.

John Morgan and Nicholas Spreckley, successive British ambassadors to Seoul, and their families, gave more assistance than they ever realised. In London, Pat Barnes and Nigel Bowie have valiantly read the manuscript and made helpful comments. Robert Darroll also read part of the manuscript. Julie Sailing drew the maps. We received help with illustrations from Jo Roberts, Olive Peirera, the Hillier family and the Embassy of the Republic of Korea in London. Above all, we owe special thanks to Joanna and the cat, who endured it all.

None of the above is in any way responsible for the book's contents. The opinions expressed are the authors' own and do not necessarily represent those of the Foreign and Commonwealth Office.

S.P. J.E.H
London, 1987–1988

Note: In transcribing Korean words, we have generally followed the McCune–Reischauer system of romanisation, except in cases where a different method has long been established, such as Seoul, Park Chung Hee, and so forth. For Chinese, we have used a modified Wade–Giles system, again except in cases where a different system has become standard. We have used modified Hepburn for Japanese. East Asian family names generally come first, and we have followed this usage, except where the person concerned used a different one; thus, *Kim* Il-sung, Syngman *Rhee*.

Section One

The Land and the People

In ten years, even the mountains and rivers change

Chapter One

The Geographical Framework

The Korean peninsula hangs on the edge of continental Asia, linked to and cut off from the Chinese landmass by mountains and rivers. The whole area is both a geological and a climatic frontier between the Asian landmass on the one side and the Pacific island rim on the other. This frontier position has been reflected in Korea's place in zoology and botany, as well as in its historic role as a bridge between the Asiatic continent and the islands of the Pacific. Although the peninsula has been cut in two since 1945 by politics and war, this division makes little sense. For all Koreans, North and South, there is one geographical entity, and both governments treat it as such in handbooks or other forms of publicity. It is a sensible approach and one we too will adopt.

The peninsula lies between latitudes 43° and 33° north, and between longitudes 124° and 130° east.It is some 1000 kilometres (620 miles) long, with a total coastline of over 17,361 kilometres (11,000 miles), divided between roughly equal parts of mainland and islands. There are well over 3500 islands. The total area of the peninsula is some 221,000 square kilometres (85,242 square miles), about the same as mainland Britain. The political division of the peninsula has given North Korea about 55 percent of the landmass, and South Korea 45 percent. Both North and South are steadily adding to their respective land areas — and reducing the number of islands — by land reclamation projects. Although the northern border with the People's Republic of China (PRC) and the Soviet Union (USSR), is over 1000 kilometres (620 miles) long, the peninsula has an average width of only about 250 kilometres (170 miles)

The shortest distance from South Korea to Japan is 206 kilometres (130 miles), while it is 1900 kilometres (just under 1200 miles) to the nearest point in China, on the Shantung peninsula.

The east coast is marked by deep waters, rocky outcrops and a lack of islands; the only island of any note is Ullŭng-do, far out in the East Sea (the Sea of Japan), a pirate haunt in times past and now a major squid fishing centre. The east coast tidal range is not great. The west coast has relatively wide plateaus and the sea is shallow and muddy — the somewhat unromantic origin of the name 'Yellow Sea' in both Korean and Chinese. There are huge tidal ranges and many islands. The southern coastline is a characteristic drowned valley system, with what were the hills now forming the many islands that dot the sea. These southern waters are an area of fast currents and much beauty. It includes the peninsula's largest island, the province of Cheju-do. There are some important rivers, most flowing east to west. Apart from the Yalu in the far north, they are shallow except for brief periods in the rainy season, and none have been of much use for transportation, except for shallow-bottom boats. In South Korea, only the Naktong river north of Pusan can really serve as a navigable waterway. In recent years, many rivers have been dammed for hydro-electric schemes, which has also provided lakes for boating, fishing and other pastimes.

Korea is fortunate in that the ocean currents that wash the peninsula provide good breeding ground for fish. There are three main currents. The Kuroshio, which comes from the east coast of the Philippines, splits into two near Cheju. The western section flows into the Yellow Sea, a warm, weak current with little effect. The eastern branch, however, is strong and warmer than the waters into which it flows. It in turn meets a cold current flowing south along the eastern side of the peninsula. Where these two currents meet, fish breed and accumulate in great numbers, since there is an abundant supply of food.

The most distinctive feature of Korea is mountains. In one sense, this is too grand a name for what in height are mere hills. There are none high enough to be permanently snow-capped. Many, even among the tallest, have trees or shrubs growing to the very top, a feature lovingly reproduced in many traditional paintings, and one that, to western eyes, is perhaps the chief characteristic of 'Chinese-style' art. Yet, as in Ireland or Scotland, closer acquaintance with the Korean hills justifies the grander term. Korea's highest mountain, Mount Paektu, lies in North Korea, on the border with China. It was the birthplace of one of Korea's founders, Tan'gun, whose origins are described in the next chapter, and is much celebrated in poetry and song. Such are the magical powers attributed to it, that in North Korea it has been appropriated into the Kim Il-sung family legend. Its real importance is that it is the source of both the Yalu and Tumen rivers, which are the main features of the northern border. Mount Paektu is just over 2700 metres (about 9000 feet). In South Korea, the highest mountain is Mount Halla on Cheju-do, at 1950 metres, (6400 feet). like Paektu, it is a long-defunct volcanic crater. On the South Korean mainland, the highest peak is found in the Chiri range in the south west. The most dramatic of South Korea's mountains, however, are the T'aebaek range, the southern extension of the famous Kumgang or Diamond Mountains, now mostly in North Korea, and the related Sorak range, currently being developed as a winter sports area.

Some 70 percent of the total landmass of the peninsula is mountainous. The distribution is not uniform. The north and east generally have the highest mountains, which run north to south, with spurs running to the west. In the south and west, the countryside is gentler, made up of low hills and a few small plains. Nowhere escapes the dramatic effect of the mountains, visible on all sides. The effect is of rugged ridge upon rugged ridge, ever receding into the distance. Much of the mountain region is heavily eroded, with dissected granite being common. The exact cause of this is not known, but it is generally accepted that it is not the result of glaciation. The ice ages did not touch Korea, except in the very far north. The mountain ranges have left few channels along the peninsula, and these have served as invasion routes right up to the present. Today, South Korean forces pay particular attention to the same openings north to south as did their ancestors; modern methods of transport and new weapons have not altered the importance of routes such as the Munsan or Chŏrwon corridors, used by the North Koreans and the Chinese in 1950 and 1951 as they had been used by other invaders in the past.

The presence of so many mountains has affected the Korean people in many ways. They have been a major factor in allowing them to preserve their self-identity in the face of pressures from strong neighbours, but they have also served to encourage internal division, especially between east and west. They have inhibited the development of an effective communications system until very recently. Today they continue to cut off sections of the country from some of the benefits found in the new areas of prosperity.

The peculiarities of the Korean landmass have had a very profound effect on where people have lived. There are few areas of settlement in the mountain regions. People clustered in the small valleys of the west and the south, which provided shelter and soil, rather than on the east. In the west is found the characteristic Korean brown earth, mostly derived from granite and gneiss, with some limestone and volcanic soils added. Even these areas, however, have not provided rich land. The soil is often acid. Korean plains have thin alluvial deposits, even at their mouths. The high tides of the western coasts have prevented the formation of deltas except on the smallest scale. Nevertheless, these areas were better than the mountains, and were the basis of the development of the Korean state. Although, as we shall see, a most successful political entity, unified Silla (pronounced 'Shilla'), based itself on the south east and from there united the peninsula over a thousand years ago, this was a relatively short-lived phenomenon, never repeated. The centre of political power has generally been in the western valleys, whether at Seoul, Kaesŏng or P'yŏngyang.

The Korean peninsula is not well-endowed with mineral deposits. Gold, silver, iron ore, tungsten, graphite, and coal are found but none in great abundance. Early western hopes of a land covered in gold proved false, though gold mining was one of the few successful western business activities in the late nineteenth and early twentieth centuries. Coal is low-quality anthracite. Most of the minerals were exploited to a greater or lesser extent by the Japanese, with gold production again being especially important. The division of the peninsula in 1945 left the best deposits in the North. In the South, existing sources have been more fully exploited than they were before 1945, but mining has not played a major part in the South's economic development. In recent years, all mineral production has fallen because of declining world demand, excessive exploitation costs, and the ready availability of alternative supplies.

In climate, the peninsula varies notably from north to south, though there are certain common features. Spring is short and there is up to six weeks' difference in its beginning between the Yalu and Cheju. By April, the winter thaw has generally set in all over Korea, and the land, hitherto brown and dead, quickly begins to show traces of green. Early spring is marked by gusty winds, which often bring choking yellow dust from the deserts of central Asia. Under the influence of the summer monsoon, the weather gradually gets hotter. By mid-June, all of Korea is hot and humid and the rains in early July at first provide welcome relief. The summer months are marked by bouts of heavy rain, interspersed with clearer skies with continuing high humidity. Extra showers from passing cyclonic storms, sometimes accompanied by thunder and lightning, are periodically added to the ordinary heavy rainfall. The amount of rain varies markedly from year to year, with the highest recorded in Seoul, over 2135 mm (8.4 inches) in 1940, and the lowest 634 mm (2.5 inches) in 1949. Under 1000 mm (4 inches) is regarded as a 'failure' of the rains, since this is the minimum required for rice cultivation without irrigation. Summer temperatures can be very high, especially in the bowl around Taegu-Ulsan, where over 40°C (104°F) have been recorded. Late September sees the beginning of autumn, Korea's most pleasant season, when 'the horses are fat and the sky is high.' Clear skies, warm days, and cool evenings gradually give way to early frosts. The first snows fall in the mountains in October, though they do not settle. By mid-November, the characteristic winter pattern of three or four mild days followed by a similar number of cold — or rather, colder days, especially in January and February — has established itself and persists until March. Winter is the dry season. Heavy falls of snow are sometimes recorded, especially on the island of Ullŭng off the east coast and in the T'aebaek mountains, but they are not common in the southern half of Korea. Snow rarely stays in towns, and in South Korea at least, fewer rivers now freeze over. A combination of embanking, dredging and chemical pollution has ended what was once a notable aspect of Korean winters. Very cold temperatures have been recorded in northern Korea, with Chungangjin recording the lowest ever temperature of −43.6°C (−46.5°F) in 1933. Seoul hovers around 1°C (34°F), while Cheju-do remains about 4°C (39°F) even in the depths of winter. Most people feel colder, however, because of the dry polar winds, which have a high windchill factor, and because of the prevailing bleakness of the winter countryside.

In vegetation, and to a lesser extent animal life, the Korean peninsula in the past acted as a bridge between Asia and the Pacific. The traditional vegetation pattern was divided into three zones: in the north of the peninsula were coniferous forests; in the centre, mixed forests; and in the south and on the islands, broadleaf forests. Koreans continue to refer to large tracts of the countryside as forest, but the old forests have long disappeared. This is sometimes blamed on the Japanese colonial period, and especially the wartime demands for fuel. But there is ample testimony to wholesale deforestation long before the Japanese colonial period. The great Victorian traveller, Isabella Bird Bishop, noted in the 1890s the 'denudation of the hills in the neighbourhood of Seoul, the coasts, the treaty ports and the main roads,' and others told the same story. Behind this loss of woodlands lay periodic forest fires and, far more important, the widespread use of wood for cooking and heating. The Japanese began a programme of reafforestation and defended it strictly, as they did most of their colonial policies, and it was these new woods that were sacrificed to the war effort between 1941 and 1945. What survived was heavily depleted during the Korean War. Since the end of the Korean War, governments both North and South have encouraged replanting, and have also promoted the search for alternative fuels, especially for domestic use. The most common trees today are pine, oak, maple, willow, juniper, larch, spruce, elm, and many fruit trees and bamboo is also widely found. Government planting, as in so many countries, tends to concentrate on quick-growing pine trees. Korean ginseng is much prized; the best is produced in North Korea. The discovery of a wild ginseng root, which is usually revealed to the finder in a dream, is a matter of great rejoicing, the wild root having greater medicinal properties than the cultivated variety.

Extravagant claims are sometimes made about Korean fauna. Those who fought against the French and the Americans in the 1860s and 1870s included many described as 'tiger-hunters'. Mrs Underwood, in *Fifteen Years among the Topknots*, published at the turn of the century, wrote of tigers and leopards in the hills, and Mrs Bishop reported the unwillingness of Koreans to travel at night for fear of tigers. Until well into this century there were still anti-tiger guard posts on the road north out of Seoul, though few people seem to have actually seen a tiger. Perhaps the Manchurian or Korean tiger was once common, but it has long disappeared from the South and probably has not survived in the North. Leopards, lynx, and other even more exotic creatures sometimes mentioned must always have been rare. Hunting, war, and the destruction of the forest environment have all contributed to the disappearance of these and other animals. Various deer flourish and some species of bears exist still, much-prized for their gall bladders, which feature in traditional medicine. There are many smaller mammals; those in the northern part of the peninsula are generally related to species found in northern Manchuria and eastern Siberia. Further south and on the islands, species linked to those found in southern Manchuria and Japan are common, though a few are uniquely Korean. The Chindo dog, found on the island of that name in the south, is now a protected species. In the past hundred years, some 370 species of birds have been identified in Korea. Some of these were vagrants, appearing once only, and two-thirds are migrants. Among birds regularly seen are herons and cranes, and large magpies are everywhere.

Chapter Two

The Korean People

The Koreans, despite today's political divisions, are a homogeneous people. In recent years, the presence of American troops has introduced a small element of racial mixing, but this has had no real effect on the basic unity of the people. Since the late nineteenth century, there has been a small Chinese minority, mainly concentrated in Seoul, but otherwise Korea is inhabited by people who display few regional differences, either physical or cultural. Only in Cheju are there speech patterns and cultural practices noticeably different from those elsewhere, and even these are minimal, when compared with differences between, for example, the Welsh and the Scots, or the Bretons and the rest of France. Few Koreans have any problem with answering the question 'Who is a Korean?'

How the Korean people came to be the Korean people is less easy to answer. The question has been studied and debated, with issues of scholarship obscured by political needs. There is no Korean written evidence on the matter until the thirteenth century, and much of what was written in Korea was clearly inspired by older Chinese accounts. Both the Chinese and the Japanese have pronounced on the issue, but for many Koreans these are tainted sources, whose compilers were out to prove points, rather than to provide disinterested contributions to knowledge. Subjects that in the west would today seem of little current interest except to scholars, in North and South Korea are of much wider concern. The modern history of Korea, and since 1948 the claims of two states for political recognition, mean that references to 'five thousand years of Korean civilisation' are not just useful political catchphrases, but definite statements about the Korean people and the Korean state. Readers should be aware that no account of the likely origins of the Korean people is likely to go unchallenged.

One Korean legend, now to be given a new lease of life in South Korea by government decree, traces the origins of the Korean people to Tan'gun, who, it is said, lived some 2300 years before Christ. In the legends Tan'gun's role varies. Some tell of him as a law-giver and founder of the first Korean kingdom. Others are more exotic. In these he is semi-divine — the offspring of a divine father, Hwan-ung, the younger son of the heavenly king, and a woman who had begun life as a bear. Longing to be human, this bear and a tigress had petitioned the gods for assistance. Only the bear followed the simple instructions given, which were to eat a bunch of mugwort and 20 pieces of garlic, and to keep out of the sunlight for 100 days. This bear-woman then married Hwan-ung, and their offspring was Tan'gun. Tan'gun established his capital at P'yŏngyang (now the capital of North Korea) and gave the name 'Chosŏn' — 'Morning Freshness' — to his kingdom. This legend is still marked today at the altar on Mani-san, the mountain on Kanghwa island near Seoul, where Tan'gun is supposed to have first worshipped on earth. The famous shrine to Tan'gun in P'yŏngyang, which was often mentioned in older accounts of Korea and Korea's religions, has probably long disappeared, though the myth still continues to have a place in North Korean historical works.

Like all such legends this contains a number of clues to the origins of the Korean people. Though the modern promulgation of the myth seems to be based on the idea that Tan'gun was somehow more an indigenous hero than those credited in the Chinese myths with the foundation of Korea, some hold the view that Tan'gun was clearly an outsider who established his rule over people already on the Korean peninsula. The bear cult elements point to links with similar cults in what is now Siberia, and perhaps also to those of the Ainu in northern Japan. It seems probable that the ancestors of most Koreans were part of the expansion of peoples outwards from central Asia that occurred some 800–1000 years BC. They reached Manchuria, where some moved south to what is now Korea and others into Japan. They did not enter empty lands. An aboriginal people were already established in both Japan and Korea, related to the present-day Ainu and to the original peoples of Kamchatka and Sakhalin. One theory is that these early inhabitants were driven out to the less well-endowed lands of the north and east; another postulates considerable intermarriage. Both probably represent part of the truth. It seems highly probable that there was intermarriage with Chinese, especially given the close cultural links between China and the Koreans. There is also evidence of more southerly influences, linking Korea to the Pacific islands.

Archeological evidence can be found for these various theories, and it is growing as more and more sites are excavated. Linguistic evidence, too, provides support both for the central Asian origins and for links between Koreans and Japanese. In colonial days these linguistic links were used to 'prove' that the two peoples were closely related and that therefore it was right for them to be united. It is not necessary to accept that self-serving argument to concede that there are clear links between the two.

None would now deny that, whatever their complicated origins, the Koreans had emerged as one people some 2000 years ago. Today, though clearly related to their Chinese, Japanese, and other East Asian neighbours, they stand apart. There are Korean minorities in China, Japan, and the Soviet Union, but they are all recent emigrants. The great majority of Koreans still inhabit the same land as did their ancestors. Physically they are generally taller and somewhat broader than either the Japanese or the Chinese, though some northern Chinese are similar. Compared with westerners the majority of Koreans were in the past long in the body and short in the leg, but changes in diet are beginning to alter this. They remain, as Mrs Bishop noted nearly a hundred years ago, 'a handsome race.' Others have frequently written of their grace and dignity, qualities today not always in evidence in city crowds, though seen more often in the quiet rural areas. Koreans claim to be able to detect differences between people of different regions. Those from the northern provinces were supposed to be belligerent, hard-working, and aggressive, for example, while those from Chŏlla are treacherous. People from the predominantly rural Kangwŏn province are poor and solid. Few outsiders have been able to discern these characteristics.

There are no reliable population figures before the Japanese colonial period. Such attempts as were made to count the population in old Korea were generally connected with taxation, and the local officials who compiled the lists were more interested in increasing revenue or their share of it than they were in accurate figures.

Returns compiled in this way showed a population around 5 million at the turn of the century, with that of Seoul, the only major town, estimated at 250,000. The Japanese were also conerned with taxation, but the authorities did want accuracy. The first attempt at a census under Japanese auspices was compiled in the early years of the protectorate, and gave a figure of around 7 million. After the annexation all the colonial apparatus was available, and far more accurate results were obtained. In 1910 the population of Korea was said to be 13,313,017, while in the early 1920s, it was just over 17 million. Included in the later totals were up to about 400,000 Japanese and a small number of other foreigners. The last census under the Japanese, carried out in 1942, gave a figure of 26,360,000. Again, only a small proportion would have been non-Koreans.

The division in 1945 left two-thirds of the population in the South. A census held in 1949 gave the population of South Korea as just over 20 million. War and general disruption contributed to a slow growth in the early 1950s, but peace brought steady increases. At the end of 1987 South Korea's population was estimated at just over 41 million, of whom over 13 million live in Seoul and the surrounding area. Seoul itself is said to have over 10 million people; in 1975, it was under 7 million. Pusan was reported to have reached 3.6 million in November 1987, and several other cities are over 1 million. The current age structure is similar to that of many developing countries, with a high proportion of young people, but is changing in line with South Korea's economic development. An energetic birth control campaign since the mid-1960s has reduced population growth, but Korean demographers are still concerned at the rate of growth. Many towns now have 'population clocks' that, by regularly showing the rate of population increase, are supposed to help slow it down. Population density is high. The poor quality of much of the land means that people are even more crammed together than a simple comparison between land area and population would indicate. It is currently about 416 people per square metre in South Korea; this average hides large variations between urban and rural areas.

North Korea has produced few statistics since the early 1960s. Current estimates put the population of the North at about 21 million, with a density of around 165 per square metre. As in the South this figure bears little relation to the ratio of usable land to population. P'yŏngyang is the largest city; it had 1.5 million people in the mid-1970s. No other city is believed to reach a million people.

Section Two

Historical Background

The shrimp's back is broken when the whales fight

Chapter Three

Ancient Korea

The earliest written Korean records are very late — thirteenth century — and not very reliable. It is from Chinese records that we have the earliest accounts of Korea, but these writers were attempting to make political points, not least about China's central role in the world, or at least the East Asian world. Thus to the Tan'gun myth, which Koreans claim as their own, can be added the Kija myth, based on an account in the *Records of the Historian* of Ssu-ma Ch'ien, in which the origins of Korea are traced to a member of the Shang ruling family who fled to Korea from China with thousands of his followers. Korea also features in early Japanese texts, and some of these have been used to justify later Japanese involvement in the Korean peninsula. If we add in the complications created by assertions made by North and South as an essential part of each one's claim to political legitimacy, then it will be readily understood that Korean history is a minefield into which the writer and the reader venture at peril.

Prehistory

The prehistory of Korea is becoming better known as archeological evidence grows. Modern archeology in Korea began under the Japanese. While some research was undoubtedly influenced by the need to prove the existence of long-established links between Japan

21

and Korea, good work was done, though not always of a standard that would pass today. After 1945, archeology was for obvious reasons not high on the priorities of North or South. But the war itself and post-war reconstruction provided many opportunities for archeological work. This was not always in ideal conditions, but the work was and is being done. In both North and South the search for political legitimacy has also given a boost to archeological and general historical studies.

The paleolithic period in the Korean peninsula was once thought to have barely existed. Recent years have seen a considerable increase in information and new sites are regularly discovered. Little is known of the way of life of these people, although they had very rough stone tools, were hunters, and used fire both for cooking and heating. Neolithic man has left little, apart from more polished stone tools and various forms of pottery of types found also in Manchuria and Siberia. For many historians, it is these people who form the first definite link with the modern Korean people. They were hunters and fishers — possibly including deep-sea fishing, from the evidence of fish bones found at a site near Pusan — who later began to practise agriculture. The available evidence points to pit dwellers, who also used caves from time to time. Groups of dwellings have been found together, which may indicate some form of community, but the evidence is slight, much of it based on back-projection from later periods. On this basis, it has been claimed that a form of clan society existed, with elected kingship. Some have also argued for a matrilineal society, but the evidence is slight.

The Korean bronze age is much better known. It began about 800–900 BC and lasted until about 300 BC. Bronze techniques seem to have come from the north and were first practised in the Liaoning region, now part of China. Bronze artifacts found include weapons and mirrors. This period also shows highly-developed pottery. Bronze age man in Korea was probably mainly an agriculturalist, and tools for harvesting rice now make their appearance. He lived in groups on the slopes near flat areas suitable for rice cultivation. It is to this period that many of the extensive dolmens found around the peninsula can be dated. The existence of these elaborate tombs, and surviving grave furnishings, point to a well-developed social structure, with a powerful and possibly hereditary aristocracy, able to command the services of many people.

It was out of these communities that states began to emerge, probably towards the end of the bronze age, as iron-working began alongside the older technique. The earliest Korean states straddled what is now the China–North Korean border, not a difficult task in a region where rivers freeze in winter and are shallow for much of the rest of the year. Later governments banned movement across these rivers, but in the earliest days the borders between Chinese culture and embryonic Korea were much less clear. In this area of forests there developed around the third century BC the first entity to which the name 'Chosŏn' was given. The meaning of this name — 'Morning Freshness' — points to Chinese links, since the area lies east of China. There is a theory that this state was organised, or at least heavily influenced, by Chinese refugees from the upheavals in China proper as the Ch'in gave way to the Han.

The Three Kingdoms

From now on the Korean peninsula and its peoples feature more regularly in the surviving historical records. In fact, given the time-serving nature of the records available, this apparent clarity hides many obscurities. No doubt real events lurk behind the tales of heroes as in other cultures, but they are equally hard to sort out. The Chinese records note that in 194 BC, a general called 'Wiman' or 'Weiman,' variously given as a Chinese or as a Korean in Chinese service, fled from China and established 'Wiman Chosŏn,' with its capital on the Taedong river, near to modern P'yŏngyang. Later legend has it that Wiman brought with him the topknot, a style of hairdressing that the Koreans were to wear until the twentieth century. While this is bad history, because the topknot did not come into use until probably the fifteenth century in China and Korea, the existence of the legend points again to Chinese influence. Wiman's kingdom did not last long. After alleged insults the Emperor Han Wu-ti of China attacked and destroyed Chosŏn in 109 BC, replacing it with four Chinese military colonies, known as the commanderies. These were established in what is now Manchuria and in north and central Korea. The most important was Loyang (*Nangnang* in Korean), which was to outlive the others, surviving until about 313

AD. Loyang's capital was also at P'yŏngyang. Through these colonies, Chinese influence flowed into the Korean peninsula. The ruling class, while originally Chinese, probably became Sino–Korean in the course of time, but appear to have remained heavily Sinicised in outlook and culture. Trade brought goods from China, and probably further away, which have been found in tombs around the former capital of Loyang.

Long before the final fall of Loyang, the peoples of the rest of the peninsula had begun to organise themselves, possibly using China or at least the Loyang shadow of China as a model. The Chinese texts give precise dates for the emergence of Korea's 'Three Kingdoms.' Silla was dated to 57 BC, Koguryŏ to 37 BC, and Paekche to 18 BC. These dates probably have more to do with the compilers' need for symmetry than with reality, and now it is generally agreed that Koguryŏ was probably the earliest established. For some time it was the most powerful. Its origins were in the north and its territory stretched far to the north of the modern division between China and Korea and south to the Han river — the exact extent of its territory in the north is still a matter of controversy. It appears to have been heavily influenced by Chinese practices, and its rulers began to use the Chinese title *wang*, meaning king. This Chinese influence did not stop it from overthrowing Loyang, which found itself unable to obtain help from a China itself in turmoil. Koguryŏ's leaders formed a military aristocracy around their king, and acquired an understandable reputation for warlike activity. Their first capital, after the fall of Loyang, was based in the area of modern P'yŏngyang.

To the south of Koguryŏ emerged two kingdoms, Paekche and Silla, whose territories roughly followed the geographical divide of the southern half of the peninsula. Paekche's origins, like those of Koguryŏ, lay far to the north of modern Korea, in a tribe called the Puyo, who lived south of the Sungari river. Under Kogoryŏ influence they gradually moved south, settling south of the Han river, with a capital based first in the area of Sŏngnam city, one of modern Seoul's dormitory towns, and later at Kongju and Puyo in present-day South Ch'ungch'ŏng province. Silla emerged from the various tribes of the south west, probably around the middle of the fourth century AD. In addition a small group of tribes in the south remained outside Silla control, looking across to the Japanese islands for assistance against their more powerful neighbours. This was the small Kaya kingdom, eventually swallowed up by the more powerful Silla.

Although for much of the period of the Three Kingdoms, China was in disarray — indeed, it was this very disarray that helped their emergence — Chinese influence continued to have a major impact in Korea. Even Silla, the furthest of the three, followed Chinese patterns of government and state organisation, as well as drawing much cultural inspiration from China. It was at this period that the Koreans began to use the Chinese writing system, having none of their own. This in turn introduced them to Chinese literature, which was to have a profound effect on Korean thinking. It was now that the Confucian model of government and behaviour came to Korea and began to exert an influence that persists to this day. It was also the beginning of the belief that the truly literate person wrote in a foreign language rather than Korean; the contemporary Korean fixation with the foreign Ph D perhaps springs from this historical source. The Three Kingdoms period also saw the introduction of Buddhism to Korea from China.

It would be wrong to think, however, that the peoples of the Three Kingdoms period accepted what China had to offer in an uncritical fashion. The idea has long persisted that the Koreans took both culture and political systems from China without modification. In fact, much of what came from China was adapted and altered to fit Korean needs. Silla, for example, may have used the Chinese structure of government, but it was superimposed on an older indigenous structure. The Confucian civil service coexisted with a tribal aristocracy and a warrior class. Korean Buddhism, like its counterparts everywhere else, took over older local deities and incorporated them into the Buddhist pantheon. Neither was it just Chinese culture that was absorbed by the Koreans, for Buddhism was already a universal creed, which introduced many ideas in both literature and art from traditions far to the west of China.

The seven hundred or so years that mark the Three Kingdoms period (37 BC to the fall of Koguryŏ to Silla in 668 AD) were ones of great cultural importance. Much evidence has survived to provide testimony to this. The rulers of the various kingdoms erected stone monuments, or steles, to mark their achievements, some of which can still be seen. The most famous, the 'great Stele of Kwanggaet'o,' erected by King Changsu of Koguryŏ to show the extent of his predecessor's successes, still stands in modern Manchuria. They are witness to an elaborate system of government. So too are the many royal tombs that have survived from the Three Kingdoms and from Kaya. The contents of these tombs point to the possible central Asian origins of these rulers. The arrival of Buddhism led to the foundation of many monasteries and to the erection of pagodas and other monuments. Many tombs have yielded Buddhist statues, or have shown the use of Buddhist symbolism. From Paekche Buddhism was carried to Japan, as was the Chinese writing system and Chinese literature.

None of this took place in a vacuum. China may have been in confusion, but its rulers tried from time to time to reassert control over Korea. From the Japanese islands, too, came regular pirate attacks on the Korean peninsula. The Three Kingdoms also fought each other, sometimes alone, sometimes in alliance wth the current Chinese dynasty or with the Japanese. Shifting alliances became the standard pattern. Koguryŏ drove Paekche further south, where in 660 Silla, aided by the newly-established T'ang dynasty in China, defeated and absorbed it, an episode made famous by the Paekche ladies who drowned themselves rather than suffer dishonour. It is claimed, somewhat fancifully, that burnt ears of rice from the final fateful day can still be found around the site of Paekche's capital.

The allies then turned their attention to Koguryŏ, which in turn fell in 668 AD. For the T'ang rulers of China this was merely the prelude to re-establishing Chinese hegemony over the peninsula. This they proceeded to do, planting military commanderies in parts of the defeated kingdoms, and attempting to extend their control over Silla by appointing its King Munmu as one of the governors-general in Korea. Silla had not fought as the T'ang ally to be reduced to the same level as its former opponents. Thus there began further conflict, which culminated in Silla's defeat of the Chinese forces and the establishment of a 'unified Silla' kingdom south of the Taedong river about 670 AD. Silla was not able to claim all the former Three Kingdoms' territory, but its achievement was considerable. Beyond the Taedong river there emerged on the ruins of Koguryŏ another successor state, *Parhae* in Korean, *P'o-hai* in Chinese. It did not occupy all the former Koguryŏ territory, some of which was absorbed by the T'ang, but it held a sizeable proportion. It displayed strong Chinese influence and was perhaps more closely meshed into the T'ang world order than Silla. Eventually, after some two centuries of quasi-independence, it fell before the Khitan early in the tenth century AD, and was absorbed into their Liao kingdom.

Unified Silla and Koryŏ

From unified Silla developed the modern Korean state, but it is too early yet to speak of 'Korea'; some accounts speak of unified Silla as the 'proto-Korean state,' which is probably as accurate a description as any. It was rich and powerful, still run on tribal lines, with a heavy overlay of Chinese culture in part absorbed from defeated Koguryŏ and Paekche. Its capital Kŭmsŏng, the modern Kyŏngju, in the south east of the peninsula was comparatively remote but became a byword for wealth, rivalling the contemporary T'ang capital at Ch'angan. Buddhism flourished. Temple remains testify to this, as do the many examples of sculpture and other artifacts that have survived. The heavily-restored Pulkuksa temple and the nearby Sŏkkuram cave are the best-known, and archeological finds add regularly to our knowledge of Silla. From this period also date the first known examples of indigenous rather than Chinese literature, recorded by using Chinese characters to represent the phonetic values of the native language. Silla occupied an important trading and cultural position in East Asia, dealing with both China and Japan. In the Chinese case the reality of Silla's independence was concealed by the tribute system, which allowed a considerable trade to develop under the guise of Silla tribute to the T'ang court. From Silla there flowed to Japan much Chinese culture and Korean artifacts, as well as scholars and craftsmen to teach the skills required to master both. Silla also had contacts as far afield as India, in the search for new sources of Buddhist enlightenment.

The wealth and culture of Silla were not achieved without cost. A huge slave or semi-slave population supported the ruling class, created during the years of fighting that had led to the establishment of unified Silla. Here was one possible source of trouble. Another lay in the increasingly authoritarian rule of the Silla kings, who asserted a paramount position at the expense of their fellow aristocrats. The creation of subordinate capitals to compensate for the comparative remoteness of Kŭmsŏng, while in many ways a sensible administrative arrangement, also provided alternative centres of power to the capital. From the late eighth century the kingdom was torn by rebellion. Aristocratic groups conspired to place their own nominees on the throne or set up rival kingdoms. The common people too rebelled, either openly or by leaving the estates of the nobility. Many fled from Korea altogether, while others played a prominent role in the trade with China and Japan. By about 890 AD Silla was on the point of collapse, with new kingdoms emerging in the old Paekche and the southern Koguryŏ areas.

These Latter Three Kingdoms not only fought amongst themselves, but they too were prone to internal rebellion. It was one such rebellion in 'neo-Koguryŏ' that led to the emergence of a soldier, Wang Kŏn, as king in 918. Wang Kŏn established his capital near his own home at Songak (modern Kaesŏng) and called his kingdom Koryŏ. In the following years, by a judicious mixture of war, bribery, alliance, and good luck, he succeeded in recreating a unified kingdom, which embraced not only the Latter Three Kingdoms but parts of Parhae as well. His generosity towards many of the former ruling classes of his disparate kingdom helped him to portray Koryŏ as the legitimate successor to the traditions of the former kingdoms, especially those of Silla, the unifier.

The Koryŏ period occupies a special place in Korean history. For the first time the majority of modern Korea came under one ruler. From Koryŏ derives the western name Korea, or *La Corée*, and the variations on this. In addition Koryŏ faced major foreign threats, which have often reminded Koreans of their subsequent unhappy experiences with outside powers. But the immediate effect of uniting the country was a revival of the trade and crafts that had been so prominent under Silla. According to some accounts, the splendour of Koryŏ matched that of the contemporary Chinese Sung dynasty. Koryŏ papermaking and printing with movable type, well in advance of Europe, were famous in East Asia, as were Koryŏ celadons.

Yet there were problems from the very beginning of the dynasty. The founder, Wang Kŏn, or King T'aejo, to give him the name bestowed on him posthumously, faced a difficult task. A marked feature of the final days of Silla and the Latter Three Kingdoms period was the emergence of castle towns controlled by local nobles who were reluctant to give up power. The court was faced with a constant and ultimately unsuccessful struggle to control these powerful subjects and to bring them under central authority. It was a task made more difficult by the great numbers of former Silla and Parhae nobles who had to be accommodated in the new kingdom. As a counter-balance, from 958 the Koryŏ kings reinforced the Chinese concept of an examination system and of advance by merit to create a bureaucracy. It was a concept that was to survive in Korea long after Koryŏ, but under local conditions it became much modified from its Chinese original, serving to endorse the superior position of the aristocracy rather than providing an alternative to it by providing a path for the poor but able scholar to positions of authority. King T'aejo also encouraged the growth of Buddhism, and this too became a further cause of difficulties. Buddhist institutions acquired great wealth from gifts given by the king and the nobility, with a view to earning merit. With wealth came a desire for power, and the result was the growth of intrigue on the part of the great monasteries.

These difficulties were compounded by external pressures. The Korean peninsula was continually subjected to raids by Japanese pirates along its eastern and southern coasts. More important, however, was pressure from the north. Strong rulers in China always turned their attention to Korea, continually trying to bring it under their control. The advent of the Mongols in China at the beginning of the thirteenth century was no exception. The invaders soon turned their attention to Korea, which they found weak and ripe for takeover. There was some ineffective resistance. By fleeing to Kanghwa island, near present-day Seoul, the court for a time escaped the Mongols, but for real protection it relied less on its armies than on the carving of Buddhist scriptures on wooden blocks. This impressive if not very effective undertaking took sixteen years, but brought little succour.

The Mongol invasion caused much disruption and economic damage. Later Korea was also dragged into its new overlords' unsuccessful attempts at invading Japan. Even as the Mongol power collapsed, the Koreans found themselves still involved, as Chinese armies periodically retreated into the peninsula during the fighting that marked the transition from Mongol to Ming in the second half of the fourteenth century. This confusion in the last years of the Mongols led to the end of Koryŏ in 1392, though by then power had long since slipped away from the court to the gentry, to the Buddhist abbots, and, increasingly, to the generals. One of these generals, Yi Sŏng-gye, of modest gentry background, sent to campaign in the north on behalf of the Mongols against the increasingly successful Ming, decided that enough was enough. Abandoning his hopeless campaign against the Ming forces on the Yalu river, he brought his forces back to the capital and deposed the king. For a time he ruled through a puppet. Then in 1392 he decided to take the throne himself. Yi T'aejo, as he is known to history, thus founded Korea's longest-reigning and best-known dynasty.

Chapter Four

Yi Dynasty Korea, 1392–1910

The establishment of the dynasty

Koreans often refer to the Yi dynasty as though it was an unchanging whole. Korean museums and art history books will often describe a building, an object, or a painting simply as 'Yi dynasty' or 'Chosŏn dynasty,' from the name by which Korea was known from 1392 to 1897, when it became the 'Taehan' empire. Adding the dates '1392–1910' is hardly more illuminating. Yet it all fits in with the Korean belief that Korea has been unchanging, a 'hermit kingdom,' happily isolated from the world, until outside interference shattered its tranquillity. Another variation of the seamless whole myth is a form of back projection from what is seen as the shameful end of the dynasty at the hands of the Japanese. This 'failure' is seen as present in the Yi dynasty from the beginning. Many North Korean accounts follow this line, but it is not unknown in South Korea. In the past Japanese historians and many early western writers have tended to produce variations on this theme. But Yi Korea was no less prone to change than other societies, and Korea at the beginning of the fifteenth century was very different from Korea at the beginning of the twentieth.

Yi T'aejo began, as all good rulers did, by moving the capital to break literally and symbolically with the past. He settled on a small city, Hanyang, near the Han river in the centre of the country. Here he built his new city, and it is this city, 'Seoul,' a native Korean word meaning simply 'capital,' the chief city of unified Korea from about

1394 to 1945, which is today the capital of the Republic of Korea. Although much altered in subsequent years, it remained recognisably Yi T'aejo's capital until about 1900. Now, though war and growth have changed much of what once seemed unchangeable, there still remain shrines, palaces, walls, and gates to remind today's Koreans of the original Yi city. The central position that Seoul quickly assumed as the source of power and influence in the country has also persisted in South Korea to the present day.

The determination to begin anew was seen in other ways. There was a major land reform, in which most land was deemed to belong to the state, to be used to reward those who served the state. The power of the old gentry, with their vast tax-free estates, was thus broken. The land in the capital region, the province of Kyŏnggi, was used to reward Yi T'aejo's principal followers. They were to be called 'merit subjects,' and were bound to their leader, while the followers of the former dynasty were dispossessed. Later another class of 'minor merit subjects' was created, with lesser grants of land, equally bound to the new dynasty. This was the beginning of the *yangban* class, the 'two groups,' civil and military, who were to govern Korea under the Yi. Administrative reform, which went together with land reform, was to further consolidate the position of this group. Yi T'aejo emphasised the Chinese examination system and a Chinese-style civil service, which were to be important factors in the spread of Confucian ideas. The study of Confucian texts and commentaries, especially those of the neo-Confucian school, was to form the main basis of the examination system. The examinations themselves, though superficially egalitarian, provided no open road to the top. The ruling class quickly monopolised access to them, and a further firm line was drawn between the *yangban* and the rest. The victory of neo-Confucian thought in Yi Korea was not achieved overnight. Rather, it was a steady build-up of ideas over some 200 years, with now one aspect of doctrine, now another being emphasised by the Confucian scholars who were the allies of the Yi kings. One early stage was the downgrading of the military examination and the role of the military: a useful means of checking any other soldier who might have ambitions about becoming king. Control of social customs and the exclusion of Buddhist influence took much longer, not being achieved fully before the sixteenth century.

It was again to Chinese tradition that Yi T'aejo turned for the administrative framework for his new government. The restoration of links with the Chinese court, the re-establishment of regular embassies to China, and the related tribute system, all helped to give legitimacy to the new regime. Here, too, the Koreans adapted and altered what they took from China, turning it into something Korean. Central government consisted of a Central Council and Boards of Personnel, Revenue, Rituals, War, Justice and Works. These boards gradually developed the right of direct appeal to the throne. Various censoring bodies were also established to check both the King and his administration, which they were to do with relish. Provincial government, too, was modelled on China, with eight circuits, or provinces, remaining the basic structure until the nineteenth century. Provincial governors came from the centre and were moved every two years to prevent them building up local power bases. Below that level local government was in the hands of the local gentry, checked with varying degrees of effectiveness by inspectors, and by the requirement that their sons should serve — that is, be hostages — in Seoul.

The power of the Buddhist monasteries was curbed. As in contemporary Europe, these religious foundations had acquired much land, often as gifts from devout followers. Wealth in turn bred wealth, and led to the acquisition of further land. Most of this slipped from under the central government's tax control. It also caused problems in other ways. Those deprived of land by the avaricious habits of the monks were a threat to the peace of the state, while the monks themselves were staunch defenders of what they held, either by fighting where necessary or by intrigue at court. Yi T'aejo was already a follower of Confucian doctrines, and this may have made him further suspicious of the Buddhists. The monks were therefore stripped of much of their wealth and banished both from court and from the cities. Buddhism was not proscribed, but it was no longer encouraged. Monasteries continued to exist, but only in remote areas.

Another major problem was that of the Japanese pirates, the *wakō*. (Depending on the character with which *wa* is written, *wakō* means either 'Japanese pirates' or 'dwarf pirates.' Understandably, the Japanese prefer the former; the Koreans and the Chinese, who were on the receiving end, the latter.) These raiders had long been a menace to both Korea and China. In the fourteenth century there was a breakdown in law and order both in Japan and on the mainland, and a big increase in Japanese raids. Mongol restrictions placed on its Koryŏ vassal had limited the ability of the Koreans to deal with the problem, but the Mongol collapse ended that restraint. In the later years of Koryŏ there was a determined effort to rid Korea of them, helped by major innovations in naval warfare. These efforts had been successful until troops were moved away from the south to engage in the Mongol–Ming conflict and central authority had collapsed. The Japanese then returned to what seemed a soft target. As the Yi leader moved to take over the throne, he turned his attention to the Japanese, launching raids on the pirate bases in Tsushima and destroying their boats and settlements. Many islands that provided tempting targets were evacuated during these campaigns, some remaining empty for several hundred years. These efforts were successful and the pirate raids on Korea had largely stopped by about 1420. Strenuous efforts were also made to pacify the northern frontier, which was very unsettled following the Mongol collapse and was subject to frequent cross-border raids. To stop these, and to contain unruly frontier tribes, a system of forts and military outposts was put in place by about 1450. The frontier between Korea and Manchuria was now firmly established. Just as islands were cleared to discourage the Japanese, so large tracts along the river frontier were cleared to discourage further attacks by land.

The Yi dynasty's momentum for change and consolidation was kept up for over a hundred years; administration and land reform, for example, were continuous processes rather than one-off events. The new capital was given extra defence works, and palaces and other buildings proliferated. Elsewhere, too, years of neglect were now put right. Scholarship flourished in the return to comparative peace and with the encouragement of Confucian studies. Confucian schools *sŏwŏn*, an essential requirement for the examination system, were established throughout the country. Chinese influence was strong, especially in the first half of the Yi period, and it replaced many of the native, Buddhist-inspired traditions of earlier years, especially in art. There were a number of major literary undertakings, including a Chinese-style history of the fallen dynasty, the *Koryŏ-sa* (History of Koryŏ), completed in 1451. Movable type printing became particularly well-established. The Korean alphabet, *han'gŭl*, was introduced in the mid-fifteenth century. Later, in reaction against the excessive Chinese-oriented nature of much literature, there was to be a revival of native Korean forms, such as *sijo* poetry. Applied science and technology showed some major advances, especially in weaponry and naval design, but also in more peaceful ways, such as various forms of weather gauge.

Political affairs under the Yi could fill many books. They would not make edifying reading. Confucian ideals were one thing, practice often far removed. Respect for kings, though accorded the highest position in the Confucian scale, was not a marked feature of Korea under the Yi. Yi T'aejo's successor, his brother Chŏngjong, was rapidly replaced by T'aejo's fifth son in 1400, and the pattern continued in later years. Difficult or critical ministers were also disposed of, with little concern for the niceties of Confucian ethics. The Confucian schools soon acquired a similar status to the Buddhist temples in Koryŏ times: they received gifts of land; they obtained exemption from taxation as a further mark of respect; and they began to encourage their students to form groups to arrange for further advancement both of the school and its alumni. These groups formed factions at court, competing for influence and office. Within the royal family, too, there was an early tendency to form factions, with the families of royal consorts playing a particularly prominent role. There was little to distinguish one of these groups from another: power was their interest and the bond between the members of a faction.

The structure of society

Such matters concerned only the *yangban*, who at the most were perhaps five percent of the population. The term hid many gradations, from powerful ministers at court to small local gentry, barely distinguishable from their tenants. The novel, *Tale of a Yangban*, by a reforming scholar, Pak Chi-wŏn (1737–1805), refers to the *yangban* as 'above consorting with the king, below with the common people.' Whether above or below, certain standards were demanded of them. Avoidance of all but intellectual work was chief among these. Below the *yangban* there were officially three classes: farmers, artisans, and merchants. These together made up the common people, the *sangmin*. In practice, society was more subdivided than that. Between the *yangban* and the commoners was a class of technicians, including physicians, interpreters, certain military officers and some categories of local officials. Members of this group were often illegitimate sons of *yangban*. Below the commoners were certain despised occupations and slaves or serfs. Among the former were sorcerors, actors and Buddhist monks and nuns. The slaves or serfs were usually criminals or descendants of criminals, though some were supposedly descendants of the captives of ancient wars. They were often servants of the *yangban* or the state. While officially despised, they were sometimes better off than either the poorest *yangban* or many commoners, and in times of trouble farmers and others would nominally take serf status under a friendly local landlord for protection.

This was the theoretical structure of society. Like all such outlines, it would be hard to find one point when things actually operated as they were supposed to do. In times of unrest, or in areas remote from direct central control or influence, things were very different. When oppression grew too much, the common people would rise in revolt in Korea as elsewhere, and on such occasions an early target was the genealogical records where status was recorded. It was not easy to reconstruct these. It was not unknown, either, for *yangban* down on their luck to sell their status to others. On the whole, as time went on, the tendency was for a breakdown of the formal rigidities of society. Slave households were often established separately from the master's house, and in time became indistinguishable from tenant farmers. In certain circumstances slaves could purchase their freedom, and there was merit to be gained by freeing slaves. Slavery was to continue until the end of the nineteenth century, but it was by then very much a shadow of its former self.

The Japanese and the 'Imjin' War

The successful anti-pirate campaign and the restoration of correct relations with Ming China allowed the Koreans nearly 200 years of freedom from external concerns. The tribute missions to the Ming allowed a certain amount of trade to take place, while trade developed, too, with the Japanese, mainly through the island of

Tsushima. The Japanese were allowed to establish trading settlements in the south. These could be a source of trouble, and following one disturbance in 1510, all trade relations were broken off by the Koreans. Entreaties from the feudal lords of Tsushima eventually succeeded in persuading the Koreans to sign a new treaty in 1512, but the amount of trade was much reduced, and the Japanese were limited to one port, Pusan.

That Korea could remain at peace was not entirely due to its own efforts. For much of the fifteenth and sixteenth centuries, Japan was in political turmoil, with no strong central government and feudal lords fighting each other. Apart from a few easily-repulsed pirate raids, the Japanese were too preoccupied to concern themselves with their neighbours. This convenient state of affairs came to an end in the 1580s, when Hideyoshi Toyotomi brought an end to the fighting. Seeking an external diversion, he turned his attention to China. It may be that his intentions were not entirely warlike; there was some interest in Japan in re-opening and expanding trade relations with China. But the Ming court, which had increasingly cut off links with the outside world since the mid-fifteenth century, was not receptive. Hideyoshi therefore resolved to force them to deal with Japan. He demanded Korean agreement for his troops to pass on their way to China. Given the Korean attitude to China, such a request was refused. Hideyoshi therefore launched an invasion of Korea in 1592. Thus began the 'Imjin War,' so called from the Korean name of the year.

Peace had taken its toll of the Korean military, who were looked down upon by the scholar aristocracy. The martial traditions of the founders of the Yi dynasty had long been allowed to lapse by the late sixteenth century, but there was no naval or military structure that could be immediately used against the Japanese. The Korean defence collapsed and the court fled north, to the outrage of the commoners of Seoul, who tried to prevent this weakness before the Japanese. The latter fought their way north until they were held at the Yalu by a joint Korean and Chinese force.

Meanwhile, Yi Sun-sin, a naval commander in Chŏlla province, had organised naval forces in the south and was able to inflict heavy defeats on the Japanese using a new type of ship. These were the famous 'turtle ships,' whose iron-covered decks made them the world's first armoured vessels. Equally important was his use of cannon, which enabled him to use heavier fire power than the

Japanese ships. Korean guerrilla bands also successfully harassed the Japanese. These defeats and vastly extended supply lines led the Japanese to begin peace negotiations with the Ming. These came to nothing, and while they went on Japanese armies remained in Korea, living off the land. In 1597 Hideyoshi again attacked Korea. Admiral Yi was not there to stop him. He was in disgrace, victim of factional in-fighting. He was quickly recalled, however, when the Korean fleet suffered a major defeat. Under his guidance Korean fortunes were again restored. The Japanese were pinned down by land and by sea. Hideyoshi's death in September 1598 settled the matter, and the Japanese withdrew. Yi Sun-sin did not live to see his success, for he was killed in battle just before the end of the war.

Hideyoshi's invasion has seared into the Korean collective memory and is seen as the forerunner of the Japanese takeover in 1910. The country did suffer greatly. Every province was affected, with those in the south especially badly hit. The population fell and whole villages disappeared. Palaces and temples were burnt, books and historical records destroyed. The general devastation and the government's need for funds pressed heavily on the population, as did the presence of three large armies for some six years. There were numerous uprisings, some serious. The destruction of official records made proper government difficult. Many Koreans were taken as prisoners to Japan, including many skilled craftsmen. Korea's loss was Japan's gain, for among the craftsmen were potters who introduced new techniques to Japan and who helped develop Japanese ceramic traditions.

Peace with Japan was restored in 1606, and thereafter the countries regularly exchanged missions; as in the Chinese case, these provided opportunities for trade. Trade also revived through Tsushima. The Tokugawa policy, instituted in the 1630s, of avoiding unnecessary involvement with the outside world, suited the Koreans, who were content to keep their contacts with Japan to a minimum. They were less fortunate with other external contacts. Even as Korea recovered from the Imjin War, a major new threat was in the offing, this time from the north.

Hideyoshi's invasion of Korea had helped to weaken the Ming and had prevented them dealing effectively with another threat, the growing power of the Manchus. The Ming–Manchu wars spilled over into Korea, with a major Manchu invasion of the north of the peninsula in 1627. As the Manchu consolidated their hold on China in the following years, so they turned their attention again to Korea, demanding a Korean acknowledgment of suzerainty. This was refused by King Injo and the Manchus invaded. The King sent his family to Kangwha island and himself retreated to the South Fortress near Seoul. But the Manchus quickly succeeded in defeating the Koreans in 1636 and the King accepted the Ch'ing, as the Manchu conquerors now styled themselves, as overlords. It was not the ideal way to ensure loyalty, and the Koreans never fully accepted the Ch'ing as the heirs to the Ming. Ming ways continued to be favoured in Korea.

New influences and pressures

There followed some 200 years of comparative peace. Korea recovered from the devastation of the wars. The court and the *yangban* returned to the pursuit of factional quarrels. At the same time there were those who tried, while operating within the Confucian system, to break away from the sterile arguments about minor points of doctrine that had become the staple of Korean Confucianism. But these advocates of new learning made little impact. For most of those near the centre of power, what mattered was to be 'in' rather than 'out,' to control the king rather than reform the administration.

Under the pressure of events some of the earlier certainties began to break down. The government experimented with coins and notes as a means of paying its way, since old means of exchange had collapsed in the war. On the edges of Korea cross-border private trading began to develop in spite of all government attempts to stop it. The eighteenth century saw the growth of economic guilds. A further sign of change was the emergence of self-help groups, known as *kye*, set up among ordinary people of the villages and quite outside official control. The destruction of records, together with new-found economic independence, enabled many former slave households to establish themselves as commoners. The troubled times and the destruction of records led some *yangban* to sell their status. To further add to confusion, new and disturbing ideas began to reach Korea.

Korean interest in Catholicism dated almost from the beginning of the Jesuits' links with the Chinese court in the sixteenth century, as those on the tribute missions learnt of the new teaching, but it was only at the end of the eighteenth century that the new teaching, generally called *sohak*, or western learning, began to have a wider appeal, especially to those deprived of power. The new religion was soon a target of official disapproval and persecution. As in China an important reason for such concern was Catholic opposition to the ancestral rites, a matter of fundamental importance in Confucianism. If people failed to honour their own ancestors, they might soon question all other rules for the well-ordering of society. The first restrictions on Christianity came in the 1780s, as did Korea's first Christian martyr.

These outside influences began to affect Korea at a time when it was facing considerable internal problems. It is now generally agreed that the devastation of the Hideyoshi and the Manchu invasion was not as great as older writers described it. Korea recovered, albeit slowly. But the experience of those years and the violent changes in China tended to reinforce Korean conservatism. The Korean ruling class saw themselves as the true guardians of neo-Confucian tradition, at a time when there were usurpers in Peking. Preoccupation with factional politics left little desire for innovation. The ordinary people, passive most of the time, were occasionally goaded into fierce rebellion. There were many small uprisings and a major one in 1811–1812. An additional cause for concern was the willingness of disaffected *yangban* to throw in their lot with the discontented peasants.

From the 1790s onwards, there were new pressures. After years of invasion and interference, the Koreans had no wish for foreign entanglements. Yet Roman Catholicism continued to percolate into the country from China, and to find a domestic following in spite of persecution. Developments in China and Japan brought the western powers nearer and nearer to Korea, and at the same time provided graphic warnings of the threat these outsiders posed. The Koreans were well aware of the intermingling of Christianity and politics. The arrival of missionaries on what seemed like warships and visits by British and American survey vessels mapping the country's coasts and bays, were not reassuring. And, though almost invariably treated with hostility, if not always with actual violence, these interlopers returned. Nothing seemed to warn them, whether it was the execution of French missionary priests in 1839 or the attack on the American merchant ship, the *General Sherman*, at P'yŏngyang in 1866.

It was unfortunate that as Korea faced major difficulties in the 1860s, King Kojong was a minor and the country was effectively governed by his father, the Taewŏn'gun, or regent. The Taewŏn'gun was a man of ability and honesty but a rigid believer in the old ways. His administrative skills were used not to change Korea in the face of the new challenges, but to try to restore it to Confucian purity. For some time he succeeded. A further massive persecution, with many martyrs, including several foreign priests, seemed to check Catholicism. Rebellion in the south west, led by followers of another new religion, the Tonghak, which borrowed from east and west, was put down in 1864. Factionalism was restrained, and many of the Confucian *sŏwŏn* closed down. Taxation was extended to some categories of *yangban* in order to meet increased military spending, and some of the tax burden on the peasants was alleviated. Fortifications were rebuilt and the military reformed. American and French expeditions sent to demand redress for the killing of their nationals were driven off in 1866 and 1871. The Koreans took heart from these successes. To remind people of the dangers posed by foreigners, warning steles were put up at various points in the country in 1871 against anyone who might 'advocate peace and sell out the country.' The old ways appeared successful. But the victories were hollow. Elsewhere in East Asia the old order was collapsing under similar pressures. The Koreans could not expect outside support. China, the traditional mentor, was negotiating with the western barbarians, even if reluctantly. Japan, having at first resisted, by the late 1860s seemed to have gone over completely to the foreigners' ways.

It was this that prompted the Taewŏn'gun to make another stand for the old order. The Japanese announced to the Koreans that the Tokugawa family, who had governed Japan since 1603, had been overthrown, and imperial rule restored. The Koreans professed to know nothing of a Japanese emperor. The Japanese then attempted to communicate with Korea in standard western diplomatic terms and notified the Koreans that the old trading arrangements at Pusan and the links through Tsushima were to be replaced by a more modern arrangement. These overtures were rudely rejected by the Korean government as the behaviour of 'a country with no law.' It was not an approach likely to endear the Koreans to the new dynamic government in Tokyo, eager to prove that it was a full member of the western 'family of nations.'

This Japanese concern with Korea might have been counter-balanced by the involvement of other countries, for there was undoubtedly western interest in Korea. Regular naval visits to Korean waters — two or three a year by the early 1870s — had aroused interest in the strategic value of Korea's many islands, and there were proposals from both the British and the American navies that Kŏmun-do (Port Hamilton), near Cheju island, should be occupied. There was also some Russian interest in the same group. Western missionaries were keen to enter Korea. Some western diplomats in China and Japan also took an interest in the country, and efforts were made to collect information and study the language. But Korea did not occupy the attention of the west as did China or Japan. It lay off the main shipping lanes in East Asia. While once there had been stories about Korea's great wealth, recent visits had tended to produce a picture of a drab and poor country with little to offer. In strategic terms, Korea was not widely seen as important by western countries until late in the nineteenth century. It was left to the Japanese to force Korea's opening.

The opening of Korea

Intrigues at court and the end of King Kojong's minority led to the Taewŏn'gun's impeachment and banishment in December 1873. At first there was no change in the new government's attitude to the outside world. Warnings from China about possible Japanese plans to attack Korea were seen as yet another sign of a Ch'ing fall from Confucian grace and ignored. However, other counsels began to prevail, and attempts were made to repair the relationship with Japan. Although for a time these looked as though they might bear fruit, ultimately they were unsuccessful. When Korean batteries on Kangwha island fired on the Japanese warship *Unyōkan* in May 1875, they set in train events that led to the Japanese extorting a western-style treaty from Korea the following year, and ultimately to the complete Japanese takeover of Korea in 1910.

'Japanese imperialism' arouses strong feelings among Koreans. The events of 1875–1876 are seen as part of a long-term Japanese plan to absorb Korea. The reality is that there was no long-term plan, but the coming together of a number of strands that pushed Japan towards involvement in Korea. The Meiji restoration of 1868 and the subsequent reforms in Japan left large numbers of samurai without useful occupations. Some of these sought foreign outlets for their energies. Given the historical links between Korea and Japan, it was not surprising that some of them saw in Korea opportunities denied them at home. Japanese industrialisation, begun well before 1868, also sought outlets for goods that could not all be consumed at home. Most importantly, Japan in the 1870s was attempting to prove to the western powers that the treaty arrangements forced upon the country in the years 1854 to 1869 were unequal and unworthy of a country willing to accept westernisation as a goal. It did this in a number of ways. Major reforms were undertaken in Japan's domestic laws, to bring them into line with western practice. The Japanese adopted western clothes — which convinced the Koreans that they were now little better than pale imitations of their western mentors — and western practices, all in an attempt to reverse the unequal treaties. If Japan behaved like the western powers, so the thinking seemed to go, then Japan would be treated like one of them. The Japanese hoped that they would be seen as playing a similar role in Korea to that played by the west in China and Japan. They were careful to keep the western powers informed of their policy towards Korea, and to follow a similar pattern of treaty making as the western powers had done elsewhere in China and Japan. The treaty therefore granted the Japanese extra-territorial rights, and Japanese nationals were to be allowed to settle and trade at specially designated treaty ports. Because of the ambiguity of Korea's relationship with China, Korea's independence was specifically written into the treaty.

The old relationship with China thus appeared at an end; a sovereign state that could conclude a treaty could not at the same time be under the suzerainty of China. In fact, the Chinese and the Koreans continued to act as though the old arrangements still continued, with the Korean court turning to China for advice and assistance. That the Japanese did not accept this view was obvious from the 1876 treaty, but this was of little consequence to the Chinese, who set out to undermine the Japanese position by encouraging the Koreans to dilute the effect of the Japanese treaty by negotiating treaties with the western powers. Thus, from 1882 onwards, the Koreans signed treaties with the United States, Britain, France, Germany, and other countries. Here was an interesting mix of eastern and western diplomatic practice being used to outflank Japan.

The treaties brought mixed benefits to Korea. Trade remained minimal, the western merchants finding little in Korea to tempt them. The small-scale nature of local commerce, mainly dependent on the packhorse and the pedlar, promised few profits. Western trading houses such as Jardines, long established on the China coast and in Japan, tried the Korean market, but quickly withdrew. For Chinese and Japanese traders, however faced with fewer overheads, the new treaty framework that kept duties low and trade restrictions few proved a golden opportunity. By the 1890s, even trade in western goods such as matches and kerosene was wholly in the hands of Chinese and Japanese. Such westerners as did establish themselves as merchants generally traded on a small scale.

The treaties brought other changes. The Korean customs service, established as a branch of the foreign-dominated Chinese service, established new standards of administration. Under the Ulsterman, John McLeavy Brown, the customs provided a regular revenue for the government, and set in train a series of schemes to clean up and modernise Seoul. Under Japanese and western pressure, other economic changes were under way. A banking system was introduced in the 1870s, and a postal service in 1884. Goldmining began to use modern methods. At the end of the century, railways made their appearance. American Protestant missionaries arrived under treaty protection and introduced western-style schools and medicine. A number of Korea's present-day universities and medical schools can trace their origins to missionary enterprise in the years after 1882.

Korea in the late nineteenth century was in ferment. The ruling class was divided. A minority were eager to learn new ways, but the majority rejected all that was new. The first group tended to be pro-Japanese and, by extension, pro-western; the latter pro-Chinese. For a time the reformers were dominant. Fact-finding missions went to Japan, and modern scientific and military training began under both Chinese and Japanese auspices. Inevitably, these moves led to further factional fighting, which burst into open revolt in 1882. Tensions among various groups of soldiers in Seoul, in part caused by new methods, and in part by the grievances about not being paid on a regular basis, led to an attack on the Japanese mission in Seoul. The Taewŏn'gun seized the opportunity to regain power, hoping in the turmoil to destroy the Queen and her family's influence at court, which had supplanted his own. The Japanese minister, meanwhile, forced to fight his way out of the capital, returned with more troops, demanding compensation for the earlier attack.

At this point the Chinese decided that developments in Korea were becoming dangerous, and that they should take action. Basing their position on their 1871 treaty with Japan, under which the Chinese government had pledged to protect Japanese citizens in the Chinese empire — an interesting twist in the suzerainty question — they sent 2000 troops to Seoul to restore order. The Taewŏn'gun was removed to China and the rebellious troops disarmed, executed or dispersed. Peace was restored, but a dangerous precedent had been set.

For twelve years, from 1882 to 1894, Korea was under strong Chinese influence. Large numbers of Chinese troops remained in the country, and China played a major role in domestic and international affairs. When British naval forces occupied Kŏmun-do from 1885 to 1887, to counter an alleged Russian threat, it was the Chinese who conducted the negotiations leading to their withdrawal, with the Koreans barely consulted. It was perhaps not surprising, given Chinese predominance and Chinese conservatism, that to many Koreans reform or modernisation became firmly linked with the Japanese model, and it was those with ties to Japan who were the most fervent advocates of change. In December 1884 a group of them tried to stage a coup d'état on the occasion of the opening of a modern post office. They failed, despite Japanese assistance, and their failure and the Japanese involvement only served to increase Chinese influence. In the meantime, Japanese commercial interests continued to grow in Korea, thus increasing the importance the Japanese government attached to the peninsula. Since the Chinese, too, were important traders in Korea, here was another possible source of tension. At the same time, the consolidation of the Russian position in East Asia after 1860 brought a new dimension to East Asian strategic thinking. Russia now bordered Korea.

The Tonghak rebellion

In 1894 the tensions caused in Korea by domestic and external developments came together in a major outbreak of rebellion. The opening of the country to foreign trade seemed to bring little benefit to the Korean peasants. The more efficient Japanese destroyed both the Korean fishing industry and the small-scale coastal trade. The export of rice, provided for in the treaties, caused domestic hardship. Mass-produced Japanese goods were cheaper than hand-made domestic products, but their arrival put many artisans out of work. Attempts by local officials to stop the export trade, or to restrict imports, led to Japanese protests and appeals to the letter of the treaties. Discontent grew, fuelled by disquiet at the way the old customs were being abandoned. Modernisation demanded increased taxation, from a population already poor. There was a steady growth in banditry and minor local uprisings. Gradually, these coalesced in the south west into a revival of the Tonghak movement, which sought a vaguely-defined reform and the expulsion of foreigners, especially the Japanese. Out of office *yangban* allied themselves with the peasants and provided leadership and organisation. Beginning in February 1894 in Chŏlla, the rebellion quickly spread into the neighbouring provinces. By June 1894 the rebels were pressing on Seoul itself. The threat seemed so serious that the government turned to the Chinese for assistance, and the Chinese responded by assembling a fleet to send to Korea. It was a fateful move.

To the Japanese, this Chinese intervention in Korean affairs seemed a major threat to their own political and commercial interests. Japan by 1894 was far more confident than had been the case in 1873, or even in 1876 or 1882. The unequal treaties with western powers had been renegotiated. Japan had real and substantial interests in Korea, which were growing year by year, and were well worth defending. Japan's rulers, and even more Japanese on the ground in Korea, were in no mood to brook either Korean 'insolence' or Chinese claims to superiority. When informed of China's intentions, as required by agreement, the Japanese assembled their own forces for an expedition to Korea, though no Korean appeal had gone to them. Some attempt was made to engage in a joint Sino–Japanese reform programme in Korea, but the Japanese who mattered were not interested. The Korean government then announced that it had been able to cope with the rebellion itself and that there was therefore no need of any outside assistance. It was too late, for the Japanese government was now determined to assert full control over the peninsula and to oust the Chinese. In July 1894 the Japanese navy struck at the Chinese fleet without a formal declaration of war and full-scale hostilities began.

The Japanese victory was swift, despite widespread expectations to the contrary. In the process they destroyed the Tonghak movement as a political force. Defeat shattered Chinese prestige and ended their influence in Seoul. It also allowed the Japanese to begin empire-building in East Asia, with the acquisition of Taiwan in 1895.

The Japanese now controlled Korea. In order to give the appearance of legitimacy to their position, the Japanese chose as their front man their old enemy, the Taewŏn'gun, now brought out of retirement. (Before long, however, they dropped him, claiming that he had been stirring up anti-Japanese feeling.) A major series of government reforms was set in hand, designed in theory to bring Korean administration into line with the best modern practice, but in fact to ensure Japan's dominant role. The currency, long in chaos, was standardised. Slavery was ended, and other far-reaching social changes were introduced. Many of these were in line with what Korean reformers had been calling for, but the way in which the Japanese forced the pace of change was much disliked. Many of those who had welcomed the Japanese, including the King, now resented both their methods and their policies. Some began to intrigue with the Russians, hoping that the firm attitude Russia had shown towards Japanese acquisitions in China would be repeated in Korea. Prominent among the opposition to Japan's dominance were the Queen and her faction. The Japanese resolved to get rid of her, and in October 1895, she was murdered in the Kyŏngbok palace in Seoul. Japanese involvement in the Queen's murder was admitted privately although official responsibility was denied. The King was forced to downgrade his late wife's rank to the lowest level.

There was outrage in the country, which added to the turmoil already provoked by the continued reform programme. The Koreans were particularly incensed by an order that they should cut off their topknots. By early 1896 there were small scale revolts in many parts of the country, which the Japanese firmly suppressed.

The Japanese then suffered a setback, for the King escaped from the Kyŏngbok palace and took refuge in the Russian legation. Anti-Japanese feeling now reached a further peak. Those associated with the Japanese were attacked and a number, including the Prime Minister, were killed. Some of the reforms were rescinded.

The King remained in the Russian legation for over a year. During this time, Korea seemed to enter a new phase, with Japanese influence destroyed. There was a growing movement centred around the first Korean–American, Dr Philip Jaeson (Sŏ Chae-p'il), who had fled to the United States after the failure of the 1884 coup. He returned to Korea in 1896 and soon attracted a following among those who wished to see the country free of all foreign influence. In April 1896 he started to publish a bi-lingual newspaper, *The Independent*, using *han'gŭl*. A proposal in the paper that the old arch on the road north out of Seoul where the Chinese envoys had been greeted in the past should be replaced by an 'Independence Arch' was widely supported and the arch duly erected. (It still stands, on one of the main roads north out of Seoul.) This in turn led to the emergence of an 'Independence Association,' dedicated to the creation of an independent and modernised Korea, with democratic institutions. For a brief period even the government supported the Association.

One of the Association's principal aims was to persuade the King to leave the Russian legation, which he did in February 1897. He did not go back to the Kyŏngbok palace, with its unhappy associations, but moved into the Kyŏngun palace (now the Tŏksu palace) in the legation quarter. Here he could feel safe, especially as he had gates cut from the palace to the Russian, British, and American legations, in case he should need to flee again. In October 1897 King Kojong proclaimed himself the emperor of *Taehan Cheguk*, the empire of the Han people, and thus the co-equal of the emperors of China and Japan. Korean envoys were sent abroad, a flag adopted, and a national anthem commissioned. Worried by the Independence Association's attacks on all foreign influence, which seemed likely to invite the very attention it sought to avoid, the government banned the Association in 1898, but did not stop the reform programme, which was also designed to reduce opportunities for foreign interference. A new currency law, nominally putting Korea on the gold standard, was proclaimed in 1901. The same year saw the beginning of the Seoul–Pusan railway. Military reforms, long a preoccupation of the court, were again set in hand, so that by 1903, on paper at least, Korea had a modern army.

But the Korean empire's moment was shortlived. Although it was to survive in theory until 1910, its fate was sealed by the Russo–Japanese war of 1904–1905. Once again events outside Korea were to be more important in determining the Koreans' future than any wishes they might have.

Chapter Five

Korea under Japanese Rule, 1910–1945

The Japanese takeover

Despite occasional setbacks, such as followed the Queen's murder, the Japanese position in Korea was growing stronger. Their hold on the Korean economy, in particular, was steadily increasing. There were many Japanese, therefore, who were concerned that Russian influence, apparently so strong after 1896, might work against them. They were eager to see it curtailed. At the same time, strategic interests were beginning to play an important part in Japanese government thinking about Korea. Russia's steady consolidation of its Siberian and East Asian possessions was one factor in this. Another was growing Russo–Japanese rivalry in Manchuria, especially after the end of the Boxer rebellion in China in 1900. That event, and the international force sent to quell it, had left the Russians and the Japanese with large detachments of troops in north China, neither of which showed any intention of moving. The 1902 Anglo–Japanese alliance, drawn up with Russia in mind, gave the Japanese a powerful ally, and led them to seek a Russian acceptance of Japan's dominant position in Korea and the departure of the Russians from Manchuria. The Russians were willing to accept the former, although their military forces in Manchuria had allowed them to establish a strong position in the north of Korea, but they were unwilling to give up their position in Manchuria. The result was war in February 1904. The Japanese won, and Russian influence in Korea was destroyed until 1945.

The Korean government had declared its neutrality at the outset, but to little avail. The Japanese landed troops at Inch'ŏn, who promptly moved up to Seoul and established control over the government. 'To secure the safety and repose' of the Korean imperial family, the Japanese compelled the Korean government to agree to virtual freedom of movement for their forces in Korea. In August 1904 Korea's independence was further curtailed by an agreement under which Japan was to be consulted on all matters relating to foreign affairs. While the fighting with Russia continued, the Japanese obtained a series of further agreements that gave them control over most aspects of the Korean government. Some Koreans hoped that the treaties with the western powers signed in the 1880s would help them, but they were disappointed. Although in 1885 Britain had been prepared to occupy Korean territory to preserve Korean independence, by 1905 it needed Japan to preserve its position in East Asia, and was therefore willing to allow Japan a free hand in Korea. British officials had long since decided that Korea would never successfully reform itself and that some form of foreign guidance was necessary. In British eyes Japan was a better choice for this than Russia of China. The United States, too, once seen as the disinterested friend of Korea, had other concerns that made it acquiesce to Japan's policies in Korea.

Thus the Japan–Korea treaty of protection, signed in Seoul on 17 November 1905 and effectively implemented in February 1906 with the establishment of the Japanese Residency–General, drew no international objections. Within Korea it was very different. A number of prominent officials committed suicide. The Emperor made it known that the treaty had been signed under duress, and belatedly sought outside support. A number of foreign residents rallied to the cause of Korean independence. Many Koreans fled, either because they feared they would be imprisoned or, especially among the poorer, because they had lost land and possessions to the Japanese. Throughout the country there emerged 'Righteous Armies,' who fought the Japanese. Some of these were drawn from the old Korean army, disbanded on Japanese orders in 1907; others came from the tradition of the peasant uprisings of the past. Contemporary photographs show ragged groups, dressed in a motley mixture of eastern and western uniforms. Many operated from remote Buddhist temples, deep in the mountains, while some struck at the Japanese from bases established in north east China. Exact details of these forces will probably never be known, but Japanese police records noted 1451 incidents in 1908, involving some 70,000 men. By 1910, the number of incidents had dropped to 147, involving some 1900 men. Korean opposition was not confined to these desperate groups. In 1907 Emperor Kojong made another attempt to attract world attention to the plight of Korea by sending a group secretly to the International Peace Conference at The Hague to plead Korea's cause, but without success. Denied a hearing, one of the group, Yi Chun, joined the growing list of suicides. Other Koreans took violent action abroad. In California in March 1908, two Koreans assassinated D. W. Stevens, a former Japanese-nominated adviser to the Korean Foreign Office.

The Japanese response to all these moves was repression. The first Resident–General was the veteran Japanese statesman Itō Hirobumi (1841–1909), who may have meant well by the Koreans, but who was in no position to restrain his fellow countrymen, who saw Korea as ripe for plucking. Even Itō regarded Korean opposition as treason, to be dealt with firmly. Large numbers of troops and gendarmes were drafted to Korea from 1905 onwards and Japanese rule was enforced with brutal firmness. The Japanese authorities published, apparently with pride, pictures of Korean peasants being executed by firing squads for resisting the takeover of their land. Other pictures also appeared, without Japanese approval, of Koreans being tortured in Japanese prisons. Kojong's attempt to have Korea's case heard at The Hague led to pressure on him to abdicate in favour of his son, Sunjong, in 1907.

Since continued Korean opposition seemed likely as long as the concept of a separate Korean state continued, a growing number of Japanese argued for the annexation of the country. In this they were supported by a Korean pro-Japanese and nominally reform-minded group known as the *ilchinhoe*. The decision to annex seems to have been taken in July 1909, and any Japanese doubts were removed by the assassination of Itō by a Korean at Harbin railway station in October 1909. In August 1910 the Korean Prime Minister, head of but a shadow government, signed the treaty of annexation. Although the Korean government was not formally dissolved until October 1910, old Korea came to an end on 29 August 1910, when the last Korean imperial ordinance proclaimed the annexation treaty. The empire of Korea was replaced by Japan's new territory, to be known again by the old name, Chosŏn, or *Chōsen* in Japanese.

All political organisations were banned, including the *ilchinhoe*. In November 1910 the Japanese announced that opposition had ceased throughout the country.

The Japanese administration

The Japanese set about the task of governing their new colony with great self-confidence. The Director of Foreign Affairs of the newly-established government–general told a meeting of the Korea Branch of the Royal Asiatic Society in 1911, 'Japan has now made the country an integral part of her dominion and has set upon herself the work not of improvement but of rejuvenescence of the territory.' The Japanese were comparative newcomers to the colonial field, having acquired their first colony, Taiwan, only in 1895. Their experience there coloured their approach to Korea, for while they had been faced with considerable opposition to their rule, this had come either from a largely unsophisticated population with little cultural background of its own or from illiterate tribal peoples. They were not prepared to make any concession to Korea's cultural inheritance or tradition of independence. Whatever the cause of opposition, it had to be firmly put down. Local culture and language might, just, be a curiosity, but it could in no way match Japan's superior culture and should be repressed.

This determination was reinforced by Japan's own growing self-assertion. In spite of all predictions to the contrary, the Japanese by 1910 had successively defeated China, the great repository of East Asian tradition, and Russia, a major world power. They had, alone of all the countries in the world subject to 'unequal treaties,' overcome the stigma that had denied them complete jurisdiction and tariff autonomy. These factors, taken with a belief in Japan's divine mission — in itself a product of a combination of Japan's military and diplomatic successes and Japanese legends about the divine origin of the imperial line — meant that the Japanese approach to governing Korea was little tempered with liberalism. Korea was there to be exploited for the good of Japan. In the process Koreans might benefit, but that was a secondary matter. The apparent indifference of countries such as Britain and the United States, whose

earlier attitudes towards Korea might have led them to take an interest in Japan's policies, only added to the Japanese conviction that
what they were doing was right. The apparent excesses of the 1905–
1910 period were excused or glossed over as a necessary preliminary
to the establishment of a proper government in Korea. A few challenged this bland explanation, but they were not powerful voices
and were largely ignored.

If the period from 1904-5 to 1910 was the period of establishing
control, that from 1910 to 1919 was one of restructuring the Korean
economy and social system. The Japanese erected a powerful
bureaucratic machine, efficiently staffed. At the top was the
Governor-General, always a military officer. In all, seven generals
and one admiral governed Korea in the years 1910 to 1945. The
Governor-General was the chief executive and commander-in-chief.
He could issue decrees and appoint judges and provincial governors. He ran an administration that was more powerful than any
Japanese home minister, for he was, in theory, answerable only to
the emperor, since the 1910 treaty had been one between equal
sovereigns. Below the Governor-General was a dual system, involving Japanese and Koreans. The senior posts were for all practical
purposes a Japanese monopoly, and such Korean officials as were
appointed tended to occupy the lowest rungs of the ladder. Even
where there was in theory equal ranking, salaries for Korean officials
were lower than those for Japanese.

At the same time as the governor-general acted without control
from Tokyo, he was equally unchecked locally. A central council
was established in 1910, composed of Koreans of 'ability and reputation,' to advise the Governor-General, but it was left to the latter to
decide on what matters he wished to consult it and consultation normally only took place on matters relating to Korean custom and
practice. There were also local provincial councils from 1920. They
were at first composed of appointees, but elections were introduced
in the early 1930s. This made little difference. The composition of
the councils was biased towards Japanese representation, with a
high proportion of seats allocated to the urban areas where the
Japanese were concentrated. To make sure of inbuilt control, the
provincial governors could also nominate non-elected members to
sit on the councils. In any case, power remained firmly in the hands
of the appointed provincial governors, who were also the chairmen
of the local councils.

Probably the feature of Japanese rule that affected most Koreans was the large police force, which was supplemented by a separately-organised gendarmerie until 1919. Although the armed resistance that had marked the years after 1910 had largely disappeared by 1911–1912, the police force continued to expand all through the colonial period. In 1910 the total force, including gendarmes, was some 7700. By 1918 it had reached over 14,000. By 1930, over ten years after the abolition of the gendarmerie, it was just under 19,000, and by 1937 it was approaching 21,000. From 1937 onwards the picture is less clear, as Japan and Korea moved more and more on to a war footing, but police numbers continued to increase. In 1922 there was one policeman for every 800 inhabitants of Korea. By the early 1930s there was one policeman for every 400. As the police force grew, so the percentage of Korean to Japanese members in it dropped. It remained at about 57 percent during the first ten years of Japanese rule, but after the events of 1919 it fell steadily. By 1930 just under 40 percent of the police force was Korean. By the late 1930s the colonial authorities had ceased to list the Japanese and Koreans separately, but there is no reason to believe that the general picture changed. Senior ranks were entirely Japanese.

The police force was important not just as a sign of colonial power, but also because it could and did exercise summary juris-diction. In the early years of colonial rule, this allowed the police to flog or fine for 'minor' offences. Flogging, justified by the Japanese on the grounds that it was a 'traditional' Korean punishment, was widely used by the police. Virtually all those who were accused of political offences were so treated, for example. The practice became less widespread after international outrage as the extent of arbitrary flogging was revealed in 1919. Thereafter, police powers to fine or imprison for an ever-lengthening list of offences became the more usual exercise of summary powers. Often the misdemeanours for which these penalties were imposed included infringement of the many administrative rules issued by the Government-General. Pen-alties appear to have been much heavier than for the corresponding offences in Japan. Since Koreans generally were much poorer than Japanese, this put a powerful weapon in the hands of the police. In theory there was a system of appeals, but since an appeal lay on a Japanese policeman's decision to a Japanese court, and since any court appeal was likely to be expensive, few bothered. Even those sympathetic to Japan drew the line at the Japanese police system in

Korea. One such, the former British consular officer Joseph Longford, writing in 1923, described the lower-grade Japanese civil servants and police in Korea as being not 'wholly free from the Prussian spirit,' and that they believed that 'no matter what they do, they can never be wrong.' The result of this 'orgy of tyranny' was that Korea was 'now the Ireland of Japan.'

Economic and social development

Major economic and social changes took place under the Japanese, continuing and extending developments that had begun in the last years of the nineteenth century and that reached a peak in the years from 1904 to 1910. The banking system was consolidated, and the vagaries of the old Korean currency came to an end. Large-scale exploitation of Korea's natural resources and the development of both light and heavy industry were put in hand. An economic division emerged between the north and south of the peninsula, with mining and heavy industry concentrated in the north, while the economy of the south continued to be mainly an agricultural one, though there was also some light industry. A major programme of land registration was carried out from 1912 to 1918, echoing the practice of all new rulers in Korea. The Japanese were more efficient than their predecessors, and the new registration provided the basis for the main source of colonial revenue. Taxes were more regularly collected, which in turn provided the incentive for landholders, whether Korean or Japanese, to make more efficient use of the land. Much Japanese effort up to 1939 went into improving Korean agriculture, and the Korean chemical fertiliser industry dates from this period. The main beneficiaries of this policy were not the Koreans, whose rice consumption actually fell, but the Japanese home islands. Korean rice went to feed the Japanese, who flocked to the cities of Japan as a major industrial revolution got under way.

After the 1929 slump, when Japan's agricultural production became less export-oriented and available for home consumption, the colonial authorities in Korea encouraged both the Japanese settlers and the Koreans to begin moving out of agriculture into the production of raw materials and semi-finished goods to help Japanese industrial production. There was also some development of small-scale consumer industries, such as textiles, designed to take pressure from Japan. In this process, as in agricultural development earlier, there was some spin-off for Koreans, but the main interest of the colonial power was in the benefit for Japan.

The same was true of all other aspects of development. New roads and railways were built, hydro-electric schemes developed, and in many parts of the country, new towns established. Among modern Korean cities, Taejŏn, Chinhae and Mokp'o are Japanese creations. Existing cities were transformed, especially in the centres and in those areas where most Japanese lived. Seoul became a modern city, with fine if recognisably 'colonial' buildings, and broad boulevards. Streets were kept clean and sewers functioned. But since much of this economic activity was linked to Japan's needs, it had some lop-sided results. Commercial and industrial development was concentrated in those areas closest to Japan. Communications were designed less to improve links between the various parts of Korea than to connect Korea with Japan; or, as the Japanese advanced into Manchuria, with Japanese possessions in China. The result was a distortion that has persisted to this day.

In other areas, too, development under the Japanese led to distortions. The education system provides a good example of this, since it reflects clearly Japanese attitudes towards Koreans. Education in Japan had received a high priority from the Meiji reformers. They had seen the promotion of a comprehensive modern educational system as one of the keys to transforming Japan and they had introduced western-style education, mainly modelled on the German system, to Japan. Primary education was compulsory and attendance was enforced. A comprehensive system of technical schools and modern universities was introduced. In the early years the emphasis was very much on acquiring technical skills, especially foreign languages and military sciences. As time passed, however, equal importance was given to training the minds of those who would be the administrators and functionaries of the Japanese state and its colonial possessions. Scholarships enabled the brightest to benefit. None of this operated in a vacuum. Education was designed to make good citizens of the Japanese empire, accepting the state and the imperial system. It was highly central-ised, with administrative control exercised by the Ministry of Education over the curriculum, appointments, and many other matters.

Much of this was superficially reflected in Korea. The colonial education system in theory provided for six years of primary school, followed by six years of secondary school and four years of college. There were new schools at all levels, including many technical schools, and from 1923 a university in Seoul, similar to the existing Japanese imperial universities. The main beneficiaries of this system were not the Koreans but the children of expatriate Japanese. For the Koreans, the Japanese envisaged an educational system that would, in the words of the Japanese-owned Bank of Chōsen in one of its publications, 'make them economically useful.' The Koreans were to learn practical skills in vocational schools, if they were to learn anything at all; in practice, periods of schooling for Korean students were shorter than those for Japanese until 1922 and the authorities saw no need to enforce school attendance.

Although the proportion of Japanese to Koreans in Korea was small, the proportion of Japanese receiving education at any level was much greater than that of Koreans. In 1939, at what was in effect the height of Korean advance under the Japanese, even if few realised it, 58 Koreans per 1000 were in some form of education; for Japanese in Korea, the figure was 195.9 per 1000. (These figures hide another discrimination: even in primary schools, there were three times as many boys as girls; while at the higher levels, there were up to five times as many boys in colleges or teacher-training establishments in 1939 as there were girls. Girls were not allowed at all in the state-run university. The pattern was similar to that in Japan, though more extreme.) Until the later 1930s, Koreans attended separate schools from the Japanese, and the Japanese schools were much better equipped. Less than 13 percent of Korean children eligible for primary education were at school in 1930. By 1942, the figure had improved, to around 40 percent, but still fell far behind either Japanese in Korea or in Japan proper, where there had been compulsory school attendance since the 1870s. Instruction in all schools, whether government, private, or missionary, was required to be in Japanese, and Korean language, history and culture received little emphasis. Korean levels of literacy remained very low; after 35 years of Japanese rule, in 1945 only 22 percent of adults were literate in Korean or Japanese. When turned into figures reflecting employment, this meant that the 1940 census showed only one quarter of the technical, professional, or managerial positions in

Korea occupied by Koreans. Higher education was severely restricted. Keijō (the Japanese name for Seoul) Imperial University, the only state university in Korea and the forerunner of Seoul National University, limited Koreans to 40 percent of the total intake. Private universities, such as Chosŏn Christian College, now Yŏnsei university, provided an alternative channel of advance, and a small number of Koreans studied abroad.

The same pattern was repeated in all fields. Whatever the resource, whether it was a hospital, a library, or a cinema, the Koreans lost out to the Japanese. Here again, as in education, the efforts of foreign missionaries sometimes remedied the defects, whether through large hospitals, such as the Severance Hospital in Seoul, or the small clinics that the Anglican church organised in some rural areas. Such measures helped, but they did not deal with the basic injustice of the system. Despite early commitments to preserve Korea's distinctiveness, the practice was rather a determined attempt to change Korea. Korea's archeological heritage, for example, received much attention from the Japanese, but often the purpose was to prove that there were long-standing political and cultural links between the two countries. The Korean language was disregarded. After 1919 a Korean press was tolerated but never favoured. During the 1920s, the main newspapers were regularly suspended. The 1930s saw a more tolerant approach, largely because the newspapers themselves avoided controversy. In 1940 all Korean language newspapers were closed down.

Japanese influence was of course not wholly negative. It benefited all when marsh land was drained, or other health measures were taken. It was clearly better to enforce the use of cemeteries than to allow those killed by epidemics to lie unburied. The new railways and roads made travel easier for Koreans as well as Japanese. The Koreans did learn about modern administration and how to run industries. New concepts in literature and art were introduced, sometimes directly from Japan, sometimes from the west via Japan.

As Japan moved steadily on to a war footing after the outbreak of hostilities in China in 1937, so the situation in Korea deteriorated. The Korean economy was more and more geared to supporting the Japanese war effort. Students were compelled to join various 'volunteer' corps, for example, and eventually all students were ordered to wear khaki uniforms. Women were registered for road repair work and other heavy tasks. The Japanese became steadily less tolerant of any signs of deviance from the Japanese norm. The colonial pressure was deliberately stepped up, to make the Koreans into Japanese. Now Korean children were at last educated alongside Japanese and followed the same curriculum. The study of Korean was abandoned in schools, and before long the Korean language and the use of Korean names was banned. All were expected to learn Japanese and the penalties for not using it became increasingly severe. It was not only the Japanese language that was forced on the Koreans. From 1936 onwards pressure was applied to make Koreans take part in Japanese *shintō* ceremonies, to prove loyalty to the emperor. It was an issue that put many under severe strain, and led to splits among Korean Christians on how to deal with those who participated in such ceremonies (see Chapter 11). As the war progressed, many Koreans were pressed into service for work in Japan and elsewhere in the Japanese empire to release manpower for the armed forces. In addition, some Koreans were able to join the Japanese military, and a small number became officers, among them the future President Park Chung Hee.

Korean resistance

The long Korean tradition of accepting oppression passively helped the Japanese to impose their rule. But the heavy-handed nature of the colonial government proved too much for many Koreans. Large numbers fled the country before 1910, including remnants of the disbanded Korean army. Many settled in Manchuria or the Russian far east, joining already-established Korean communities. This exodus continued after 1910. The land tax system in particular led many to abandon Korea, since they were unwilling or unable to comply with the new rules. Some of the earlier reformers, joined by new arrivals escaping from the colonial regime, settled in places like Hawaii or Shanghai, where they attempted to organise opposition to the Japanese. Like all such exile groups, they were much given to infighting, to which they added a peculiarly Korean dimension in the form of incessant factionalism. Many Koreans gathered in Tokyo, There the discrimination practised against them at home was absent and the opportunities for advance, especially in the field of education, were much greater. A number of Korean students in Tokyo drew up their own declaration of independence in February 1919, which foreshadowed and indeed encouraged the much bigger uprising and declaration of independence in Seoul a few weeks later.

Many of these small bands of exiles schemed for the end of the colonial regime. From Manchuria, raiding parties crossed the frontier and fired on police stations. Some were communists but others were nationalists, more interested in Korea's independence than its ultimate social structure. After the Japanese takeover of Manchuria and the establishment of the puppet state of 'Manchukuo' in the 1930s, these groups came under increasing Japanese military pressure. Some moved into China proper, joining up with the nationalists or the Chinese communists. Others were forced into the Soviet Union, especially during a major Japanese campaign in 1940–1941.

The Japanese professed to see plots everywhere, a position that rested somewhat uneasily with the oft-repeated claim that the majority of Koreans accepted the new order. Right at the outset of the colonial period, the Japanese brought to trial over 100 Koreans who were allegedly members of a group called *shinmin-hoe* ('New People's Association'). According to the indictments brought against this group, they had organised the *shinmin-hoe* as early as 1905 in order to assassinate Japanese officials. Following the annexation, they decided to assassinate the Governor General. Whatever the Japanese intention was in staging this trial, it backfired. Although six of the accused were sentenced to various periods in prison, few were convinced that those charged were really guilty. The evidence was poor, wild accusations were made about foreigners being involved, especially missionaries, and many of the accused claimed to have been beaten or otherwise tortured. The Japanese authorities refused to back down, but a few years later the six were quietly released. If the *shinmin-hoe* trial was meant to deter Koreans from opposing the new regime, it failed. All through the colonial years the Japanese regularly uncovered groups of Koreans organising to restore their country's independence. Such groups were harshly dealt with, but others always took their place.

Most of the resistance activities within and without Korea did not pose any real threat to Japanese rule, and later rhetoric notwithstanding, were unimportant to the Japanese. The events of March 1919 could not be ignored in the same way. The First World War made little direct impression on Korea. News of the peace-making process did have an impact. Korean exiles in the United States made an unsuccessful attempt to attend the proposed Peace Conference, rather as some had tried to attend the 1907 Hague Conference. Korean students in Japan saw the end of the war as a possible way of focusing world attention on their country's plight, believing that President Wilson's principle of self-determination should apply to Korea along with other small nations. Within Korea, news of the Peace Conference and of the activities of the exiles coincided with an air of unsettlement following the death of the former Emperor Kojong in January 1919. Two days before his funeral, fixed for 3 March, a group gathered in a Seoul restaurant. They had drawn up a 'Declaration of Independence,' which they proceeded to read out in Seoul's Pagoda Park. The group's motives were mixed. Most sought a peaceful demonstration, to attract world attention. Although the occasion of their protest was linked through the Emperor's funeral to the old order, they could be seen as representing a new Korea; none of the signatories came from the old ruling class, for example. What they unleashed was the pent-up bitterness of the Koreans, who came out in their thousands up and down the country, denouncing Japanese rule and calling for independence. The March First (*sam-il* in Korean) movement was under way.

The Japanese reaction was swift and typical. There was some Korean violence as the movement spread, and this was used to justify Japanese actions. The demonstrations were suppressed with a savagery sufficient to attract outside condemnation and to force the Tokyo government to intervene. Once the *samil* movement had been suppressed, the Japanese authorities moved to remedy some of the grievances of the Koreans. The gendarmerie was disbanded, though the police force was increased. Measures were adopted to increase educational opportunities for Koreans. The publication of vernacular newspapers, forbidden since 1910 except for one government-owned paper, was permitted. As a result, both the *Dong-A Ilbo* and the *Chosun Ilbo*, still two of the principal South Korean newspapers, first appeared in 1920.

These moves did not go far enough for many Koreans. One exile group in Shanghai proclaimed Korea's independence and in April 1919 appointed a government. Its head was Syngman Rhee (Yi Seung-mun), who had suffered imprisonment in the last years of independent Korea. He had subsequently left for the United States, where he had studied for a Ph D and had become a prominent member of the Korean exile community. In Manchuria the events of 1919 led others to step up armed resistance to the Japanese.Within Korea the events of 1919 made a lasting impression.There were later demonstrations, such as that by students in the southern town of Kwangju in 1929, which served to keep alive the Korean sense of grievance, though none reached the intensity of 1 March 1919.

By 1945 the war had taken its toll of Korea as it had of Japan proper. The demands for increased production, especially of food, to meet Japan's war needs put a severe strain on the Korean economy. Machinery was worked flat out, with little chance of repair. The newly-planted forests of which the Japanese had been most proud had largely gone for fuel. Even the wooden seats from the Seoul tramcars had been taken for the same purpose. Some Koreans had volunteered for military service. Many of those who had not done so had been conscripted for the military or for war work. By 1945 few could escape the demands of the Japanese military machine. By then, however, many Koreans realised that Japan could not win. Now hope began to emerge that Japan's defeat would lead to the restoration of Korea's independence.

The colonial period in retrospect

The colonial period is one of the most difficult of all periods to handle for the people of South Korea. It is still part of the recent experience of many. Most Koreans, even those who have lived and worked abroad, remain remarkably Korean-centred, and are unaware of other peoples' experiences of colonialism. Korea's experience is seen as somehow 'unique,' and its past sorrows and current difficulties in coming to terms with what happened under colonialism as somehow much greater than those of other colonial peoples. The knowledge that Korea lost its independence partly because of the actions of some Koreans is a matter of bitterness, yet it has to be faced. So, too, does the fact that, after 1910 and after the failure of the 1919 protests, many Koreans assumed the Japanese were there for the foreseeable future, and, whatever views they held about the rights and wrongs of this, it was better to work with the system than against it. But while organising Korean businesses or Korean schools and universities could be seen as upholding Korean values or providing opportunities for Koreans that would otherwise be denied, it could also be presented as collaborating with the hated colonial oppressors. Those who joined the Japanese police or the Japanese military pose a special problem. That some Koreans went so far as to praise the Japanese and to express contempt for Korea and Korean culture is only now being examined, albeit in terms of the 'literature of national betrayal.' The fact that not everything the colonial regime did was entirely bad also taxes Koreans, some of whom will deny the benefits of new roads or railway building because these were carried out by the Japanese. Others, too, find a problem in the survival of many Japanese practices in the life and work of contemporary South Korea; and indeed, though sometimes more disguised, in what we see of North Korea. These are often very obvious to the outsider who has lived or worked in Japan, but are denied, sometimes vehemently, by many Koreans — though less so by those who have themselves spent some time in Japan. The fact that Korea gained its liberation from Japan in 1945 at the hands of outside forces rather than by the efforts of the Koreans themselves has added to the difficulties of coming to terms with the colonial period. These are all painful subjects, not easily aired, especially by outsiders. But even at the most difficult periods in recent history, there have always been some Koreans who have tried to look at these issues. As time passes, and those with direct experience of the colonial past disappear, so more Korean scholars will try to assess the recent past in discussion terms.

Section Three

Development since 1945

Even the Diamond Mountain must be seen on a full stomach

Chapter Six

War and Politics

The emergence of separate regimes 1945–1948

The sudden arrival of liberation in August 1945 led to turmoil in Korea and among Koreans abroad. The Japanese gone, it was assumed an independent Korean state would soon be re-established. In the peninsula itself, at least sixty political parties had been formed by November 1945. Koreans soon knew that Japanese forces would surrender either to Soviet or American troops, and that the 1943 Cairo Declaration had said that Korea 'would in due course be independent.' Most Koreans probably thought that this meant Korean independence once the war was over. By early September, a 'People's Republic of Korea' had been proclaimed in Seoul by the Korean National Foundation Preparatory Committee. But already this group had ceased to function north of the 38th parallel, and the proposed president of the new 'republic,' the veteran exile Syngman Rhee, turned down the nomination.

Before 1945, the allies had given little thought to Korea. At Cairo, the main concern had been to punish Japan by destroying the empire created since 1895. It was not clear what would happen to Japanese territories, and the British were concerned about precedents for the independence of colonial territories. Some post-war planning on Korea was carried out in the United States' State Department and in the British Foreign Office. It was hampered by lack of material, and tended to reach the convenient conclusion that Korea was not yet ready for independence. The speed of the

Japanese collapse caught the allies by surprise, and disrupted whatever thoughts they had about the orderly occupation of Korea. In addition, by August 1945 other considerations were at work. American suspicions of the Soviet Union grew fast at the end of the war, and American planners were thinking of how to limit Soviet influence in the world. It was against this background that Korea was divided at the 38th parallel to effect the surrender of Japanese forces. The Americans eventually settled on the 38th parallel because it placed the capital in their area and it was the furthest north they could expect the Russians to accept.

When American troops landed at Inch'ŏn in September 1945 they were ill-prepared for their task. There had been little time to select staff or prepare proper briefings. Faced with the huge political ferment, with seemingly left-wing groups clamouring for power and with memories of claims about the readiness of Koreans for self-government, General Hodge and his men opted for the continuation of law and order. To the fury of many Koreans, they were pushed aside and the Japanese retained in authority. Indeed, there was a tendency to treat Koreans as defeated enemies rather than new allies. The Japanese were not used for long, but the American occupation had got off to a bad start.

From the Korean point of view, matters worsened. The Japanese were replaced by an American military government, and the Koreans learnt that 'in due course' meant a period of trusteeship. In December 1945 the USSR, the USA, and Britain signed the Moscow agreement, to which China would later adhere, which provided for a five-year trusteeship. A joint USSR–US commission would work with Korean democratic parties and organisations to establish a provisional government. Even before the Moscow declaration, Koreans north and south of the 38th parallel were protesting at the denial of their claim to govern themselves. All the major political groups north and south now opposed the Moscow proposals and the end of the year saw massive demonstrations throughout the peninsula. Opposition in the north quickly ended (see Chapter 14); in the south it continued, to no avail.

The USSR—US joint commission met in Seoul in March 1946. It was to function spasmodically until adjourned *sine die* in October 1947. By then, any hope of cooperation had ceased and two distinct entities were emerging north and south of the 38th parallel. There were many reasons for the failure of the joint commission, some local, some international. The Russians would only allow organisations that had not opposed trusteeship to be consulted over the provisional government. The Americans resisted this, since only leftist groups susceptible to Soviet influence adopted this stand. Fundamentally, however, the division of Korea was institutionalised because of growing Soviet-US tensions worldwide rather than because of any real consideration of Korea. Once again, the big powers disposed of Korea for their own purposes.

In September 1947 the United States referred the question of Korea to the United Nations General Assembly, confident of being able to influence that body towards the solution it favoured in Korea. This proved to be the case. In spite of Soviet objections, the General Assembly passed two resolutions on 14 November 1947 that called for the participation of the Korean people in the political process; for the swift independence of Korea and the withdrawal of occupying forces; and for free and independent elections. It appointed a United Nations' temporary commission to carry out these terms and to oversee the elections. Although the Soviet Union and its supporters did not vote against the resolutions, their clear opposition made it unlikely that they would allow the commission to operate north of the parallel.

This proved to be the case. The May 1948 elections only took place in the south, though a hundred seats were reserved for the north. The new assembly held its first session on 31 May 1948, adopted the name *Taehan Minguk* (Republic of Korea) and drew up a constitution, proclaimed on 17 July. The assembly came near to adopting a parliamentary system of government, but opted instead for a presidential system based on the American model. On 15 August 1948 the Republic of Korea (ROK) became independent. The move was condemned by the Soviet Union and the North Koreans, and in September 1948 the Democratic People's Republic of Korea (DPRK) was established, also claiming to represent the whole country. In December 1948 the United Nations General Assembly passed a further resolution, again at US prompting, by which the ROK was recognised as the only legitimate government on the Korean peninsula. A further resolution set up a new UN commission to promote the unification of Korea. From January 1949 the US and its allies began to establish diplomatic relations with the ROK, while the Russians and their allies did so with the DPRK.

Characteristics of the South Korean state

The southern half of Korea was probably more conservative than
the north by the middle of the twentieth century. Most big landlords' holdings were in the south. Seoul, the capital, had long been
the focus of those seeking power. By and large those who had
gravitated towards the centre under the Japanese had been those
least in favour of change. They might not have liked the Japanese
system, but for most it was a regime with which they could work and
from which some at least benefited.

By 1945 the reputation of the Soviet Union was such that none of
these people would have contemplated going north to live under a
Soviet-organised system. In the north those of a similar conservative
cast made the related decision, and fled south. Their experiences
and fears helped to reinforce anti-communist sentiment south of the
parallel. Before the end of 1945, the conservatives were well-
established south of the 38th parallel. Their numbers steadily
increased in the next five years. From 1945 to 1947, there was movement across the parallel, sometimes open and sometimes in secret.
The majority of southern radicals moved north, either because they
preferred the society that was emerging there, or because the pressures in the south were too great. Each uprising and rebellion in the
south saw a trickle of survivors to the north. Land reform and other
changes in the north, including the attacks on religious leaders and
office holders under the Japanese, pushed more and more to the
south. It is difficult to give exact numbers because there were further
movements during the Korean War, but some one and three
quarter million people appear to have travelled south by 1950;
figures for those who went north are less easy to obtain, but no
source suggests that there were more than a few thousand.

The Americans did not set out to create a conservative state in
Korea south of the parallel. During the war policymakers in
Washington had kept at arm's length the various Korean exile
groups and leaders who demanded a voice in Korea's future. Even
after August 1945 American planners had not wanted Dr Syngman
Rhee in Korea at all. But as the division of the country forced them
to look to the question of government in the south, so they came to
favour the conservative groups. It was a shift that seemed natural in
the context of the mid-1940s, with the disappearance of the mild

leftish euphoria of the New Deal and of wartime enthusiasm for the Soviet Union.

Since the Americans tended to work with what was there already, the state that emerged in August 1948 bore many of the characteristics of that which it replaced. It was highly authoritarian and highly centralised. The power of the police was very great, as was that of the bureaucrats. The state expected to take decisions and did so with the minimum of consultation. Opposition, even to draw attention to legitimate grievances, was seen as akin to treason, especially since it could be increasingly linked with the North Koreans and communism.

By 1948 the kingpin in this system was Syngman Rhee. He had lived abroad for many years, learnt much about political infighting and scarcely anything about democracy. He believed that his anti-Japanese record and his links to the 1919 'Korean Republic' gave him political legitimacy beyond mere votes. While he remained publicly pledged to a unified Korea, he indicated early on that he would be willing to head a state based only in the south. As problems grew with the Russians, this willingness to compromise made him more acceptable to the American Military Government and Washington than other conservative leaders such as Kim Ku or Kim Kyu-sik, whose claims to legitimacy also went back to the 1919 Shanghai government, but who argued for national unity above all else, and who were willing to talk with the North Koreans right up to 1948. As well as establishing his position with the Americans, Rhee devoted much energy to organising a power base within South Korea, built on the police and on quasi-legal para-military bodies. His style was authoritarian, brooking no opposition. Partly this was temperament, perhaps made more extreme by old age and the respect accorded to one with a long revolutionary tradition; partly it was the old Korean political tradition, from which Rhee came, reasserting itself.

The Korean War

The 'origins of the Korean War' is a subject that has produced many books and much debate. Some see the war solely as a product of international tensions in the period 1945 to 1950. In this interpretation, Korea and the Korean people figure as surrogates for the Soviet Union and its satellite, communist China, on the one hand, and the United States, as the vanguard of the capitalist world, on the other. The other view sees the Korean War as a further stage in a Korean struggle between the forces of reaction and those of reform, unleashed at liberation, and interrupted in 1945 by the division of the peninsula. The result of that division was to turn the north into a bastion of reform, and the south into one of reaction, challenged by frequent uprisings and rebellions, which indicated that the majority of the people sought change. In this interpretation, the war was a civil war, as the reform-oriented north tried to aid the dispossessed in the south and at the same time undo the division of the peninsula.

The emergence of separate regimes in Korea was followed by the withdrawal of first Soviet and then US military forces from the peninsula. Both left behind embryonic armed forces and military advisors. The Soviet forces appear to have gone further in organising the North Korean military than the Americans did in the south, and certainly left more and better equipment. With the return of battle-hardened veterans from the guerilla groups in China, the North Koreans had a basic corps of officers and NCOs. The numbers of these increased rapidly as the Chinese civil war came to an end in 1949. In South Korea there was a small trickle of soldiers returning after service with Chinese or Japanese forces, but nowhere near the numbers who went to North Korea. There was much talk of reunification, by force if necessary, on both sides.

There was much social unrest in the Republic of Korea after the establishment of the new state. Some of it was minor, involving small groups in sporadic local unrest. There were also major incidents, such as a mutiny in Cheju island in early October 1948, and a more serious outbreak at Yŏsu and Sunch'ŏn later the same month. The following year there were further signs of unrest, with the assassination of Kim Ku in June, and more military mutinies in the autumn. Communist and left-wing parties were outlawed in August 1949, and arrests and executions of many alleged communists followed. In May 1950 President Rhee's nominee for prime minister was rejected by the National Assembly, and the general election the following month saw a major setback for Rhee's party. To the North Koreans, it may well have seemed that a regime in the last throes of its existence was lashing out at the forces of 'progress'

President Rhee's government. But there was also a widespread feeling that whatever the faults of the ROK government, they did not justify North Korea's actions.

By early August 1950 the effective territory of the Republic of Korea had been reduced to the region around Pusan. Within the areas occupied by North Korean forces, some attempt was already under way to repeat the social revolution that had taken place in the north. Many deemed collaborators or class enemies were killed. In Pusan, President Rhee and his supporters were concerned as much with their own political position as with fighting the North Koreans. The UN forces, at first mainly American and such ROK units as could be regrouped, but gradually supplemented by other arrivals, were dispirited and unwilling to break out of the 'Pusan perimeter.' Then in early September General MacArthur, the UN commander, launched an attack behind North Korean lines at the west coast port of Inch'ŏn.

The tide now turned with a vengeance. With superior equipment and elated by Inch'ŏn, the UN forces broke out from the Pusan perimeter and fought their way north. Seoul was re-taken on 28 September 1950, and Rhee announced the crossing of the parallel the same day. Although there were some doubts expressed about the wisdom of this move, since the People's Republic of China had warned against such a development, these were swept aside. The UN General Assembly on 7 October approved the crossing of the parallel and set up a Commission for the Unification and Rehabilitation of Korea. Rather than returning to the position of 25 June, the UN forces now seemed committed to the forcible reunification of Korea, something that they had not allowed the North Koreans to do, and about which the Chinese were passing increasingly serious warnings.

On 19 October UN forces entered P'yŏngyang and pressed on towards the Yalu. ROK troops reached the river on 26 October, with other UN forces not far behind. They soon encountered Chinese patrols, followed by growing signs of Chinese intervention in large numbers. By the end of the year the high hopes of September were gone, as Chinese 'volunteers' and North Korean units pushed the UN forces south. The UN advance deteriorated into a 'bug-out,' with men fleeing as fast as they could, discarding weapons and equipment in large quantities. Seoul was abandoned without a fight at the end of December, and the ROK government returned to

and must be stopped. The southern military were weak, demoral
ised by mutiny and ill-equipped. The departure of American force
and subsequent statements excluding Korea from lists of countrie
or territories vital to United States' security suggested there woul
be no trouble from the United States. The fact that the America
has stood by while the Chinese nationalists were defeated by t
communists in autumn 1949 also indicated that they would not
over Korea.

During the years 1948 to 1950, the 38th parallel had not be
peaceful. Neither side accepted it as an international frontier. Th
were periodic exchanges of fire along the line, and each side c
ducted raids. There were also clashes at sea. Each side accused
other of planning war, and both talked about unification. On
June 1950 North Korean forces launched attacks along the par
of an intensity never seen before against South Korean forces nei
equipped nor prepared for attack.

The North Koreans swept all before them. Some indivi
South Korean units put up a brave fight, but most collapsed b
the armour and ferocity of their attackers. Seoul fell within
days. The government fled south, abandoning its capital a
appeared, the will to fight. Rhee established himself brie
Taejŏn, then at Taegu and finally at Pusan in the far south,
where there was nowhere else to go. Behind the government
what remained of the armed forces.

What saved the ROK was the American belief that the
Korean attack was part of a worldwide communist move agai
'free world' that must be stopped. US military forces
despatched to Korea. In the United Nations, the America
advantage of the absence of the Soviet Union from the S
Council to get international assistance for the Republic of K
series of resolutions were passed in the Security Council in la
and early July. They called for the end of the conflict and tl
drawal of the North Koreans, recommended that UN
states send forces to help the ROK and set up a Unified
Nations Command, under a commander to be designate
United States. Sixteen countries responded with forces,
number of others sent medical teams. The main motive be
decision of the United States' allies was to make sure
Americans would respond in similar fashion to commu
lenges elsewhere in the world, and there were few illusi

Pusan. The retreat only stopped south of Seoul in the early spring. Under General Ridgeway, the UN forces slowly fought their way back to Seoul, and to the region of the parallel. They crossed it at the end of March, but this time there was no push north. The war moved back to the political front.

The collapse of the winter had led to a great debate about whether to use the atomic bomb against the Chinese. MacArthur's wish to do so, and his evident unwillingness to be bound by orders, led to his dismissal and replacement by General Ridgeway in April 1951. On the South Korean side, Rhee and his colleagues believed that they had been robbed of reunification by the refusal to use atomic weapons, which they blamed on weak-willed liberals in the United States and allies soft on communism. Further 'betrayals' followed. Instead of advancing, the UN forces talked, first at Kaesŏng and then at P'anmunjŏm. Though the line of battle was stabilised by May–June 1951, sporadic fighting continued right up to the armistice in July 1953, but the UN refused to take the war north again. When an armistice was finally in sight, Rhee attempted to jeopardise it by releasing thousands of Chinese and North Korean prisoners-of-war whose repatriation had been demanded. He refused to allow his representatives to sign the armistice agreement, and talked of the ROK going north on its own. Instead of a unified Korea, July 1953 saw the peninsula still divided, an uneasy truce and huge dislocation of population, considerable destruction of towns, villages, and industry and thousands — perhaps even a million — dead or missing. South Korea was dependent for survival, for reconstruction, and for security on the United States, and yet its leader and many of his supporters had very mixed feelings about the American role in Korea. To them, Korea had again been sacrificed to great power interests.

Politics under Rhee

In the 1948 presidential election Rhee had enjoyed overwhelming support from the National Assembly, acting as the electoral college. He represented a link with the past. His American experience, and his Princeton doctorate in a country that prized education, were also valuable assets. He represented independence, liberalism, and democracy. To a fledgling state, with some demanding wholesale reform and others nervous of change, and all unsure of how to proceed, he seemed to offer much.

The reality was different. Rhee believed that he had a right to rule and that none should interfere with that right. By 1950 he had alienated many of his supporters. The May 1950 National Assembly elections, in which many of those who had boycotted the 1948 elections took part, overwhelmingly rejected Rhee's followers, returning a majority of independents. The coming of war prevented an immediate crisis, but did not stop the President from running the country as a private kingdom. Supporters were bought, opponents were crushed with a heavy-handed use of strongmen, just as pedlars' guilds had been used in Yi dynasty Seoul. When the Assembly would not do his bidding, the President did not hesitate to use the same methods. Constitutional amendments were railroaded through in 1952 to allow direct election of the president and in 1955 to enable Rhee to stand for a third term.

The 1956 presidential election saw Rhee returned, but with only 55 percent of the vote. More worrying to his supporters was that the President was now 81 and his Liberal Party running mate had been defeated by Dr Chang Myŏn (John Chang) of the opposition Democratic Party. (In terms of policies, there was nothing to distinguish these parties; both were anti-communist and for the preservation of the status quo.) There followed four years when most of the effort of the government went into protecting Rhee and ensuring his re-election in 1960. Pressure on the opposition grew steadily heavier, especially when the Liberal Party lost heavily in the 1958 assembly elections. At the same time, since it could not be expected to do the President's will, the National Assembly was ignored or bypassed. The power of the central government, especially of the police, increased. Salaries were low, inflation high, and corruption was widespread. Influence and connections were a better way of getting things done than official channels. The press, despite its conservative outlook on most issues, was also subject to government pressure greater than at any time since the Korean war.

Rhee and his supporters were determined that there would be no upset in the 1960 presidential election. All the resources of the state were deployed again to make sure Rhee and his proposed vice-president were elected on 15 March 1960. There had already been demonstrations in schools and universities against police pressure, and the election results, which were clearly fraudulent, were greeted by widespread student protests. The police reacted with determination, firing on crowds in several cases. Following the discovery of a student's body in Masan on 11 April, students all over the country came out, with the biggest demonstrations in Seoul on 19 April. As the students marched on the presidential palace, the police opened fire, killing one hundred. Before the end of the day, the police had lost control and had largely fled the streets. The students, now joined by office workers and other people, attacked government buildings and the government-owned newspaper, the *Seoul Sinmun*. That night martial law was declared and troops moved into Seoul and five other cities.

Opposition to Rhee did not stop, however. University professors now joined in, apologising for their absence when their students were being killed. The troops kept order but did not interfere. In Seoul, at least, the police disappeared. The cabinet resigned on 21 April. Rhee clung on, claiming that it was 'unbelievable that any element of the patriotic Korean people . . . could act in such a way.' But on 26 April he accepted the inevitable and resigned. On 29 May he went into exile in Hawaii, where he died in 1965.

All this, to one later writer, showed that Korean democracy was '. . . alive and healthy, and none doubted that it would continue and prosper.' So it seemed to many within and without Korea. Following the constitution, the Foreign Minister, Hŏ Chŏng, became acting president. A new constitution was adopted, providing for a ceremonial president, a bicameral assembly, and an executive prime minister. The former opposition Democratic Party leaders, Yun Po-sun and Chang Myŏn, became, respectively, president and prime minister. Later claims notwithstanding, the ROK had now had its first peaceful transfer of power.

If Rhee had died in 1959 there can be little doubt that he would have been seen in a different light from the broken figure who fled from Kimp'o airport on 29 May 1960. He was a bully and an autocrat, who did not mind using violent methods to get his way. His prejudices and preoccupations had led to squandering of aid and to a bureaucracy that spent much of its time protecting the President and lining its pockets. He had allowed the freebooting entrepreneurs who emerged in the post-war turmoil a more or less free hand, in return for political support. He had been an exasperating ally.

But he had been one of those who had doggedly kept the idea of an independent Korea alive all through the Japanese period. He had pulled the Republic of Korea into existence, and whatever his failings as a war leader, he had battled hard on the political front for the survival of his state and for the re-unification of the peninsula. The South Korean people were undoubtedly poor in 1960, but they were less poor than they had been. The dislocation and destruction of wartime were growing less. Literacy and education were increasing.

Yet in the end Rhee's legacy was a poor one. His apologists might speak of Rhee as a 'Jeffersonian liberal,' but there was no trace of democratic principle in Rhee's approach to government. His rule reinforced the Japanese colonial tradition of a strong centralised bureaucracy, with token assemblies that could be ignored. The people were there for the government, not the government for the people. That had just worked in the old rural Korea. In the new Korea of the late 1950s, with the end of the limitations on education, relatively uncensored newspapers available to all, with more people living in cities, with the praise of democracy and the free world all about them, and with the 'threat from the north' no longer seen as an immediate danger, many Koreans were eager for change. Democracy had been too long postponed. Now they would have it.

The lost democracy, April 1960–May 1961

The months after the upheavals of April 1960 were filled for many in the Republic of Korea with a great sense of exhilaration. The students in particular saw themselves as pioneers and guardians of the new order. The press, freed from the restrictiveness of Rhee's latter years, ran riot. New journals appeared full of revelations about political and financial scandals. 'Democracy' was again the keyword, as in 1945. For many Koreans, however, democracy was a vague concept, primarily related to the end of the hardship suffered since 1950. Demands for a fairer share of the national wealth became more frequent. This the political system was not able to deliver. The opposition, thrust into power, quickly revealed its patched-up nature and its lack of direction. In the limited range of options allowed in South Korean politics, its main reason for existence had been to oppose Rhee. Deprived of that focus, it was quickly in difficulties. Even before the new constitution was in operation, the factions in the Democratic Party had split. The president and the prime minister could not agree. In the wings, the students made more and more radical demands. No policy was sacred, even that of hostility to North Korea. The government under Chang Myŏn appeared to have no solution to the growing pressures that faced it.

On 16 May 1961, the government's problems were solved. A group of army officers, with forty-four year old Major General Park Chung Hee at its head, and Colonel Kim Jong Pil as its organising genius, seized power in a bloodless coup. The chief of staff threw in his lot with the new junta, and President Yun was persuaded to stay on long enough to give the appearance of legality to the move. The justification for intervention was presented in grand language: domestic turmoil put the nation in danger; the student demands for an opening to North Korea could lead to an attempt at reunification by force. These themes were to be built upon and expanded in the eighteen years that followed, while the undoubted economic successes of the Park Chung Hee years (described in the next chapter) were later used as an *ex post facto* defence.

By 1961 the ROK military formed the most 'modern' and powerful element in Korean society, commanding the largest share of resources, familiar with modern technology and methods of organisation. The officer corps, especially those trained in the Korean Military Academy, had a high sense of purpose and group unity. This was particularly the case with the first group to complete the KMA two-year course, of which Park Chung Hee was a member. Rhee had been able to exert control over the military as he did in other areas by means of his prestige and ability at intrigue. The Chang government was unable to do so. Many soldiers disliked what they saw of the political scene. The 'disorder' of democracy offended their sense of what was right, while student slogans appeared close to the communist ideology they were taught to oppose. They felt that with the ROK facing a particularly hostile enemy, the military had a special role as defenders of the state.

Some contemporary observers saw less exalted motives at work. The democratic chaos of Korea was hardly worse than that in many other countries in the world. Far from a coup forced upon an unwilling group of soldiers faced with the imminent collapse of their country, the evidence pointed to long-laid plans, perhaps originally directed against Rhee, connected with disgruntlement about promotions and military funding.

Politics under Park Chung Hee, 1961–1979

The army enjoyed high prestige in South Korea in 1961. Whatever the early reverses in the Korean war, individual units had often fought well, and the army had built a good reputation subsequently. The soldiers' unwillingness to support Syngman Rhee in 1960, especially their refusal to fire on unarmed civilians as the police had done, was an important factor in their favour. The general belief in a real threat from North Korea was another, as was the acceptance that the military represented progress. Many civilians were, like the soldiers, disillusioned with the Chang government and with the apparent chaos that seemed to go with democracy. The majority may well have been happy to see order restored.

From 1961 to 1963, the country was ruled first by a 'Military Revolutionary Committee,' and then by the 'Supreme Council for National Reconstruction,' made up of twenty generals and colonels. The military junta had no special programme or solution to the country's problems, apart from a dose of military discipline and a 'fresh and clean morality.' Students were sent back to their classrooms. All political activity was banned, and the National Assembly dissolved. Many politicians and others were blacklisted, some generals were retired, and a number of industrialists investigated on corruption charges. Army officers took over key posts in the administration. Another important step was the establishment under Kim Jong Pil of the Korean Central Intelligence Agency, the KCIA, in June 1961. Modelled in theory on the United States' CIA, its functions included internal security. In particular, it was to make sure that no other group of soldiers followed in Park's footsteps.

Park claimed that the soldiers would return to barracks once they had sorted out the country's problems. A new constitution was drawn up and accepted in a national referendum in December 1962. It provided for a strong executive president, elected by direct popular vote. The president would appoint the prime minister and the cabinet, and could invoke emergency economic measures. Park firmly disclaimed any intention of taking part in civilian politics in February 1963, but a month later he proposed a further referendum to seek public agreement for another four years of military rule, arguing that political parties and political debate would not benefit Korea. Strong opposition at home and from the United States persuaded him to abandon this plan. Instead, he left the army in August 1963 and announced he would be the newly-organised Democratic Republican Party's presidential candidate at the election.

His campaign was fought against an inauspicious record of economic faltering, persistent reports of corruption involving the KCIA, and factionalism among the junta. Against Park, Yun Po-sun stood as the candidate of a hastily-organised New Democratic Party. The election was close-run, with Park obtaining 46.1 percent of the votes against Yun's 45.1 percent. Much of Park's support came from the south east, especially from his home province of North Kyŏngsang; Yun carried Seoul and the northern part of the country. In the Assembly elections, Park's Democratic Republican Party won 110 out of 175 seats.

Park now began a policy of rapid economic development. He remained impatient of politicians and political parties, bypassing the Assembly where possible, and concentrating power in the bureaucracy. His cabinets and the presidential secretariat were staffed by technocrats, who shared his wish to get things done. Many military or former military men occupied positions in the bureaucracy or in the developing industries. Although these people were officially civilians or quickly shed their uniforms, they retained their military links, often through KMA class associations, and shared a common outlook. The KCIA became a powerful force, able to investigate virtually anybody. Its powers were not confined to an anti-communist role. It established a presence overseas, where it watched the activities of South Korean dissidents, especially students, and North Korean embassies. A number of opponents of the regime were spirited back to Korea. In general, however, although the government was authoritarian, the political process was not completely circumvented. A fair amount of press freedom was allowed. Park's opponents could voice their views. Student demonstrations over contentious issues such as the normalisation of relations with Japan were broken up, but without fatal casualties.

In the 1967 presidential elections, Park again defeated Yun, with a higher share of the vote. He was now constitutionally barred from a third term, but an enabling amendment was forced through the Assembly so that he would be allowed to stand in 1971. After the amendment had been accepted, he pledged that he would not stand beyond three terms. In 1971, facing a new opponent, Kim Dae Jung, his share of the vote dropped. Kim got 46 percent, and claimed that he had been defeated by fraud. In the face of the steady erosion of the Democratic Republican Party's position in the National Assembly, Park introduced severe control measures in December 1971. Less than a year later he effectively staged a coup against his own 1962 constitution, using as justification the uncertain international situation and the current North–South talks. He declared martial law, dissolved the Assembly, banned political activity, closed the universities, and introduced complete press censorship. Soon afterwards, another constitution was adopted, again following a referendum.

This constitution, known as the *Yushin* (Revitalisation or Restoration) constitution, allowed Park to succeed himself indefinitely, to adopt emergency powers when he considered it necessary, and to appoint one-third of the National Assembly. The president would no longer be chosen by direct vote or by the National Assembly, but by a newly-constituted and supposedly non-partisan National Conference for Unification. In December 1972, this college duly elected Park for an extended six-year term.

Succeeding years saw Park's rule become more and more authoritarian. In the countryside the *saemaŭl* (new community or new village) movement, whose economic role is described in the following chapter, was used as a means of simple ideological influence. Apologists for the government maintained that Park had devised a special Korean form of democracy, which appeared to be based on bureaucratic dominance. The strong opposition within the country made it clear that not all accepted this concept. For much of the period from January 1974 onwards, the ROK was under what were effectively variations of martial law. The opposition was harried. Kim Dae Jung, who had fled to Japan, was kidnapped, almost certainly by agents of the KCIA, and brought back to Korea in 1973. He claimed that his captors had intended to kill him. Many opposition figures, including Yun Po-sun and Kim Dae Jung, were given prison sentences in 1976 for organising a declaration calling for the restoration of democracy. Several prominent religious leaders were also jailed for opposition activities. Some less prominent opponents were executed. Student dissent was ruthlessly suppressed, and press censorship reached levels not seen since Japanese days. Independent newspapers, such as the *Dong-A Ilbo*, were put under great pressure, with government and other advertising withdrawn and editorial staff threatened. Matters were made worse by the increasing remoteness of the president from what was happening about him. From August 1974 onwards, when an assassination attempt on him by a Korean from Japan killed his wife, Park avoided public exposure and uncongenial advice.

The justification for 'Korean democracy' and for the repressiveness of the government had been economic advance, but by the mid-1970s this had begun to slow down. Inflation and unemployment became new ingredients in the growing dissent. The government's unpopularity was reflected in the December 1978 National Assembly elections, when Park's Democratic Republican Party failed to win a majority of the popular vote, doing especially badly in the urban areas. The president's power to appoint one third of the Assembly, plus pressure on independents, meant that the DRP did not lose control. But its position was shaky, and when challenged on the government's failure to deal with unrest by the leader of the New Democratic Party, Kim Young Sam, in the summer of 1979, it panicked. Kim was expelled from the Assembly, an act which united the opposition — no mean feat — who all withdrew in October. Students and workers were joining forces on the streets of Seoul and several other major cities. Martial law was declared in Pusan. A major split now emerged between those who favoured compromise, including the head of the KCIA, Kim Jae-kyu, and those who wanted further repression. Park was persuaded to attend a dinner in a KCIA restaurant on 26 October 1979. An argument developed and Kim shot and killed the President and his bodyguards. At his trial Kim claimed that he had seen the need to get rid of Park since 1972.

Park's economic achievements were great, and much flowed from them. South Korea was a far richer and stronger country in 1979 than anybody would have thought possible in 1961. So successful were its development policies, that by 1979 South Korea was in economic terms on the verge of leaving behind third world status. In political terms, however, there had been little advance. The state was more powerful than in the past and the means of control were more extensive and efficient than those available to earlier rulers. Otherwise, little had changed. Koreans were still told by their rulers that they were not yet ready to govern themselves.

Politics since 1979

Following the constitution, the Prime Minister, Choi Kyu Hah, became acting president. He was a cautious man, who was to follow a cautious programme, refusing to give in to demands for the immediate end of the *Yushin* constitution, under whose terms he was elected 'interim president' in December 1979, while at the same time committed to greater democratisation. On the surface, the dismantling of *Yushin* went forward. The emergency decrees were repealed and political prisoners released. Political activity began again, with the three Kims — Kim Jong Pil, Kim Young Sam and Kim Dae Jung — the most prominent, but not the only contenders for power. But there were widespread demands for early constitutional reform and protests at what seemed delaying tactics by the government. Choi's problem was that behind the scenes the military were again emerging as a factor on the political scene.

The controls established after the 1961 coup had worked well; for eighteen years no second group of officers followed Park's example. October 1979 had left Park dead and the KCIA leaderless and disgraced. For six weeks the soldiers remained quiet, though hints were dropped about the dangers of dismantling the *Yushin* system. Then on 12 December Major General Chun Doo Hwan, commmander of the unit responsible for army security, staged an internal military coup. Some forty generals, including the chief of staff, were forced to retire, some accused of complicity in Park's death, others of corruption. To effect the coup, key troops were pulled out of the frontline without consultation with the commander of the ROK–US Combined Forces Command. As in 1961, 'national security' provided the justification for the move.

Spring 1980 saw growing ferment, with student demonstrators, seeing themselves as the heirs of 1960, voicing political demands, especially the need to keep the military out of politics. Labour unrest increased as workers demanded the wage rises they had been denied under Park. Following massive student demonstrations in Seoul, Chun moved on 17 May 1980, tightening martial law and press censorship, banning strikes, and closing universities and colleges. The National Assembly and political party offices were closed. There were widespread arrests of leading political and governmental figures the next day. Most were charged with corruption. The charge against Kim Dae Jung, however, was sedition. His arrest sparked off demonstrations in Kwangju, capital of his home province of South Chŏlla. This region had long been disaffected, especially resenting the way in which industrial and infrastructural development had been concentrated in Park's home region. When the 'Special Forces' trained for use against North Korea were used against Kwangju students, the resentment burst out in nine days of rioting, in which the government lost control of the city. Order was only restored when the army moved in with tanks. The opposition claimed up to 2000 died in Kwangju. The government denied this, but at one time admitted to 170 deaths. The truth may never be known, but 'the Kwangju incident' became a potent symbol of resistance to Chun and military rule.

Following Kwangju, General Chun's move to political power was swift. In August 1980 he left the army and took over as interim president. There were sweeping reforms in the political system. All political parties were dissolved and their assets confiscated; most existing politicians were banned from political activity; the press and private broadcasting were brought under closer government control; some papers were closed and prominent journalists dismissed; university staff were also purged, and a graduation quota system introduced to force students to study rather than demonstrate. There were widespread investigations for corruption among the bureaucracy and industrialists. Kim Dae Jung was tried and sentenced to death for his alleged role in the Kwangju incident, although he had been in jail when it began. International protests led to a commutation of the death sentence, and he was eventually permitted to go to the United States.

A modified version of the *Yushin* constitution was accepted at a referendum in October 1980. It still provided for indirect election of the president, but allowed only one seven-year term of office. Chun was duly elected in February 1981. New political parties appeared, with government encouragement. In theory they represented a wide range of political views, including socialism, but they had no grass-roots base. National Assembly elections were held in March 1981. The government party, the Democratic Justice Party (DJP), had many well-known candidates, and won an overwhelming victory, which President Chun presented as an endorsement of his rule. There was some truth in this; as in 1961, many South Korean voters were glad to get away from political upheaval. But most opposition candidates were unknown and were unlikely to be influential if elected. There were restrictions on campaigning, which tended to be enforced on opposition parties, and on the subjects to be discussed. President Chun and his record were taboo, for example. As in the past, the state apparatus worked for the government party.

Much of the *Yushin* apparatus continued under the new system. The KCIA, renamed the Agency for National Security Planning, monitored a wide range of activities, as did a number of other, mostly military, agencies. Left-wing views continued to be suppressed. The press was forced to follow a system of self-censorship, which journalists claimed was more far-reaching than anything under Park. The *saemaŭl* movement, under the President's younger brother, became more involved with spiritual training, especially for the bureaucracy, than it had been before, and a number of other institutions were established for the same purpose. But claims about a new morality in public life were dented by allegations of corruption in high places. A new generation of military officers were found posts in the bureaucracy or in industry.

President Chun set about establishing his position as a statesman, with many overseas visits and a proposal for a 'Pacific Summit' meeting. He repeatedly pledged that he would step down in 1988 at the end of his term of office, arguing that what the ROK needed was a period of stability and a peaceful transfer of power. His calm and control at the time of the Rangoon bombing in September 1983 were widely noted. There were signs of a more liberal approach to questions of politics and security. In January 1982 the curfew that had been in force over most of the country since 1947 was generally lifted. School uniforms were abolished. There was some relaxation of the rules for foreign travel. The political ban was steadily relaxed, although few really prominent figures benefited. There were signs that the National Assembly, and even the DJP, were not prepared always to rubber stamp executive decisions. Student demonstrations on campus were not disturbed. Foreign journals no longer failed to appeaı if they carried hostile comment on the ROK or its leaders. The decision to hold the 1988 summer Olympic Games in Seoul was presented as a sign of the political and economic maturity of the ROK.

The signs of political liberalisation led to the formation of a 'Council for the Promotion of Democracy' in May 1984. Kim Young Sam, still technically banned, was a leading figure. In January 1985 members of the Council organised a 'New Korea Democratic Party' to contest the National Assembly elections due the following month. Despite the lateness of its formation, its lack of resources or a clear programme, and government and DJP hostility, the new party did well, aided by the return of Kim Dae Jung after two years' exile in the United States.

Politics after February 1985 reverted to earlier patterns of confrontation, with the opposition in the National Assembly demanding an end to repression and a restoration of civil liberties. Outside the Assembly the events of early 1985 encouraged the students to challenge the government on a wider range of issues. There were calls for radical reorganisation of society and for a new approach to North Korea. Demonstrations became increasingly violent, as did the police response. Kim Young Sam and Kim Dae Jung, still officially banned and ignored in the media, were influential with the opposition within and without the Assembly. Religious leaders of a number of denominations, including the Roman Catholic Cardinal Stephen Kim, expressed concern at the government's unyielding approach to political reform.

President Chun continued to insist that the most important political goal was a peaceful handover of power under the 1980 constitution. When the opposition's demands did not abate, he agreed in April 1986 that there could be constitutional revision before 1988 if the parties in the National Assembly reached agreement. As well as domestic considerations, the overthrow of President Marcos in the Philippines may have prompted him to a more conciliatory line. Various proposals were aired, with the DJP favouring a cabinet system and the opposition increasingly concentrating on direct election of the president. A year later no agreement had been reached, and Chun announced on 13 April 1987 that there would be no change in the constitution until after the 1988 Olympics.

This announcement did not defuse the issue. In January 1987 the death of a student under torture while in police custody created an angry mood on the campuses, which led to further demonstrations. They had subsided by April, but revelations about the extent of police involvement and dissatisfaction at political developments led to further outbreaks in May 1987. These intensified in early June when President Chun nominated his close associate, and fellow KMA graduate, Roh Tae Woo, as the DJP's candidate for the 1988 presidential election. The students were now joined by workers. Scenes of violent demonstrations and police tear-gassing appeared all over the world, as television crews flocked to Seoul. The world's press, having woken up to Korea, began to editorialise on a threat to the Olympics. Government officials made ominous noises about the possibility of 'something serious' happening, and the United States' government indicated concern.

On 29 June Roh Tae Woo intervened. He proposed a package of reforms that conceded many of the opposition's demands, including the direct election of the president. President Chun accepted it two days later and the political crisis was over. There was industrial unrest, however, with workers demanding pay increases and managerial reforms. The government generally kept out of this issue. Summer and autumn 1987 saw a frenzy of political activity, as the parties negotiated over a new constitution, which was accepted at a referendum in October. The constitution provides for direct election of the president, strengthens the National Assembly against the power of the executive, and contains detailed guarantees for personal liberty. All efforts were then concentrated on preparations for a presidential election on 16 December 1987. Kim Young Sam and Kim Dae Jung had in April formed a new political party, pledging that there would be only one opposition party candidate; in the event, neither would concede and both stood. In another echo of the past, Kim Jong Pil announced he would be a candidate.

The campaign was marked by strong regional animosities, and by allegations from the three Kims that the government machine, especially state-owned radio and television, was used to favour Roh's candidacy. There were also claims that the military vote had been marshalled for his support. Roh won by a margin of some two million votes, with Kim Young Sam second, and Kim Dae Jung third. Allegations about electoral fraud continued, and there were some rather half-hearted demonstrations. In the end, even Kim Young Sam and Kim Dae Jung admitted that their split had damaged the opposition cause. The press, now largely free of government 'guidance,' did not seem disposed to accept the claims of fraud. Roh Tae Woo became the seventh president of the Republic of Korea on 25 February 1988.

Korean politics at a watershed

In the forty years since the Republic of Korea was established, the face of the country and its economic standing have changed beyond recognition. Few think that its political development has kept pace, however. The state structure, centred on a powerful president backed by a strong, efficient and virtually unchecked bureaucracy, continues much in the mould of the Japanese Government-General, with some American overlay. Since 1961 the role of the military in the running of the state echoes Japanese days, though now the soldiers wear Korean uniforms. The justification for this has been the need for a strong country to face the threat from North Korea. It is hard to deny that there is such a threat. North Korean forces sit close to Seoul and there is real tension between the two Koreas.

Yet the repression that has characterised South Korean politics since 1948 cannot be justified on these grounds alone. Other countries have faced threats to their very existence without the need to curtail civil liberties or political activities in the way successive ROK governments have done. Many Koreans, often very conservative in their general political outlook, have found it hard to accept these restrictions. To outsiders, it is difficult to see in the sober-suited political figures of the South Korean opposition, with party platforms that would seem ultra-cautious in Des Moines or Surbiton, the dangerous radicals who it is claimed threaten the fabric of the state. The ROK has an additional guarantee for security, in the form of the US military commitment, not available to many other countries that feel threatened, which should allow greater opportunity for political freedom, not less. Unlike some armies, that of the ROK has a real military task to carry out.

It may be that South Korean politics are now approaching a watershed, and it will be accepted that there is no longer a need for its elite officers to take on the additional task of running civilian affairs. Roh Tae Woo's election has clearly not ended the pattern begun in 1961. He is still from a military background, even if it is seven years rather than a few months since he put away his uniform. But the South Korean people have changed. The voters of 1987 are different from those of 1961. There are more of them, they are younger, urbanised, better educated, and better informed than their parents and grandparents. The majority do not wish to see violent upheavals in society and very few support the more extreme student radicals in the call for social revolution. For many of them, however, the things used to justify the political system operating since the early 1960s no longer matter. The Korean War is remote, the privations of the 1950s and the 1960s distant memories. No longer are the military the main force for progress or modernisation in the ROK. The technocrats who occupy managerial positions in government and industry are coming more and more to resent it when soldiers, even retired soldiers, are brought in over their heads. Moderately rich town dwellers dislike a system that up to now has allowed them no say in where the street lights are to go, or whether a new factory is to be built in a residential area. Increasingly they will also want to be heard on wider political issues.

On 29 June 1987 Roh Tae Woo made a bid for the support of these people, offering them a measure of political reform that allows a real choice in the selection of the government. As a candidate on 16 December 1987, he offered reassurance to those with vested interests in the existing power structure that reform need not threaten them. His task on taking office is to balance these competing claims. It will not be easy to satisfy both sides, but there would be considerable merit in leading the ROK into political development to match its economic advances.

Chapter Seven

The Economic Miracle

From Nike running shoes to Hyundai Pony cars, from teddy bears to Amstrad computers: South Korea is now familiar to us all for its manufactured goods. The names of some of its leading industrial and construction groups — Samsung, Lucky–Goldstar, Daewoo, Ssangyong, Hyundai — are becoming almost as well-known as Japanese brand names. The trading element, often marked by buoyant levels of Korean exports, is an important part of the ROK's relationships with a number of countries. Among the most remarkable aspects of South Korea's economic position in the world today are the speed of its development and its general ability for sustained growth. These two qualities largely account for the term 'economic miracle' so often applied to the ROK. The expansionary period of South Korea's economy can be dated back to 1961, when Park Chung Hee directed the country on to a course of economic development to pull it out of the misery of the postwar years. The first plan was launched in 1962, and from then onwards South Korea's Gross National Product (GNP) has shown an average annual growth rate of around nine percent.

A variety of other indicators illustrate the distance covered since 1962. In that year GNP stood at US$2.3 billion, but had grown by 1986 to US$95 billion (in current prices), and is estimated at US$120 billion for 1987. Per capita GNP in 1962 was only US$87, by contrast with US$2296 in 1986 and an estimated US$2850 for 1987. Exports, which have led the ROK's economic growth, rose from some US$50 million in 1962 to touch US$46 billion in 1987, though this spectacular increase should not obscure the fact that South Korea has in many years run a trade deficit and has a large foreign debt. Foreign confidence in the economy, however, has not wavered, and investment from non-Korean sources has risen steadily during the 1980s. The country's range of manufactured products has been consolidated and expanded since the early 1960s. To the small-scale industrial plants, textile and other light industries and processing plants producing consumer goods that were restored during the 1950s were added electronics and plastics during the following decade, while the chemical, cement and ceramics sectors were reinvigorated. Steel, ships, motor vehicles, and other heavy industries including defence were introduced during the 1970s. In the present decade the emphasis has been on further development of high-technology areas such as electronics and telecommunications, and on expanding the steel, refining, and motor manufacturing sectors. To meet the needs of these industries, a technically-qualified workforce has been built up over the past two and a half decades, backed by government and private research. It operates alongside a less-skilled labour force engaged in older industries such as textiles. Since the mid-1960s some of South Korea's skilled workers have been active abroad in a variety of construction projects, largely in South East Asia, the Middle East and the Gulf.

The benefits for the ROK of the sustained economic growth of the past twenty-five years have been considerable. Stable economic expansion has contributed to social stability. The government has been able to meet the needs of national security, despite a defence budget that consumes about one third of central government budget expenditure and 5.5 percent of GNP. National pride and confidence have been boosted by economic success, and the humiliation of Japan's annexation of Korea partly assuaged. For several sections of South Korean society, in particular the new middle classes, national prosperity has brought comfortable levels of living; and some individuals have amassed great fortunes. As national wealth has accumulated, so the government has started to introduce various welfare schemes that it hopes to extend to most sections of society. Progressive expansion of the infrastructure through universal electrification and the building of dams, highways, airports and urban subway systems, has raised living standards and enhanced mobility for most of the population.

There has been a price for this economic miracle. When Park Chung Hee made the decision to go for economic development as the means of building up the ROK's strength and independence, he did so largely at the cost of the country's political institutions. The distortions inflicted on South Korean political life have been described in the previous chapter. Park's justification for his measures was initially the need to maintain stability and national harmony in defence of the ROK's integrity. As time went on, the urgency of protecting the economic advances already achieved was given as a further reason for curtailing political activity.

Basis for lift-off

The end of the Pacific war in 1945 left the Korean economy in chaos. Japan's exploitation of the country's agricultural and industrial bases and infrastructure in the furtherance of its war effort had caused great disruption. The retreating Japanese repatriated capital and withdrew engineers, technicians, and managers. The banking and financial network they had administered was severely dislocated, and inflation was heavy. The return of Korean migrants from Japan and China and the movement of people from the north to the south of the peninsula swelled the population in the south by an estimated 1.5–2 million between 1945 and 1948, and added to existing economic difficulties. The division of the country into two separate states in 1948 broke former domestic trading patterns and deprived the ROK of access to most of the peninsula's natural resources and existing heavy industry and energy supplies, but left it with more of the population. Substantial US government relief support in the form of essential commodities and grants and loans, amounting to US$525 million over the period 1945 to 1949, and augmented by contributions from United Nations funds, staved off starvation and permitted some industrial rehabilitation. The little achieved was, however, obliterated by the ravages of the Korean war. Over 40 percent of all industrial installations were heavily damaged, while property losses amounted to an estimated US$1800 million.

Once again South Korea was obliged to depend on foreign aid and technical assistance, supplied in large measure by the United

States with some support from UN relief funds. During the years 1953 to 1960 economic aid from these two sources amounted to US$2083 million. The US government in addition provided considerable military aid. The United States continued its economic aid programme beyond 1960, though from 1964 on a much reduced scale, and after 1971 only very small sums were involved. Foreign assistance during the first decade following the Korean War largely took the form of grants in aid, food imports and imports of consumer goods. Some of the funds went into the construction of industrial installations. Assistance from US sources is said to have amounted to 77 percent of capital formation. Imports under the aid programme accounted on average for some 70 percent of total imports during the period. The wisdom of these foreign aid policies came to be questioned, both at the time by Park Chung Hee and by later analysts. Especial criticism has been made of the high proportion of consumer goods imported under the aid schemes to the detriment of capital goods, which would have encouraged manufacturing, and of the provision of cheap food grains. The latter led during the 1950s to depressed purchase prices for locally-grown grains and low food prices in general. Such reduction in food costs enabled wages for urban industrial workers to be kept down (a situation that was to benefit South Korea's later industrial spurt). Low agricultural prices, however, depressed the farming sector and contributed to its stagnation. The foreign aid programme served a purpose, nonetheless, in that it permitted essential rehabilitation of the Korean economy to take place fairly rapidly and thus laid foundations for its later growth. In the early 1960s US aid was directed away from grants and towards loans requiring repayment in US dollars. The US assistance programme was eventually scaled down, partly as a result of revised American economic priorities. These developments encouraged the formation of new and more self-reliant economic patterns in South Korea.

The economic policies of Syngman Rhee's government during the years 1953 to 1960 have been much criticised. Rhee himself was more concerned with questions of security and political stability and with his own position, than with issues of development. The volume of foreign aid, moreover, blunted initiative by reducing the urgency of finding solutions to economic problems. These extended into many areas. Agricultural output was too low to meet the needs of the expanding population and had to be supplemented by imports of food grains. The ROK was left, on division of the peninsula, with a preponderance of light and processing industries. This will have accounted in part for the predominance of consumer goods, but industrial production hardly went beyond meeting the immediate requirements of reconstruction and the domestic market. Development of heavy industry was tardy, and South Korea produced very few capital goods during the 1950s. Foreign trade was a disaster area, with imports increasingly outweighing exports. By 1957 imports were valued at US$440 million, against exports valued at only US$22 million. Exports were largely of primary materials, with a small allocation for manufactured goods. To counter the imbalance and the drain on foreign reserves, a programme of import substitution — domestic manufacture of ranges of goods that had hitherto been imported — was introduced. Inflation was a considerable problem, as were low interest rates (discouraging investment), poor levels of domestic savings, and depressed foreign exchange rates leading to an overvaluation of the Korean currency. The economic weaknesses of Syngman Rhee's administration indicated clear areas for improvements and new policies. This period should not, however, be dismissed out of hand. Through reconstruction work and the promotion of import-substitution industries, the productive base was slowly built up in South Korea during the years after the Korean War, and an annual growth rate of 5.1 percent achieved.

By 1961 South Korea was in a position to draw on the benefits of one of the first policies initiated in the early years of independence: widespread provision of education. The whittling down of illiteracy, the introduction of compulsory free primary schooling, the availability of higher education and the opportunity for some to study overseas, were all factors contributing to the development of a literate, educated workforce. At the lower end of the scale, primary school enrolment was increasing (it stood at 84 percent in 1961). At the upper end, Korean graduates returning from advanced study abroad, particularly in the United States, participated in the formulation of the plans that helped to launch South Korea's economic spurt.

Other more elusive factors had also been at play during the years since the end of the Pacific war. Freed from the constraints of colonial status, and with the old administrative and social patterns of pre-colonial days long dismantled, society in the newly-formed Republic of Korea was a good deal more fluid than it had been before or was even to become in the following decades. Civil war and political division, with the consequent weakening for many of family ties, the disruption of economic activity, together with constant exposure to western influence, all contributed to a great loosening of social norms. In such an atmosphere able entrepreneurs felt able to act boldly and seized such opportunities as the economic system then offered. A 'freebooting' style developed, which, while it may have been an ill-disciplined element in the Korean economy of the 1950s, was proof of the entrepreneurial potential within society.

Characteristics of development

The outstanding feature of South Korea's economic development over the past quarter century has been the leading role that government has allotted to itself. Though the ROK's economy is often described as a free market one, official intervention in its working can frequently be discerned, and the public sector has been sizeable, even if it is now shrinking. The government is at no pains to hide its role. The authorised *Handbook of Korea* in its 1987 edition states: 'The national economy can be divided into two parts: the government sector and the private sector functioning under the government's policy.'

Private enterprise has been encouraged and supported, but on the understanding that it accepted official guidlines and even supervision. The chief indicators of government intentions have been the five-year economic development plans drawn up by the Economic Planning Board, which have been implemented continuously since 1962, backed up by specific plans directed at various sectors. The country is now into its sixth plan, inaugurated in 1987. The concept of planning had already been introduced in the 1950s and some plans even drawn up, but they never matched the comprehensive nature and determined implementation of those following them.

The earlier five-year plans aimed to lay the foundations for an independent national economy. During the 1960s this involved a re-orientation away from import substitution towards an easing of imports, devaluation of the currency, and higher rates of investment in order to encourage the manufacture of goods suitable for an export drive. The domestic market started to expand, but was kept checked in favour of exports. Expenditure on the country's infrastructure — roadbuilding, electrification, and so on — assisted economic growth. In exports the emphasis was at first on light manufactured goods, but during the 1970s planning gave prominence to the development of heavy industrial products to widen the export range. During the present decade electronic goods have been added. The course charted in the plans has led to a considerable restructuring of the national economy and a changed relationship between occupational sectors. The fast rate of growth has brought problems of heavy reliance on foreign sources of investment, budget deficits and bouts of inflation. Now, in the 1980s, the signs are that the government, while continuing to reserve the right to indicate the direction the economy should take and even intervene in its functioning, will leave more initiative, but also more responsibility, in the hands of individual firms for their development, and allow freer play to market mechanisms. Its aim is to maintain economic stability through containing inflation, balancing its budgets and reducing the volume of foreign loans.

A variety of means and circumstances have permitted successive South Korean governments to achieve a large measure of control over the course of the economy and its operation. In the early 1960s the modest scale and fairly simple structure of the country's economic institutions, compounded by lack of natural resources, gave scope for planning and reorganisation. There was the opportunity and perhaps even the need for bold initiatives. In the early stages the government's direction was accordingly effective. Its control over banking, funding, and access to foreign exchange has been a particularly strong element in its relationship with industry. Through preferential schemes of taxes, incentives, credit supplies, and so on, it has been able to promote one sector of the economy over another. Through legislation it has worked to control the activities and demands of the labour force. It has further regulated the conditions for industry and banking through protectionist measures directed against foreign imports and the operations of foreign banks. In recent years, as the economy has expanded, diversified, and grown more sophisticated, government intervention has become less efficient. It has always drawn some criticism from both Korean and foreign commentators. The first five-year plan was described at the time by the *Far Eastern Economic Review* as a 'costly failure' leading to higher imports and depletion of foreign exchange reserves. Later critics have pointed to price distortion, loss of competitiveness, and the creation of imbalances between industrial sectors and between domestic and export markets as weaknesses resulting from official planning policies. Against that must be set the part played by vigorous government leadership in indicating priorities, harnessing the entrepreneurial skill of the big conglomerates or *chaebŏl*, providing a measure of security, and creating an atmosphere favourable to development. The economic buoyancy that South Korea was able to achieve helped it to survive the two oil shocks of the 1970s and problems of world recession.

Both government and private enterprise have shown themselves alert in making use of whatever advantages came their way. From the first five-year plan onwards, either through transfer or purchase, they have sought to acquire new technology as a short cut to growth. The impetus came first from the army, which in the early 1960s was already a technically-oriented and trained organisation through its contacts with the US military establishment. The chief foreign sources for new technology have been and remain Japan and the United States. Native talent has not been overlooked, and both the public and private sectors have appreciated and made use of the well-educated labour force at their disposal. Government and industry follow a policy of co-operation in research for which considerable financial allocation is made. In 1987, for instance, the ratio of research investment against GNP rose to 2.2 percent. In the area of investment and project financing, South Korea has been ready to draw on foreign sources to make good the recurring shortfall in domestic investment funds. Again, Japan and the United States have provided the lion's share of such financing — 80 percent between them of the 1186 projects valued at US$2.65 billion authorised during the period 1962 to 1985, many of which were taken up within the private sector. The government has also been able to draw on international development funds, which it has used for infrastructure projects such as roadbuilding, and to benefit from technical aid schemes administered by UN agencies. Now, as it is pulling away from the ranks of the developing countries, the ROK is having to relinquish its status of aid recipient, a move that is the occasion for both pride and apprehension.

Elements in success

The government's commitment to development, its energetic leadership, and flexible approach to problems have played a vital part in pushing South Korea forward economically. The administrations of Park Chung Hee and Chun Doo Hwan have, moreover, shown themselves prepared to take a hard line to get their economic policies implemented. Equally important, though, has been the response from the population to the government's call. The vision, consciously nurtured by successive administrations, of a strong and independent society capable of asserting itself against former enemies and detractors, has had great appeal and much success in harnessing a spirit of co-operation among Koreans. Against a background of working for the national good, many people have also seen that their own and family interests could be well served through joining in the economic push. The speed of development and the fairly rapid spread of benefits and generally high level of employment that it has engendered have given further encouragement to support government policies. The ROK also knows it has a case to win in the wider context of the Korean peninsula. In the early decades of separate development the DPRK was ahead of the ROK on a number of economic indicators. Now, the South Korean government insists, it has fallen behind, thanks to the South's policies.

Weaknesses, actual and potential

The foundations of the South Korean economy are at many points extremely strong and have withstood the demands of rapid expansion. They have their weaknesses, nonetheless. Labour relations and big business are two areas giving actual or potential anxiety, and a number of imbalances and deficiencies threaten the economic structure.

Labour relations

In the days following the proposals for political reform announced on 29 June 1987 by Roh Tae Woo, then Chairman of the Democratic

Justice Party, a series of strikes spread across South Korea, affecting public services, large industries and small businesses alike. Company offices were occupied and officials detained or roughed up, street demonstrations and factory sit-ins organised, and property damaged. The easing of political restrictions offered by Roh clearly sparked off a desire for concessions in the workplace. Workers' demands barely touched on political issues, but concentrated on long-held grievances over wages, conditions of work, and reform of trade union organisation. There is now a general feeling among workers that the time has come to allow them a more active role in the functioning of the economy and a greater share in its fruits.

It is acknowledged both within and without the ROK that low wage costs have contributed enormously to the country's rapid economic growth and particularly to the development of successful export industries. Various factors have been at play. In the 1960s, as the agricultural sector began to lose its manpower to the cities, industrial labour was plentiful. The wages paid, though low, still provided a higher income than had been obtainable through rural work. Moreover, many of those entering industry, especially textiles, were young women whose expectations were very modest. Government exhortations to workers to help construct a strong nation generally fell on responsive ears, and in any case were backed up by measures aimed at restricting the bargaining and striking power of labour. Some of these basic conditions still obtain. Rural incomes are still lower than urban industrial ones. The female workforce is still quiescent. Trade unions still lack clout. Wage increases have been granted, but the aim has always been to keep productivity rates ahead of wage rates. In 1986 average hourly earnings over all industries were put at US$1.75, a figure that masked a considerable discrepancy between male and female average wages and between sectors. The average number of hours worked per month stood at 223 in 1985, among the highest in the world. These figures point to an average monthly salary of some US$390 in recent years. A minimum monthly wage was due to be introduced on 1 January 1988, which would lift low-paid workers above the 111,000 *wŏn* mark — about US$140 — but labour is still in dispute with government and management over its size. Workers in small firms cannot always be sure of receiving wages on time from employers whose cash flow problems may make them default on salaries. Holidays are generally limited to a weekly rest day and public holidays, and employers may oblige employees to put in extra hours before such breaks to tide production over. A paid week's holiday is gradually being offered to employees in bigger companies. Working conditions can vary greatly. The big conglomerates provide modern factories, company housing and schooling, training and adequate chances of promotion. Small firms, often under-capitalised, may operate in crowded workshops with outdated equipment and offer their employees few opportunities for advancement. The labour inspectorate is undermanned and underfunded.

Women fare particularly badly in the workplace, even though they have been part of the industrial labour force since the early years of this century and have long worked on the land. Their problems stem partly from negative attitudes among both men and women towards female participation in work outside the home (a non-working wife is a sign of a man's good financial standing), partly from the limited expectations of many women workers, and partly from past official indifference towards them. Their poor status is reflected in their low earnings, which average 47 percent of male wages, and in their general absence from managerial and decision-making grades — though there are several bright exceptions in business and public life. Women constitute some 40 percent of the workforce. In rural areas they are an even higher proportion. In the manufacturing sector they are concentrated in semi-skilled jobs in the textile and clothing trades, or electrical and electronic assembly work. Many are young women from the countryside who work, some of them for less even than the proposed minimum wage, until their mid-twenties when they are expected to retire on marriage. Other women enter clerical work, or what might be termed 'feminine' professions such as paediatrics, nursing and teaching. Few are recruited into the big business conglomerates. Employment opportunities for graduate women are generally poor. The female contribution to South Korea's present prosperity is now publicly acknowledged, but practical measures to improve women's pay and promotion are still slow to be implemented.

Continuing discontent over wages and working conditions reflect the failure of management and labour to achieve understanding in the workplace. If workers can be held guilty on occasion of resorting to violence, management can often be charged with authoritarian attitudes towards labour. For a society in which the principle of harmony is so valued, there has ironically been little sign of it in work relations. One reason for this lies in the genesis of many of today's companies. They are often the creation of an individual who has left his personal mark on the firm and perpetuated his hold through family succession. His style of management may be auto-cratic, demanding loyalty from all employees, or at best paternalist. Consultation with his workforce may not be high on his priorities. So far he has generally enjoyed official backing for such a line. From now onwards, however, he may find he cannot rely straightaway on the authorities' support in dealing with recalcitrant workers. During the summer of 1987 the government made it clear it expected employers to settle labour disputes on their own, though it threat-ened intervention if order broke down.

Apart from the disruption of the Korean War, and a period from 1961 to 1963 when Park suspended all political parties and trade unions, union activity has been maintained in South Korea since the country's liberation in 1945, when it picked up the tradition of organised labour introduced during the Japanese annexation of Korea. The incoming US Army Military Goverment, suspicious of existing left wing labour groups, favoured a closely-controlled form of union organisation, and this style has been perpetuated. Fearful that labour might develop a potential for disruption and even sub-version, the authorities have confined union activity to work issues, resisted the formation of unions outside of a permitted structure, the Federation of Korean Trade Unions (FKTU), forbidden union political involvement, and restricted intervention by third parties. Liaison between workers and students or religious groups such as the Urban Industrial Mission is discouraged. Considerable legisla-tion regulates union registration and procedures for the handling of disputes and gives the government large powers of intervention. The structure of union organisation was amended in 1980 from the system of industry-based unions instituted under Park to one based primarily on individual enterprises grouped into sixteen industrial labour unions. The right to represent workers and negotiate on their behalf was for a while vested solely in the business unions, but now the FKTU and the senior industrial unions are permitted to inter-vene in disputes. Only enterprises with a workforce of thirty upwards are entitled to form a union, and many small businesses offer no means of representation to their workers. Where a union has already been formed, it is difficult to get another one estab-lished. The freedom to set up rival organisations independent of the

FKTU, which is seen as too tied to the government, has long been claimed by workers and is only now being gradually conceded.

Union membership covers only a small proportion of workers: in 1985 1,004,398 out of a workforce of 15,646,000. They were organised into 2534 business unions. Many firms do not accept trade unions. As an alternative forum for the discussion of disputes, some of them have set up joint labour–management negotiation committees. The handling of strikes has long been the occasion for violence, with company strong-arm men attacking both male and female workers and riot police intervening. Labour disputes in the 1970s were particularly bitter. The tradition of confrontation between labour and management remains, but may ease if the government withdraws somewhat from the scene and employers and employees develop better negotiating techniques.

Big business

The visitor to South Korea can, if he likes, set up a number of mental exercises for himself. Firstly, how many big business names can he spot on office buildings and in advertisements; and secondly, and more difficult, on how many products and in how many lines of business can he find these names? A full list may surprise him by its variety: heavy industry, electronics, textiles, construction, engineering, trading, retailing, insurance, advertising, medical services, hotels and tourism, a farm, a basketball team, a cultural foundation, and a newspaper. The name bringing these activities together is Samsung, but other big conglomerates or *chaebŏl* can sport a similar range. The diversification of these companies is one of their most prominent features. Other characteristics are their family ownership and their still close relationship with government. They command large resources and considerable influence. In a style cultivated by all in positions of eminence, the heads of these concerns move with the assurance and hauter of medieval barons followed by a retinue of retainers. They keep a controlling hand even after their supposed retirement, place family members in charge of different branches of the business, encourage careful marriages for their children, and try to set up a family succession to themselves. The same ethos may lead them to adopt a 'family' style in dealings with their employees.

In concept and style these big conglomerates are reminiscent of the Japanese *zaibatsu*, some of which, such as Mitsubishi and Mitsui, established branches in Korea in the 1920s. The founder of the Samsung group, Lee Byung-chull, who died in late 1987, had his first taste of business in colonial Korea. After the country's liberation in 1945, he resumed activities and was joined during the late 1940s and the 1950s by other entrepreneurs who started up companies and factories dealing largely in the import or manufacture of consumer goods and the provision of services, all much needed in South Korea at that time. As resourceful businessmen they prospered through the acquisition of former Japanese properties and the take-over of ailing concerns, and through access to bank loans, public contracts, foreign aid funds and foreign exchange. These last advantages were offered by the government. The new administration of 1961, though ready to curb *chaebŏl* excesses (Lee Byung-chull was fined for having amassed what was regarded as an illegal fortune), was prepared to use the talents of these entrepreneurs. They in turn were willing to work with the government. The close cooperation that ensued between big business and government lasted throughout the 1960s and 1970s and undoubtedly played an important part in South Korea's rapid economic progress. Many of the particular thrusts marking successive economic plans, such as shipbuilding, heavy and chemical industries, and electronics, were made possible by *chaebŏl* willingness to develop these lines. Big business showed itself amenable to official guidance during the sixties and seventies perhaps because it realised it had little other choice if it was to flourish. In return it benefited from the continuing provision of cheap credit and other financial and fiscal incentives, and more generally from an ambiance favourable to its activities.

This era of collaboration may now be finishing. The official mood is towards greater self-reliance and competitiveness in business activities and less government involvement. A sharper eye is being turned on the *chaebŏl*. Charges of monopolistic practices, over-diversification and poor management are being levelled. Some of the groups, taking growth as their prime target, have spread into disparate ventures not all of which are thriving. To finance new subsidiaries conglomerates have resorted to cross-investment with the aim of enhancing the capital value of a subsidiary and thereby securing bank loans. The big groups' excessive branching into new fields and their dominant need of investment and loan funds are resented by smaller firms. The very basis of their organisation, their family ownership, is a further source of grievance, since they are reluctant to relinquish family control. The government, while it may have decided to withdraw from certain areas of economic activity, still asserts rights of guidance and control. It encourages *chaebŏl* to separate ownership and management and introduce more professional trained managers. It has called on them to drop unproductive holdings, reduce debts, and specialise to a greater extent; and has even shown itself willing to let an ailing conglomerate go to the wall as a warning to others.

The very extent of *chaebŏl* resources has had its beneficial effects. It has allowed them to develop and install new technologies, to build new factories, and recruit and train skilled workforces that they can pay above the average. The conglomerates absorb many of the graduates leaving Korean universities and occupy an important place in the employment market. They take the output of many smaller components firms. The government, while anxious they be taken in hand, does not want to see a string of failed *chaebŏl*. It will doubtless watch closely to see if they can regain their former vigour and initiative.

Imbalances in the system

One of these has already been indicated: the gap between large companies and small to medium ones. The divergence shows itself in several ways: scale of capitalisation, scope of activity, size of workforce and standards of equipment. Recurring worries where small businesses are concerned are their outdated machinery and generally low level of technology. The government is now concerned to improve the efficiency of such firms. The problem stems partly from earlier official policies that tolerated the growth of the big companies at the expense of smaller ones, and that in favouring export-oriented businesses may have stunted those catering for the domestic market. Other imbalances, such as that between heavy industry and other industrial sectors, also reflect past government decisions. The differing pace of development between South Korea's various regions is attributed by many to official preferences. Natural causes such as terrain account to some extent for such divergence, but political and even historical sentiments have played their part in the expansion of the metropolitan area and the rapid opening up of the south east of the country by comparison with the slow development of the south west.

A basic weakness in South Korea's economic structure is the lack of natural resources. The need to import raw materials to meet the requirements of energy production and the textile and heavy industry and chemical sectors undoubtedly puts a heavy burden on the economy. Apart from the demands it imposes on foreign exchange reserves, it renders South Korea vulnerable to price fluctuations and makes urgent a search for diversification of sources of supply. The rising share of nuclear power in the generation of energy is one response to the problem. Self-sufficiency is a slogan for many sectors, and has, we are told, been achieved in steel and chemical fertiliser production (despite heavy dependence on imports of raw materials). Other sectors such as electronics, industrial machinery, and machine tools and textiles still rely on imports to meet their needs for equipment and components.

The other noticeable area of weakness in the economy is its financial structure. The main difficulty seems to centre around the financing of enterprise. From the 1950s onwards a gap has always existed between the level of domestic savings and rates of investment. To fuel the country's economic expansion successive governments first of all drew on foreign aid, loans and trade credits, then solicited foreign investment funds. The result has been a large external debt that at the end of 1987 stood at US$35.5 billion. It must be said that this figure is much down from the US$44.5 billion recorded in 1986. The emergence of trade and current account surpluses from 1986 is taken as a further sign that the size of the external debt will gradually diminish. On the domestic front the government, through its control of the banking sector, has long rationed the flow of credit. This has thrown up some undesirable practices such as cross-investment and an informal or 'curb' finance market to satisfy the needs of investors. There was a major 'curb' loan scandal in 1982. The government has gradually loosened its hold on the commercial banks, but still controls the Bank of Korea. Official intervention in the finance sector is said to have produced distortions, but it is easy to recognise the advantages to the government's economic policies of controlling access to both foreign and domestic funds. Over the years South Korean governments have argued that the results of their strategy outweighed its weaknesses and justified both risks and restraints. The ROK's economic policies over the past quarter century indeed in some respects look like an enormous gamble that has so far paid off.

Agriculture

South Korea's main crop is rice, with barley, wheat, vegetables, maize and tobacco as important secondary crops. Mulberry, ginseng and fruit cultivation is also pursued. Tea is grown in small quantities. Around urban conglomerations, particularly Seoul, a horticultural industry is developing, aided by the introduction of 'vinyl farming' — the use of vinyl sheeting to protect vegetables during the winter cold. Vinyl also provides a cover for the rice seedbeds. Cattle are still much used as draft animals, but the livestock industry is increasing as more meat and milk enter the diet. Sheep are hardly found, mutton being repugnant to most Koreans. The predominantly rugged topography of South Korea, with mountains taking up 70 percent of the land area, leaves some 20 percent of the country available for cultivation. Much of the flat land is in the south west and around the Naktong delta. The terrain is divided into wet paddy and upland dry fields. In the mild climate and longer growing period in the southern part of the peninsula, paddy customarily supports two crops of rice a year. Dry fields can take a higher volume of double cropping in crops other than rice. Altogether some 70 percent of agricultural land is capable of double cropping. Self-sufficiency in rice and barley was achieved in 1975.

The rural sector has seen many changes since the early years of the century. A land registration carried out by the Japanese Government-General between 1912 and 1918 resulted in the transfer of much land to Japanese colonisers and the migration of Korean farmworkers to Japan and Manchuria. Following liberation, two redistributions of land were effected: one in 1948 when former Japanese-owned properties were sold to incumbent tenants; the second in the period 1950–1952, when the ROK government acquired tenanted land owned by absentee landlords, and the balance of any land held by owner–farmers in excess of 2.9 hectares (7.35 acres), a figure that came to represent the maximum size of holding. The property thus acquired was then sold to tenant farmers and those with no land of their own. By the end of the two reform programmes, some 1.5 million farmers (70 percent of total farm households) had become owner–farmers. The imposition of a maximum holding led in turn to a redistribution and equalisation of income. Land reform, undertaken in a spirit of social justice, had a beneficial effect on farming morale, but contributed to a fragmentation of the land into a large number of small holdings, many no greater than a hectare (2.4 acres), and to consequent problems of economic viability for some farmers.

The years since the Korean war have seen a reversal in the relative sectoral strengths of the Korean economy, with agriculture taking an increasingly smaller share. In the mid-1950s it provided some 40 percent of GNP and over 70 percent of employment. This ratio of GNP persisted into the first half of the 1960s, but thereafter fell rapidly, touching 23 percent in 1976 and 15 percent in 1985. Employment in the agricultural sector likewise declined from 63 percent of total employment in 1963 to 25 percent in 1985. These falls are matched by a slide in the farming population to a figure in 1985 of around 20 percent of the total population. By contrast the industrial sector expanded from a share of 13 percent of GNP in the mid-1960s to provide a third of GNP and a quarter of employment by 1985; while the service sector's contribution to GNP, showing little variation over the period 1966-1985, has hovered around 50 percent.

One of agriculture's greatest roles in South Korea's economic progress has been as a source of manpower. The drift off the land was doubtless inevitable, given the decision in the early 1960s to go for rapid industrial growth and the promotion of manufacturing industries geared to exports. A demand for labour set in, which at least until the end of the sixties could be met by surplus workers from the rural areas. The density of occupation of cultivated land at that time was very high (500–1000 people per square kilometre). The multiplicity of small holdings, many of them economically weak, left many of those working them in a marginal situation from which they escaped to the cities. Despite officially-supported programmes of financing and land improvement, the farming sector had stagnated throughout the 1950s. Low pricing policies for grains had depressed farm incomes and reduced the scope for investment. Added to the 'push' of such factors was the 'pull' of (relatively) high wages earned by those working in industry. As serious as the actual volume of migrants to the cities was the fact that those leaving were in the main young men and women, the strong and educated sections of rural communities.

The deterioration of the agricultural sector was not viewed with any complacency. Low farm output during the 1950s and 1960s, together with increases in population, prevented self-sufficiency in foodstuffs and necessitated imports of grain. The progressive backwardness and impoverishment of rural life was seen as a brake on the country's aspirations. Revised policies on pricing during the 1960s led to higher guaranteed prices for farmers. Rural migration began to have the effect of gradually increasing the size of farms as those remaining took over the land of those who had left. Then, in 1971, the farming sector was taken in hand with the introduction of *saemaŭl undong*, or the 'New Community Movement.' This aimed at encouraging self-reliance, cooperation and thrift at village level, improving rural incomes, and inculcating a positive and enlightened approach to problems. While much of the impetus on individual projects was expected to come from below, the movement was led extensively in the 1970s by *saemaŭl undong* headquarters, which offered administrative, technical and financial guidance and trained up *saemaŭl* village leaders. The basis for such an approach to rural development already existed in traditional cooperative arrangements for sharing large-scale tasks, and in the system of village headmen, but has been built upon to create an organisation charged with enhancing the quality of life of agricultural communities. So far about a third of farm households participate in projects sponsored by *saemaŭl undong*. Further government support for the rural sector will take the form of development projects aimed at remote areas, funding for various schemes and training for local leaders.

Despite such efforts, the agricultural sector remains depressed. Depleted in its strongest element, the young, it has to rely on older men and on women for its labour. By 1986 only 23 percent of farmers were aged below 35, while 42 percent were above 50. Female participation in agricultural work is high, at twice the rate for working urban women. The sector is in fact short of labour. In absolute terms the rural population is continuing to shrink, and it is doubtful how much longer it can sustain its function as a reserve of manpower for industry as well as meet its obligations in feeding the nation. There are fears that even self-sufficiency in food grains may be declining as production falls of secondary grains other than rice. Mechanisation is proceeding unevenly, and moreover cannot be easily applied to such delicate tasks as rice transplanting or in the small fields characteristic of Korea. Despite increases in rural wages, the gap between urban and rural incomes remains noticeable, and public amenities such as paved roads and piped water are slow to reach some parts of the countryside. Improvements have nonetheless come, if fitfully. It is too soon to say, though, if agriculture has reached a point of stabilisation, or whether the sector faces further weakening.

The effects of change

In all the above scant attention has been paid tò those who nonetheless can claim to be chief participants in their country's fortunes: the ordinary men and women of South Korea. Through perseverance and hard work they contribute enormously to their society's wealth and progress. Life for many of them has changed greatly in recent years as they have borne the brunt of industrialisation.

Only a third still live in rural areas. An average annual rate of 5 percent increase in the urban population since 1955 has swollen the size of South Korea's main towns and placed Seoul among the world's largest cities. While all the big towns have drawn country dwellers, Seoul has been like a giant magnet. It now houses almost a quarter of the total population of the ROK. Some 60 percent of its inhabitants were born elsewhere. South Korea's second largest city, Pusan, with a population of over 3.6 million, again has a majority of incomers among its residents. Much of the attraction has been work. During the 1970s the greater number of new jobs created were in Seoul and Pusan. Better educational and other facilities in the cities have added their lure. Accommodation, however, has not kept pace with employment and amenities, and Koreans moving to the cities may have had cause to regret the houses left behind. The gap between homes available and households to fill them has been widening since 1960. The pressure has come in part from the very rise in living standards that prosperity has brought. Former large single households have broken down into a greater number of small units as family members with the means to move out have chosen to do so.

Where the inhabitants of South Korea's big cities live is largely determined by their income. Those able to afford it, and an increasing number are clearly able to, buy an apartment in one of the enormous new complexes that are springing up especially in Seoul, where the area south of the Han river has been rapidly and extensively developed since the late 1970s to the point where it now accommodates almost half the city's population. Memories of 1950 and the threat from North Korea have been factors in persuading people to move from the districts north of the river. In attempts to ease the burden on Seoul, the authorities have established a ring of new towns around the capital. There is much to be said for moving out from the centre of Seoul, where pollution from traffic and small industry, and the level of noise, can be severe. The Han had become a dead stretch of water through pollution until a cleaning-up programme was put in hand recently. Contamination of air and water in heavily-industrialised areas elsewhere in Korea is even worse. Many urban residents in fact have no choice but to remain in one of the densely-populated *dong* or districts of tightly-packed housing put up in the 1950s and 1960s to meet urgent needs. The least fortunate may find their homes demolished around them to make way for a new development and they themselves transported to a far-off suburb, as has happened more than once in Seoul.

One of South Korea's boasts is that it has put all parts of the country within a day's travel of each other. Since the construction of the first expressway in 1968, a network of paved highways and secondary roads has come to link many places, though access to some remote spots is still over stone and dirt roads. A system of long-distance coaches serves much of the population, supplemented by trains and air transport. Within the cities fleets of rapid, if ill-disciplined, buses and taxis meet transport needs. Seoul has an underground railway system. Pusan will have one soon and Taegu would also like to build one. The extension of communications throughout the country has encouraged the growth of domestic tourism, and favourite sites see a continual procession of coaches and their occupants. The middle classes, who have shied away from this popular style of travel, are now in increasing numbers able to afford private cars. Their new independence is making them adventurous — though some still hardly leave Seoul from one year's end to another — but their vehicles are coming to clog up already busy roads, particularly in the capital.

The basic means of support for most Koreans is their income from employment. For the greater number this is a wage income, rather than the subsistence income provided by farming. Those available for work can generally find a job, but in taking note of the high employment rates quoted for Korea — in 1987 the rate stood at 96.7 percent — it should be remembered that the ROK's definition of employment for statistical purposes is work for as little as one hour a week. A small proportion of the population, under 7 percent, is regarded as destitute and entitled to public relief. The financial margin of some others is minute. They pay rent on a daily basis, and live by selling small quantities of goods in the street. Those on a salary fare better, and some receive high remuneration. The country's economic growth and educational expansion have encouraged the formation of a middle class, which in turn is creating and supporting a strong domestic market for consumer goods and services. The existence since the 1970s of a fairly wide income gap between top and bottom has been acknowledged, if deplored, by the government, which is seeking to alleviate it through the implementation of various welfare measures. Legislation authorising such measures was passed in the 1960s and 1970s, but the economic situation was never judged strong enough until now to allow all schemes to be carried through. Medical insurance provision, which presently covers about half the population, is to be gradually extended to give universal cover by 1990. Pension schemes operate at present in selected professions, but are also to be extended to other groups of employees.

What lies ahead

On 29 January 1988 the United States announced that the Republic of Korea, together with Taiwan, Hong Kong and Singapore, would be 'graduated' from the US Generalised System of Preferences from 2 January 1989. After that date certain South Korean goods will no longer be allowed duty free into the United States. The news has come as the Koreans face increasing pressure from the European Community, the United States, and other western countries to open up their markets and put an end to what are judged unfair trading practices. The ROK's very success as an exporting nation is causing general fears that it may build up the same order of surplus in its foreign trade as Japan has, and anxieties for specific partners such as the United States, which in 1986 had a deficit of US$7.3 billion in its trade with South Korea, followed in 1987 by a deficit of US$9.5 billion. The surplus on the ROK's trade with the United States is partly offset by a deficit in its trade with Japan, which in 1986 stood at US$5.4 billion, a figure barely changed in 1987. South Korea is aware it is vulnerable to protectionist moves by others. In an attempt to meet criticisms that it is itself too protective of its own domestic market, it has liberalised imports of many goods such as foreign cars, which until July 1987 could not be imported by Koreans, but has not yet reduced the often heavy tariffs on such products. The United States is also exerting pressure on South Korea to revalue its currency against the weak dollar. The ROK is unlikely rapidly to reduce its dependence on exports at a time when trade surpluses offer hope of cutting the external debt. Export industries sustain a good part of the labour force. At a more fundamental level, any re-orientation of manufacturers and public away from a sector to which they have been wedded for so long would be a protracted business. South Korea will continue as an exporting nation, and is eyeing new markets such as China and Eastern Europe, but will need to handle its trading partners carefully if it is to avoid recriminations. Overseas manufacturing ventures may be pursued as one way of circumventing restrictive quotas. Over the long term the ROK may aim for a better balance between exports and imports and encourage the domestic market as a consumer of manufactured goods.

One move it seems set to make is away from labour-intensive manufacturing, which is losing its competitive edge, to technology-intensive industries. Quality will be emphasised in place of quantity in an attempt to improve the attractiveness of South Korean exports. The rising price of raw materials and higher labour costs, fuelled in part by the strikes and pay rises of the summer of 1987, are putting pressure on industries such as textiles and forcing diversification. Some of the workforce will no doubt be retrained to new jobs; but

113

the long-term implications for employment of turning away from a heavy dependence on labour seem hardly to have been addressed. Any curtailment on openings for skilled construction workers overseas would also put a strain on the domestic labour force. Problems have already been signalled at the upper end of the market, where graduates are beginning to experience difficulty in finding work. Any interruption in the smooth progress from college to employment for South Korea's educated young and any prolonged halt to the rising expectations of the great mass of people could bring trouble.

Section Four

Korean Values

Where three travel together, one will be my teacher

Chapter Eight

Social Structure and Values

Principal among the Confucian teachings by which Koreans still set much store are the five relationships. These instruct that: between ruler and minister, there should be righteousness; between father and son, there should be affection; between husband and wife, there should be attention to their separate functions; between old and young, there should be a proper order; between friends, there should be faithfulness.

These phrases provide as good a clue as any to some of the basic tenets of Korean society.

Among such tenets is a belief in a natural order expressing itself in harmony between the various social elements, but dependent on a proper understanding of the relationship between these elements. When today Koreans deplore the pressures on their society, it is this natural order that they see as under threat, and undoubtedly the rapid industrialisation of recent decades, exposure to western ideas and fashions, the progress towards new forms of government, the impact of legislation on customary procedures, and the emancipation of women, continue to put strain on older ways of thought and action. There are three points worth making in response. One is that the Korean experience, though peculiarly Korean in its details, shares common elements with the experiences of many other societies. The passage from an agricultural and rural-based way of life to an industrial economy developing in an urban setting has taken place in South Korea over the past forty years — a rapid transition when compared with the slower process of industrialisation in many other countries. Koreans often describe their history and present situation, together with their culture and institutions, as 'unique.' Aspects certainly are, in the measure that all societies possess unique features; but an outsider listening to Korean complaints about destruction of the old order knows he has heard as much in his own country. What may be unique to Korea is the violence and intensity of the experience.

The second point is that the newcomer to South Korea may feel for a while he is in a largely westernised country, but soon he will realise there is much he does not understand as he is confronted with basic Korean instincts and responses. Change has come, but it has in many instances resulted in a change of form rather than content. Complaints about unwelcome influences have been voiced since the early days of reform and introduction of foreign modes a century ago; but despite the pessimism of Koreans that their institutions are being eroded, true rot has not yet set in and is unlikely to. A final point is that the ideal of a harmoniously-ordered society, given the flaws in any human organisation, can only be achieved with a certain amount of coercion. Confucian teaching sees nothing amiss with a society based on the subordination of some of its members to other members; indeed it sees such subordination and the hierarchies that result as essential to good order. However, such a system carries within itself the potential for disaffection and instability, particularly when authority is judged to be weak or compromised. The changes with which South Korea has had to contend are in large measure a result of pressures from within as well as without its shores.

Attitudes of government

The historical convention of government in Korea has been the accumulation of power in official hands under the rule of a leader, for centuries the king. He was judged to have received the mandate of heaven to exercise temporal control over his people and bind them together in a harmonious whole. His rule had an essentially moral basis, and he was expected to command respect by a show of virtue. All authority, whether legal or administrative, in principle stemmed from him and should be obeyed. In practice the Korean monarch faced several limitations on his powers. The condition for the exercise of his authority was that he dealt righteously with his subjects, who in return should faithfully accept his will. The unjust or immoral monarch or one who failed through weakness or incompetence to exercise effective rule, might see the mandate of heaven, that is, his right to hold authority, wrested from him by a powerful challenger or through popular protest. He was, moreover, expected to listen to comment and criticism from his advisers, men often known for their integrity and scholarship, even if he did not always heed them. He had to contend also with factionalism and intrigue on the part of wives, concubines, eunuchs and courtiers. Within the framework of such limitations, however, a combination of the moral qualities of kingship and a firm bureaucracy led to a tradition of centralised authority in Korea, commanding deference.

Much has changed in Korean political life since the abolition of the monarchy in 1910. Thirty-five years of colonial administration stifled Korean political development. War and political instability marked the early years of the new Republic of Korea. Now South Korea appears committed to a consultative form of government, however difficult the search may be for a satisfactory understanding between leading and opposition parties (the concept of a 'loyal opposition' has no roots in East Asian political traditions), and is working to adapt traditional modes of political thought to new institutions. Nonetheless, old ideals of leadership remain. Government in Korea adjudges a strong position to itself. It expects to define national goals and indicate national priorities and assumes a central role of regulator in many spheres of activity, from economic policy to education and culture. The president, still the pinnacle of the political system, expects to offer guidance and to have his words heeded. In this, it may be said, he conforms to a tradition that extends beyond the bounds of South Korea into China and even North Korea and that has its roots in a common political culture. Though both China and North Korea are moved by a very different ideology and have a different structure of government, they share a style of leadership with the Republic of Korea. This is marked by such practices as 'on the spot' guidance to workers and a liberal use of badges, medals and other awards. Party political opposition, though acknowledged now as an integral part of the political process, may still be denounced by the ruling party as disruptive of harmonious government. At the same time the administration seeks to promote social and thus national cohesion by narrowing distinctions of class and income with the intention of reducing social friction. A long tradition of primacy has led government in Korea to assume the initiative in many areas of national activity, and to concern itself with aspects of its citizen's lives that in other societies might be judged beyond its proper scope. Thus in the interests of frugality and social equality it seeks to implement modern sumptuary laws by restricting the scale of, for instance, wedding celebrations.

Family life

In some ways, a discussion of the family in Korea might claim to take precedence over anything else, such was the importance traditionally accorded it as the basic social, cultural, religious, even judicial and economic unit of society. However, the Confucian teaching that was so supportive of the family's role at the same time chose to give the greater prestige to public affairs. The family, rather, stood at the point of intersection between the public domain and the private. During the Yi dynasty the family was entrusted with considerable autonomy in the management of its internal affairs. The head of the family was held responsible for the good conduct of his household and was enjoined to observe the proper rites of mourning for his ancestors. The family also saw to it that its children were suitably married and that the male ancestral lineage was preserved. While it was generally only the wealthier families who could afford to observe closely the prescriptions on social conduct that were issued by the central authority, the essential duties of family life were familiar to all.

The status of the family remains high in modern Korea. Its autonomy has been much reduced, in part by the introduction of a Family Law following on from the constitution of 1948, which has sought to impose a measure of egality on customary family relations; but the government still regards it as basic to the well-being of Korean society in its role as the prime socialising unit for the country's young, a transmitter of national culture and a guarantee of social stability. To that end, the government is anxious to maintain the traditional authority of the family and to promote what it characterises as 'wholesome' family life, though on closer observation it is selective in the aspects it chooses to emphasise. 'Filial piety' and respect for the elderly are encouraged, perhaps because it is feared they are falling into decline at a time when the elderly are coming to form a larger portion of the population, but there is little public mention of the sharp distinction between the sexes and the subservience of women that also used to mark traditional Korean family life.

Koreans themselves set great value on family life and draw heavily on both the immediate and the wider family circle for emotional, social and often financial support. Especially close ties are held to bind parents and children together, and it is the generational link, rather than that between husband and wife, which has been regarded as vital. Family loyalty should be lifelong. In some sense a Korean may never seek to move beyond the bounds of family life, regarding an existence without family support as too fearful. Whereas the open expression of affection even between spouses is not acceptable (no self-respecting Korean man would admit to kissing his wife goodbye in the morning and indeed probably never does so), a display of violent emotion over the loss or recovery of a parent or child is permissible, even expected. This attachment to parents and siblings has made the division of the Korean peninsula into two separate entities an extremely painful experience for many older Koreans who have seen their families split asunder. In 1983 the Korean Broadcasting System (KBS) mounted a campaign to bring together family members separated during and after the Korean war. Those who had lost relatives were invited to recount on television the circumstances in which they had become separated and to give what information they could about these family members. The walls of the KBS building and the park outside were hung with notices bearing similar details. A number of reunions were effected amid much emotion, but many people remained disappointed. The effect on an outsider was oppressive, and the political aspects of the campaign could not be ignored, but for many of the Koreans involved a certain purging of the emotions will have been achieved.

Though the family retains great importance for Koreans, it is clear that as an institution it is undergoing change. The traditional pattern of a three-generation family comprising grandparents, the sons of the family and their wives and children, together with any unmarried members of the family, all living under one roof under the headship of the senior male member, has largely disappeared, though middle-aged Koreans may remember it as the style of their childhood. Three generations may still live together, even if it means only a grandfather perched miserably in the corner of a modern apartment. A better arrangement is a grandmother to do the cooking. Headship of a family still passes to the eldest son, and it is his duty to look after a widowed mother and any unmarried siblings; though again practice may belie principle, and energetic widows work to put their sons through college. The large family unit has, however, now generally broken down into a collection of nuclear families, which in turn are growing smaller in size. The number of births per childbearing woman is calculated to have dropped from 6.1 in 1960 to below 2.0 in 1986. The birth control campaign launched in 1962 with the intention of curbing population increase has encouraged this decline, but other familiar factors such as the economic advantages of a small family, changing views among women, later marriage and childbearing, the urbanisation of large sections of the population and the popularity of living in apartment blocks, particularly among the affluent, have all contributed to the reduction in family size.

Other more subtle changes have been at work as well. One function of the family that has undoubtedly diminished with the advent of a secular state is its religious or ritual one. When Confucianism provided the officially-sanctioned ethical framework of society, the family had an essential role as the forum of worship of the ancestors and guarantors of the ancestral lineage. Perpetuation of the male line was a duty lying on each new generation, as was the proper observance of mourning rites for deceased parents. Marriage was likewise a duty, though the prospective spouses had no say in the choice of a partner. A woman's chief function and desire was to produce a male heir for her husband's family. This distinct understanding of the purposes of marriage and family life has been weakened and with it the formal pre-eminence of the family; but aspects of the traditional order remain. Gatherings to express respect to living parents are still arranged, particularly at New Year, and responsibility for organising them continues to fall on the wife of the eldest son. The husband's family and its needs still take precedence over the wife's both legally and socially. The preference for sons is still pronounced among both men and women, though there are signs that even this is weakening, and a young father may admit privately that he is content with his two daughters, even if his mother or wife says she is not. With the consent of young people themselves, marriages are still largely arranged by parents, and marriage is still accepted as a duty and the sign of passage into adulthood. It no longer has its immutable character, however. Divorce is now legally permissible and is becoming more frequent, though socially it is still viewed askance.

Men and women

The nature of the male–female relationship in Korean society is not an easy one for the outsider to decipher. Its philosophical under-pinning is familiar enough in the dual concept of *yin* and *yang* — the principle of complementing forces of positive and negative, activity and passivity, strength and weakness, light and darkness, and so forth — which in turn led to the teaching that men's and women's activities and spheres of authority should be distinguished one from the other. The practical effects of this teaching in Yi dynasty times were the physical separation of the sexes from the age of seven and the training of boys and girls along quite different lines. Boys might receive a formal education and were gradually initiated into their role as members of the 'outside' world. Girls were pre-pared for their 'inside' roles as wives, mothers and household managers. Men's authority related to their position in society and extended over women and children, but within the home women were, and still are, expected to assume full charge for the efficient and harmonious running of the family. Formal segregation is no longer enforced, but a tradition of social separation persists that shows itself in a preference for men and women to eat at different tables and for men to spend the evening or Sunday in their own company. Even in the street it is rare to see an intermingled group of men and women. The persistence of the concept of separate func-tions for the sexes has made it difficult for Korean women to break into occupations judged by men to be their preserve. Women's impact on public life has so far been weak, and political parties are

123

only now showing some practical interest in women's causes, such as equal employment opportunities, on which legislation was passed in October 1987. Further revision of the Family Law, another issue close to women's organisations, is moving very slowly for fear of offending conservative opinion.

Married status and parenthood are among the common expectations of young Koreans. Their parents' willingness to assist them in the choice of a spouse removes much of the anxiety of finding a partner, but may also lower the emotional intensity of the union. Affection may well develop between husband and wife, but it has not traditionally been judged essential to the validity of the marriage. Indeed, at times an outsider may have the impression of an emotional vacuum at the centre of the family, with the husband often late home and the wife seeking companionship among female friends. Then it may be best to remember that for most Koreans the most powerful female images are those of mother and mother-in-law, and that these images are generally combined in the person of the husband's mother. The crucial link still remains the one between parent and child.

Age and seniority

To reach the age of 60 has long been a triumphant moment in a Korean's life. The celebration of *hwan'gap*, one's sixtieth birthday anniversary, shows that one has completed the full series of five twelve-year cycles and has truly crossed the threshold into old age. Respect and a large measure of personal freedom become one's due, whether one is male or female. This is the age when women start to smoke in public, and now and again an old lady can be seen puffing away at a long pipe. The sense of pride was especially strong in earlier days when average life expectancy was low. As recently as the mid-1950s it stood at 47 for men and 52.5 for women. Now, with life expectancy reaching an average of 68, the sixtieth birthday is no longer so remarkable, but still a time for congratulation.

Care of their elderly is a point on which many Asians pride themselves, contrasting their respect for the old with what they see as western callousness. Koreans also take this view; and it is undeniable that many elderly people in Korea have an alert confidence that suggests they are at ease in their status. Nonetheless, even in South Korea the situation is changing. One reason is the growing number of older people in the population. In 1985, the proportion of those aged 65 and over stood at 4.3 percent and by 1990, it is estimated, it may reach 6.2 percent of the population. Financial support of the . elderly was traditionally left to their families, but will increasingly be met now by a network of pension systems, some of them already in place, which come into effect after 55, the customary age for retirement. Not all old people can be cared for by families, and day centres and residential homes are starting to appear. In short, South Korea is beginning to experience some of the problems associated with a growing proportion of elderly people in the population.

These practical issues may have some effect on general attitudes towards the old, but it is unlikely that the Korean preoccupation with seniority will fade, especially where it is accompanied by authority. It manifests itself in many areas of life: relations between siblings; precedence in the workplace and professional relations in general; the choice of verb endings in speech; forms of address. Seniority may be based on rank and status, but it equally draws on chronological age. It is important for a Korean to be able to place himself or herself in a correct relationship with those around. This will involve knowing an order of seniority, and to this end it may be essential to find out a person's age and marital standing, even if that person is a foreigner; hence the blunt questions on one's age and the number of children one has. These reflect not idle curiosity, but a desire to gain important information.

Relations between friends

If many of the relationships that Koreans enter into seem to follow a vertical axis, those between friends are on the horizontal. They provide much of the content and animation of daily social and business dealings and act as a brake on and antidote to the demands of other relationships. In friendship, two or more people bind themselves together as equals, drawing on shared experience to construct a relationship that is expected to last indefinitely and provide

125

continuing mutual satisfaction. Many friendships date from high school and college days. Koreans explain this by pointing out that these final years of education are the last time when they can come together as equals in an undisturbed atmosphere, before the demands of work, marriage and family close in on them. The relationships formed in these relatively calm circumstances, almost invariably with those of the same sex, are expected to help the individual in his subsequent career by giving him contacts both within and outside his profession on which he can draw. In turn, he should be ready to help a friend in like manner. With increased access to higher education the prevalence of such friendships has doubtless grown. It is noticeable, and quite accepted, that an important man's classmates prosper with him. He will, after all, prefer to work with those he knows and trusts. No Korean is taken aback to know that former President Chun Doo Hwan and his successor, Roh Tae Woo, are fellow classmates from military academy days. Even dealings with a stranger are eased if a mutual acquaintance can be established. For women, who may never need to draw on their friendships for professional reasons, their friends provide companionship, a possible source of marriage partners for their children, and access, in the shape of their husbands, to men who might be able to help their own husbands. Friendship, in short, is not taken lightly in Korea, since it provides an indispensable support in meeting life's obligations, as well as bringing personal satisfaction.

Chapter Nine

Education

In December 1987 the Korean press carried a photograph of a woman standing with head bowed and hands pressed together at the gates of a school: a mother praying for the success of her child in the state college entrance examination. It is an image that expresses vividly the preoccupation of many Korean parents with the education of their offspring. Concern is not limited either to the parents of children and young people. The government, and indeed large sections of the community, take a close interest in all things related to education. Parents for their part can be much exercised by official decisions, particularly on college entrance, an issue on which, despite their general self-restraint, they can become heated. They may have made financial sacrifices to put their children through higher schooling, since only primary education is compulsory and therefore free. Their children, in preparing for university entrance, submit to an exacting regime of study that may take them away from home for fifteen or so hours each day. Yet Koreans are willing to tolerate the personal inconveniences in return for likely rewards later on and, beyond that, for the pride of knowing that their society is a literate and well-educated one that owes its economic prosperity in large measure to these very qualities.

The present enthusiasm for education derives from a number of factors, of which one is undoubtedly a long tradition of scholarship. The acceptance of Confucian and Buddhist teaching, each of which was developed in a large body of texts, led in the fourth century AD to the establishment of a Confucian college by the Koguryŏ monarchy and the dissemination of Buddhist sutras in Korea. Both

Confucian and Buddhist writings were in Chinese characters, and for that reason accessible to only a few scholars. The institution of a college or university for the training of government officials was perpetuated by the later Koryŏ and Yi dynasties, which allowed other types of colleges to be set up. A system of village schools was established from the eleventh century, intended for boys of all classes, but in practice attended largely by *yangban* children. The introduction of *han'gŭl* in the mid-fifteenth century broadened the scope of literacy particularly in the direction of women (who were excluded from any formal schooling), but a preference for Chinese texts and characters persisted. Access to education was consciously limited to male members of the upper class. They alone were eligible for admission to the national university and the examination system. This system, which was first instituted in the eighth century and called for a mastery of Confucian texts and Chinese characters, was the means of entry into the ranks of the administration. Study of the Chinese classics and language prepared a candidate for the highest qualification, but those considered for lower official posts received instruction in what were considered professional subjects such as law, mathematics, geography, calligraphy, medicine, and foreign languages. The examinations survived until 1894, by which time other moves had been put in hand to widen access to education and to introduce modern subjects and new techniques. Korean students were already being sent abroad for training. At home the Korean government had set up an institute offering a western style of education. From 1895 a regular system of primary and middle schools, teacher training college, foreign language institutes, technical and commercial colleges, medical school and other professional training institutes was established, and greater importance accorded to the Korean language in schools. Pressure for reform came from the Japanese in the mid-1890s, and the example of Christian Protestant missionary schools, which had been permitted from 1884, gave further impetus for change. Not only did the latter introduce a wider and more modern syllabus, using texts in *han'gŭl*, but they initiated formal schooling for girls and opened their doors to all children regardless of class. Against a background of such changes, the tradition of learning in Korea had, by the beginning of this century, been put on a broader basis.

Although the Japanese may have played a part in pushing through educational reform in Korea at the end of last century, their colonial administration of the country from 1910 to 1945 did not advance educational opportunities for Koreans. With the avenues to political and government activity cut and access to higher professions rendered difficult, the earlier concept of education as a stepping stone to a position of authority lost its value. The Japanese aim was integration of the Koreans as lesser subjects into the Japanese empire. Appropriate educational policies were one way in which they sought to achieve this. (See chapter 5, pages 57 to 59 for an examination of these policies.) It was not until liberation from Japanese control in 1945 that Korea was able to turn its energies to the formation of educational policies of its own choosing and to go some of the way towards meeting its people's desire for a better education.

The government of the new Republic of Korea concerned itself from the outset with the issue of education, seeing in it a means of regenerating and strengthening the country. The 1948 Constitution guaranteed the right to education and also spelt out the duty to ensure that all children received elementary schooling. The Education Act of the following year set out in some detail the aims and principles of education. Both it, and even more so the Charter of National Education published in 1968, stress the desirability of a strong moral spirit, patriotic feeling, pride in national culture, and a sense of cooperation in building the nation. The government has continued to exercise strong control through the Ministry of Education and regional boards of education over the course of the nation's schooling, aided by five-year and long-term educational plans. Official supervision and open guidance of education to meet what the government sees as ideological and material national needs are distinguishing features of the South Korean system. Moral education and instruction in national ethics form an integral part of the curriculum at all levels. The 1968 charter makes it clear that 'the love of the country and fellow countrymen, together with a firm belief in democracy against communism, is the way for our survival and the basis for realising the ideals of the free world.'

In support of this posture, student military training was introduced in the year following the charter. It is still undertaken by high school and college students, but is an unpopular duty, and less time is now spent on it at high school than previously. To meet the goals of economic construction, the government has endeavoured to turn the emphasis of education towards scientific and technological subjects. At the highest level this has meant the establishment of a range of research institutes and the encouragement of research that would benefit industrial development. At a lower level it has led to a variety of vocational high schools, some of them specially set up to meet the requirements of industrial enterprises in Korea and of construction projects undertaken by Korean firms abroad, and to the provision of vocational training centres and of in-plant training in companies above a certain size. The government's efforts to promote vocational rather than academic education have, however, failed to meet outright support. Vocational training is linked for many Koreans with manual work and so does not have the same appeal as an academic qualification.

On occasion the government has not hesitated to use compulsion. Faced in 1945 with an adult population of whom over three-quarters were illiterate (a measure of the poor spread of education under Japanese administration), it eventually placed on local authorities the obligation to institute literacy classes, at which the attendance of illiterates in the 17–43 age group was required by law. Adults received 200 hours of instruction in 70 class days. The disruption of the Korean War delayed implementation of the scheme until the mid-1950s, but progress was thereafter fast, and by 1970 the illiteracy rate had declined to 11.6 percent. In taking a firm line on this and other matters of education, the government has generally been able to rely on the cooperation or, at the very least, acquiescence of the people. In the early years of the new state, the needs of national reconstruction were so obvious as to bring acceptance of government proposals, but also a considerable amount of private initiative, and public and private provision of education up to the highest level went ahead in tandem. Constant reminders of the possibility of North Korean attack have reinforced understanding of the need for a strong society that can also, by its economic and social advances, show how much more successful its policies are. The desire to prove their worth with other countries, particularly Japan, is also a sharp stimulus for the Koreans. In other words they have been able to accept and generally identify with the government's broad objectives. A stronger reason for cooperation over education, however, lies in the overlapping of personal goals with official aims. The government wants a well-educated population; even more do Koreans want good education for themselves and their children.

The ultimate target may no longer be the higher reaches of government service, since the range of desirable occupations has broadened to include academic posts and research, medicine and the big manufacturing and trading companies, but the means of access to a good job (not to mention a good marriage later on), remains the same: graduation from university, for good measure from one of the leading institutions. The crucial link in the chain is college entrance, and the need to succeed at this level hangs like a millstone round the necks of all college aspirants and their families. The mid-teen years for families with ambitions for their children are times of trial. The volume of work imposed on the young people is enormous. Parents worry for their children's well-being, but few seem disposed to question the rigours of the system. Instead they see in this intense period of study a valuable initiation for the young into a lifetime's practice of application and hard work. It is truly a formative experience.

The desire to help their offspring succeed does, however, bring parents into potential and sometimes actual conflict with official policies. Chief among these in recent years were the prohibition in 1980 of private tutoring for both classwork and university entrance, coupled with reorganisation of the college entrance system. Since 1974 this had allowed for a preliminary state-run university entrance test, followed by a separate examination administered by the college concerned. From 1980 students were to be selected only on the basis of the nationwide state test together with an assessment of their high school work. In addition, universities and colleges were instructed to admit some 30 percent more students than their graduation quota, with the understanding that an equivalent proportion of their student intake would have to be rejected during their studies. The government's intention in curbing private tutoring and eliminating separate university entrance tests was to break the unfair advantage of extra tuition and calm the heated atmosphere surrounding college entrance. Its aim in introducing the extra 30 percent recruitment policy was to give students an incentive to apply themselves to their studies. Of the 1980 reforms this last has proved very unpopular and is being modified in the face of opposition from university administrators, students and their parents, all resentful of its unsettling effects. A measure of discretion is also being restored to universities and colleges in the selection of new students. In the main official efforts have moved towards reducing the pressure on children of examinations — tests for admission from elementary to middle school were abolished in 1968 and from middle to high school in 1974 — and discouraging the emergence of elitist tendencies.

In this respect the Korean pattern is very different from the Japanese with its open recognition of 'fast lanes' leading from kindergarten to university via certain schools and out-of-class tutoring. Korean parents and teachers are obliged to accept the government's egalitarian policies on coaching and schools, though they hint that they would welcome a measure of educational selection. The present system of admission to middle school by lottery leads to classes of mixed ability — a 'comprehensive' approach — that clearly is seen as a source of potential difficulty. The government's anti-elitist measures have reduced the prevalence of coaching, but have also cut back for many poor students a means of working their way through university. There is, in fact, no doubt that private tuition continues. Even attempts to calm the tensions of university entrance are countered by continuing intense pressure for admission. In 1987 a ratio of 4.5 applicants to every place in the upper echelon of colleges was recorded. Parents do outwit the government on one point, their persistent drive towards Seoul. For centuries the capital has sucked in the country's talent, not least in the provision and consumption of education. The aspiration of every *yangban* family, after all, was to send its best sons for their final schooling in Seoul. Such hopes endure, and the most coveted university places are at Seoul National University and several other of the capital's many universities. A reverse pattern also reveals itself in which a family settled in the capital will not take its children out of school there, but rather lets the father languish in the provinces should his work take him there. The government is aware of the gap in educational provision between the rural and urban areas, but cannot altogether close it.

Student demonstrations

There is one area that breaks with the pattern of general agreement between the providers and consumers of education, and that is student politics. If little else is known outside of South Korea about school and college life, the violent activities of student demonstrators in Seoul and provincial university cities and the equally strong reaction of riot police are now familiar to anyone with a television set. Student rioting has become a regular occurrence in South Korea in recent years, but generally has its seasons in spring and autumn. The demonstrations during the summer of 1987 prolonged the period of protest and gave the impression of considerable unrest in the capital. This was unfortunate, for the exchanges of paving stones and tear gas canisters, though alarming, were largely confined to the centre of Seoul and various university campuses, and did not spread throughout the city; nor did participation in the demonstrations extend far beyond the students. The mid-1987 clashes did, however, draw more public tolerance and even support than earlier demonstrations, and undoubtedly played their part in inducing the government to agree to a number of political reforms; and for that reason alone cannot be dismissed as the work of mere unruly elements.

It is generally claimed that the instigators of demonstrations are a small core of students within each university, motivated by leftist doctrines or strong nationalistic feeling, who draw the support of larger numbers of less-committed students for the forays out on to the streets. This scenario is probably correct. Arrests and interrogations carried out after demonstrations usually aim to isolate ringleaders among the rioters. Political activities among students are discouraged, partly out of fear of the disruption they may cause, partly out of the belief that such activities are not fitting for students, who should concentrate on preparing themselves through their studies for their future contribution to society, and leave politics to their elders. Certainly the price for dissent can be high. It may lead in extreme instances to imprisonment, and at the least to expulsion, leading in turn to difficulties in getting work and finding a spouse, and thus to a life on the margins of society. There is, however, ambiguity in the public's and even the government's attitudes towards student demonstrations. There is recognition that the majority of demonstrators are not heavily committed and are, rather, engaging in a tiresome but shortlived display of defiance before submitting once more to the controls of society. More distantly there is a recollection of the ancient role of scholars as critics of government. Nearer in time the memory of uprisings led by students tempers reactions. In 1919 the independence movement of protest against the Japanese annexation of Korea was initiated by Korean students first in Japan, then in Korea. Ten years later, in 1929, students in the southern city of Kwangju again protested against the Japanese occupiers. In 1960 students spearheaded the demonstrations against the electoral malpractices of President Syngman Rhee that led to his downfall. Bloodshed and loss of life followed these uprisings. The students who suffered are now honoured as symbols of protest against oppression and iniquity. No government, however, wishes such parallels to be drawn with its own administration and so tells the students that times have changed and that their duty now is to work, not take to the streets.

Structure of education

The educational system in place in Korea in 1945 was in great need of overhaul. Widespread illiteracy and the generally poor provision of schooling for the Korean population — it is claimed that only 30 percent of the entire group of school-age children were accommodated in the primary schools administered by the Japanese — were aggravated by a shortage of classrooms and teachers, the Japanese teachers having all left. The US Military Government that administered the southern half of the peninsula from 1945 to 1948 exerted a strong influence through its advisors on the formation of new educational structures, and the present six–three–three–four pattern of Korean schooling is based on the US model. Despite the desire to shake free of Japanese influences, some aspects of the system erected by the Japanese during their annexation of Korea were retained after 1945, notably a broader curriculum, the establishment of parents' associations, and the wearing of uniform. This last endured until 1983. Its abolition has done much to restore a more human aspect to the appearance of the nation's young people. The expansion of education in the years following liberation has been dramatic, despite the devastation of the Korean war. Pupil numbers at all levels have risen from about 1.4 million in 1945 to some 11 million in 1985 as the take-up rate of school places has increased. Near-total enrolment has been achieved in primary school, where education is compulsory but free, and the follow-on rate from primary to middle school, from which point schooling must be paid for, is also high. There has been a corresponding increase in the provision of educational institutions. The enormous classes, some up to 90 children, and the running of two or three shifts in order to accommodate demand, which marked primary schooling in particular up to the early 1970s, have largely gone, though a two-shift organisation of the day for some primary school students still exists. The government is aiming for an average primary class of about 45, but in urban areas especially this is not being achieved, and large classes still abound. Middle school and high school classes average around 60 students. Discipline is strict, but the use of corporal punishment is frowned upon. Big classes and a tradition of deference to teachers make for a lecturing style of instruction and much learning by rote.

The formal structure of education in South Korea is six years of primary school, starting at the age of six, three years of middle school, three years of high school and two to four years of tertiary education. Transfer from primary to middle school is by lottery for middle school places within the same educational zone as the primary school, from middle to high school by a qualifying state-administered examination, and then by lottery. High schools themselves are divided into two categories: academic and vocational. The government is attempting to steer more able students towards vocational high schools, but the imbalance between them and academic high schools is still of the order of two to three. At the tertiary level students may attend junior vocational colleges offering in the main two-year courses, university offering four- to six-year courses, or other colleges. At all levels a wide curriculum is insisted upon: eight subjects at primary school level and twelve at middle school; while at academic high school 27 subjects are taught over the three-year period, and at vocational high school the course is divided between theoretical and general education (30 percent) and vocational subjects (70 percent). Even at university all courses have to include basic subjects such as Korean language, foreign languages, introduction to philosophy, cultural history, general theory of science and physical education. The financing of education is largely borne by the central government which, despite provincial education budgets, parental contributions in the form of tuition fees, and the prevalence of private schools and colleges, still spends some 20 percent of its total budget on education. The tradition of private, that is, paying, education existing alongside official provision is a long one in Korea.

Its existence is a complicating factor in the government's desire to extend compulsory education, which would have to be free, up to middle school level. As it is, the government already subsidises the private sector. Other practical problems facing the government continue to be the large size of classes, shortage of teachers, and the teaching profession's dissatisfaction with its status and pay.

Chapter Ten

Cultural Heritage

The modern cultural scene in South Korea strikes the foreigner as diversified to the point of confusion. This does not mean sloppiness of execution or poverty of inspiration, but is an indication of the range of artistic traditions influencing contemporary creativity and also of the pressures and demands that are exerted on creative activity. Choices open up that would not confront a western artist with such force. In painting, music, dance and drama, for instance, one can point to a broad division between indigenous and western styles. The latter, imported into Korea over the past century, have taken root alongside traditional Korean forms. Annual art contests and exhibitions are held in two categories: the Chinese genre, and western paintings, often in oils. Western ballet in Korea is still technically and even artistically weak in comparison with western companies and with native Korean dance, but is starting to develop. Western instrumental and orchestral music have their place beside indigenous classical and folk music, and several Korean instrumentalists enjoy a worldwide reputation. In the theatre, modern experimental drama draws audiences, while *p'ansori*, a traditional form of dramatic narrative, retains its popularity. Tourist guides speak of a blend of western and traditional art forms, but such a mixture exists primarily for the spectator or listener, who is free to alternate one style of entertainment with another. For the practitioner, there is a less easy passage from one form to the other. This is not surprising, for the various categories of oriental and western art differ not only in technique but in content and spirit. Some synthesisation or fusion, a true 'blending', is, however, beginning to show itself in the hands of artists in several fields.

Not all Koreans welcome the absorption of foreign elements into the nation's cultural life, and some react with a sense of loss and contamination. Their hostility extends in many directions, to diet and dress as well as to art and language. Hamburgers and jeans may be found all over Korea, but not everybody welcomes them. It is a response with which foreigners may not often be confronted, since in general their dealings will be with Koreans who for whatever reason are prepared to mix with them. Resentment over the extent of alien influences generally expresses itself obliquely and unevenly. Aside from a determined effort to exclude Japanese influence — there has long been a ban on the playing of Japanese songs on radio and television and only recently have Japanese films been allowed — it does not appear to form part of any present government programme, though there has been a growing tendency for the use of Chinese characters in the written language to be discouraged. Official calls to uphold Korean values do nonetheless suggest that government is aware of these doubts and may even share some of them. This reaction of hostility and regret goes back to the first days of the opening up of Korea to foreign ways. The reaction of some to the new influences then entering Korea was to advocate a return to Confucian teaching and recognisably Asian modes of thought. Fears of the loss of national identity were intensified with the Japanese annexation of Korea and the eventual abasement of Korean language and culture. Liberation from Japan brought an occupying US force and exposure to vastly different cultural patterns. This was accompanied by the division of Korea into two entities that have since followed different political, social, economic and cultural paths. The mood among some Koreans, faced with so much change, has been and still is to advocate the revival of truly Korean norms of culture. This means resistance to not only western, but Japanese and sometimes Chinese influences.

The desire for a satisfactory definition of the kind of culture they would like to see emerge is probably shared by most people in South Korea. Public reference to the 'distinctive' qualities of Korean civilisation can be expected to draw a general sympathetic response. Such pronouncements when they come from government sources, however, may carry a warning note: these are qualities that need to be preserved, or may hint at a programme: the following are those aspects of national culture we intend to emphasise. The government maintains a guiding hand in cultural as in other matters. Control over the press, publishing, performing arts and the cinema is seen as an important element in official policies, though such censorship may be relaxed from time to time. It has been justified primarily on the grounds of suppressing pro-communist sentiment and preserving ethical and moral standards. One effect of such control is that delicate social and artistic issues such as the status of women or the place of nudity in painting have been approached in a circuitous fashion, by setting action in the past or using foreign models. By adding its voice, government has in some ways cleared the air by defining the bounds of literary and artistic debate, but its intervention is also a complicating factor, since it seeks not merely to discourage unacceptable thoughts, but offers as well its own interpretation of what is desirable. A basic aim is to strengthen national pride and confidence. Commemoration of national independence is an important and clearly popular theme, as shrines to heroes in the anti-Japanese struggle and the Independence Hall opened in 1987 bear witness. The excavation and restoration of ancient sites and the creation of national and provincial museums have improved people's acquaintance with their past. The government has given sympathetic treatment to past eras, drawing as much attention to the achievements of the distant Silla and Koryŏ civilisations as to those of the Yi period. Indeed, the Silla kingdom, which succeeded in achieving for the first time a measure of unity on the peninsula, is invested with a special value for a divided country.

There are other reasons for this concentration on Silla culture. One is simply the comparative richness of the archaeological remains found on the site of the former capital of Silla at present-day Kyŏngju. Another cause must lie in the high standing of unified Silla within its wider Asian region. This was an era when Korea was seen to be giving as well as receiving, exporting its learning and its artifacts as much as it was absorbing the influence of others. Modern Korea yearns to hold a similar position, to be acknowledged as a cultural as well as an economic power within its region. It is conscious of the shadow of its two stronger neighbours, China and Japan, and of the fact that in discussions of East Asian culture it is often omitted or spoken of by reference to the Chinese or Japanese models. It is particularly resentful of past Japanese ravaging of the country and of what it sees as Japanese indifference towards its culture and failure to recognise the role Korea played both as a transmitter of elements of Chinese civilisation to Japan and as a source of techniques and inspiration in its own right. One result of such anxieties is a continual effort to highlight what Japan might owe to Korea and to assert the 'uniqueness' of Korean civilisation. The Koreans' view of their own culture is largely retrospective and tends to a cult of reproduction. Points of reference are sometimes far in the past, as a glance at the hundreds of pictures and celadon vases on sale in South Korean galleries and souvenir shops, all embodying some ancient form, will confirm. The traditional acceptability in oriental art of copying a master without any of the taint of forgery that troubles western artistic ethics is undoubtedly a factor encouraging reproduction; but a fixation with past glories, and uncertainty over the kind of society art should be speaking for and to, act as a brake on artistic creativity. For daring and innovation in a new age one should turn rather to business and industry.

What to look at

In place of latterday celadon and copies of Silla gold crowns, the visitor to South Korea can go to look at the original objects. Displays at the National Museum in Seoul and its branches in Kyŏngju, Kwangju, Kongju, Puyo and Chinju, as well as in private and university museums, present many fine examples of Korean art. Some categories, notably ceramics and painting, are represented in collections outside of Korea, principally in Japan, the United States, and Europe — a dispersal that has caused some grief to Koreans. It remains, nonetheless, that much can obviously only be seen by going to Korea and then leaving the capital to visit the provinces.

Some of the richest objects from Korea's past are examples of funerary art. As well as pottery, some of it fashioned into animal and human forms, there is a range of gold metalwork and jewellery of great splendour. Many items were found in tombs of the Paekche, Kaya and Silla kingdoms, some of which have been identified as royal tombs. The technique of metalworking displayed involves the use of thinly-rolled gold sheet and gold wire. The personal ornaments made from these materials are remarkable for their delicacy and elegance. They culminate in the spectacular gold and jade crowns discovered in tombs in Kyŏngju. Pre-dating Buddhist times, these crowns, with their antler-like uprights and profuse addition of pendants, may have only been intended for funerary use. Their unusual shape suggests links with older, possibly Siberian, origins and ancient forms of shamanist worship. The tombs that yielded up these artifacts are in themselves of interest. That of the Paekche King Munyŏng (501–523 AD), at Kongju, is constructed of brick and shows the close influence of contemporary Chinese tomb design. The tombs of the later unified Silla period (668–935 AD) took the form of stone chambers covered with earth mounds — these clusters of tumuli are one of the outstanding features of archaeological Kyŏngju — some of which then had fixed around the base a series of stone slabs carved with animal figures representing the twelve signs of the oriental zodiac. Other tomb mounds have carved stone attendants in the shape of civilian and military officials or animals. The presence of stone attendants was incorporated into the tomb design of the Yi kings (1392–1910), whose vast burial mounds ring the South Korean capital.

The stiff figures at these tombs stand in contrast to the fluidity of the Buddhist statuary of the Three Kingdoms and unified Silla eras. Buddhism's influence on art and philosophy, particularly in the early centuries of its ascendancy in Korea, was immense. Little is left of the many temples built by Silla, which were later to be ravaged by both Mongol and Japanese invasions, but Buddhist reliquaries, statues small and large, rock carvings and stone pagodas and lanterns all testify to the skill of craftsmen and the devotion of their patrons. Some of the finest examples of Buddhist imagery are the seated figures of the Bodhisattva Maitreya or future or coming Buddha (in Korean *mirŭk-bosal*), where spiritual intensity is allied to and expressed through the graceful plasticity of the body and its draperies. To view what many regard as the glory of Buddhist sculpture in Korea, the visitor must go to Kyŏngju and beyond it to the eighth-century Sŏkkuram cave temple. Here the Buddha, seated in the attitude of 'touching the earth,' is surrounded by panels bearing an array of Buddhist divinities. The strength and serenity of the Buddha is matched by the vigour of the subsidiary figures. The substance is granite, but in the hands of the sculptors attains amazing movement and grace.

If Buddhism was one element in the art of the Three Kingdoms and unified Silla, another essential aspect was the coming and going and cultural interplay between the three north east Asian states, China, Korea and Japan. As well as the religious teaching of Buddhism, Taoism and Confucianism, Korea absorbed from the Chinese mainland the cultural and artistic forms of these beliefs. It was no slavish imitation, but rather an 'internalising' and 'Korean-ising' of the foreign elements to produce an indigenous interpretation and style. In turn Korea was instrumental in spreading the new teaching it was absorbing to Japan, along with its own artistic mode and techniques. This process of acquisition, followed by eventual dissemination, is well illustrated in the area of ceramics. Building on Kaya and Silla experience over several centuries in the production of unglazed ware, the potters of the Koryŏ dynasty (918–1392 AD) achieved some of the finest porcelain to emerge from East Asia. Again, the model was provided by China, whose techniques entered Korea through the south and probably also the north of the country. The first Korean glazed wares are dated to the end of the tenth century. Best known among them is celadon, so named from its fine, typically bluish-green glaze. Both white and black ware were produced, but celadon, with its wide range of colours going from grey through all hues of blue and green to olive and dark brown, held the admiration of even the Chinese. To the plain celadon was added inlaid celadon, and this technique of carving decoration on to the unglazed body and filling it with white or black slip before glazing is one of the distinguishing marks of the Korean product. Celadon ware was reserved for court and temple use. It reached its height of excellence during the first half of the twelfth century, but thereafter declined and by the end of the fourteenth century was hardly produced.

Its place was taken by a more austere tradition that evolved to meet the needs and tastes of the neo-Confucian order introduced by the Yi dynasty. *Punch'ŏng* ware, produced for popular use using techniques similar to those employed in the composition of celadon, is very different in appearance to the earlier ware, showing a more robust, even abstract, style of decoration and muted colouring. This type of pottery, with its frequent slight irregularities, was much prized by the Japanese, who incorporated some of its characteristics into their own work. It was indeed the Japanese who ended production of *punch'ŏng* in Korea when they destroyed the kilns and took the potters to Japan to continue their art there, and thus to provide the basis of Japan's famed porcelain production. In Korea itself ceramic production turned to the tradition of Koryŏ white celadon to develop a plain style of pottery for use by all classes. White remained the preferred colour within the Confucian ethic, and decoration was always restrained, but in the nineteenth century blue and white porcelain began to circulate. The plain style of Yi times persists still, and in the area to the south east of Seoul, which has long produced pottery, simple, soberly-decorated vases can be bought from local sellers as an alternative to the reproduction celadon.

It is much the same with paintings. If simplicity is prized, a sheet of calligraphy, sometimes bearing only one or two characters, will give spiritual and aesthetic satisfaction. Another kind of simplicity, that of approach and understanding, marks folk paintings with their themes of longevity and good fortune and their intuitive interpretations of legends or religious beliefs. A number of artists work in the western style using western techniques, but their paintings can seem derivative. Many others keep to the Chinese tradition in both subject and medium. Chinese influence has undoubtedly been strong in Korean painting, but it would be wrong to take the latter as a mere reflection of the Chinese model. As in many other fields of art, the Korean handling of a theme or style common to both cultures reveals a freshness, spontaneity and grace that may be absent from the Chinese treatment; while Korean painters also chose to move away sometimes from the Chinese pattern. Korean painting, and indeed Korean art in general, distinguishes itself above all by its awareness of the natural world. The main body of Korean painting on which judgements must be formed belongs to the Yi era. Very little remains from earlier centuries — paintings are vulnerable to fire, destruction, and the passage of time, and fall prey to collectors' passions. The earliest extant paintings in Korea were found in Koguryŏ tombs. Unified Silla and Koryŏ reportedly produced much Buddhist painting. What has survived is largely in Japanese collections, for the Korean products were highly valued in Japan. Buddhist painting and calligraphy made much use of gold and silver laid on blue or purple paper, to superb effect. Although Buddhist subjects were never entirely discarded, the new broom of the neo-Confucians largely swept away such art in favour of other themes, particularly landscape and the relationship of man to the universe. The long Yi period perpetuated this tradition until, in the eighteenth and nineteenth centuries, artists began to experiment with 'real landscapes' depicting views of actual places, by contrast with the rendering of often idealised landscapes, and with scenes based on observation of daily life. Particularly appealing are studies of animals. These last two categories, 'genre' and animal paintings, are widely available in reproduction nowadays. By the first decades of this century Korean artists were trying out western techniques, often learnt through training in Japan, and the existence of yet another discipline in painting had been acknowledged in Korea.

It is perhaps in the areas of traditional architecture and landscape gardening that the distinctions between Chinese, Japanese and Korean design and style are the most easy to perceive, yet the most difficult to express. As ever it is as much a question of mood and impression as of technical detail. Generally speaking, the Korean preference as revealed in palace, shrine, temple and domestic architecture is for gently-curving roof lines, a slight uptilt at the eaves, a harmonious relationship between the roof structure and the upright portions supporting it, and abundant use of natural materials, from the clay tiles of the roof to the wooden beams and paper windows of the interior. Save for Buddhist temples, which are often very brightly decorated, shades of brown, grey and white predominate in buildings in traditional style, with red much used in palace decoration. Where a similar Chinese building seeks to impress through scale and grandeur and a Japanese one strikes an austere note, a Korean structure appeals through its sense of intimacy. With both buildings and gardens, the aim is not to impose the design on the natural surroundings but to make it blend in with them. A garden should respect the natural objects within it, such as rocks, and instead of defining boundaries between it and the natural world beyond, should seek to merge with that world. At first sight a Korean garden may seem a careless affair, lacking the precision of a Japanese garden or the ingenuity of a Chinese one, but eventually the viewer comes to perceive and appreciate the careful orientation from man to nature.

A word of warning must be given about architecture. The visitor arriving at Kimp'o airport and driving into the suburbs of Seoul may be horrified by the banality and monotony of design of many of the buildings, and when he reaches the middle by the general hotch-potch style of the place. This is no city of eastern lure, but a sprawling metropolis, much of it built in a hurry since the mid-1950s round what is admittedly one of the finest city centres anywhere, a palace laid out at the foot of a mountain. The situation does not improve outside of the capital, and many of the newer houses in rural areas are strange squared-off constructions with garish roofs. Very few old private houses remain, for wood is also a vulnerable medium, and the country was fought over extensively during the Korean War. Enough public buildings survive, however, to allow some judgement on the traditional Korean style. A successful synthesis of the finest elements of this style with modern requirements marks the new national museums and Kimp'o airport itself.

The written and spoken word

Koreans are devoted to their language. They are proud of their alphabet, *han'gŭl*, and clearly savour their native tongue. Talking is a daily pleasure, from the telephone to the dinner table. Speeches at a public or private ceremony can be lengthy, and are intoned in a distinctive oratorical style that develops a momentum of its own. Radio and television shows can be taken over by the spoken word. What promises to be a programme of easy-on-the-ear light music can turn into a chat show between two disc jockeys. Even a foreigner with no understanding of the language can come to appreciate its dynamic qualities solely through listening to it, and to realise its value as part of the cement binding together the elaborate social relationships of daily life. Both the written and spoken tongue have passed through vicissitudes that have only served to make them more precious to Koreans. Under the Japanese administration, the use of the Korean language was curtailed until in 1938 Korean language lessons were eliminated from school curricula and students were forbidden to speak at any time in Korean. The present division of the Korean peninsula is deemed to be having linguistic as well as other effects, as differing policies on language are implemented and diverging political cultures leave their mark on a common tongue.

Korean is generally regarded as belonging to the Altaic group of the Ural-Altaic family of languages, and within that group to the Tungusic branch. Other branches in the group are Turkic and

Mongolian, with which Korean shares some characteristics. It also bears some relationship to Japanese. (In addition to the northerly theory of Altaic origins there exists a southerly theory of influence from some of the Polynesian languages.) Within the Korean peninsula the southern Han dialect provided the basis for the language of unified Silla and thence for the present Korean language: a case of political supremacy leading to linguistic supremacy. In its middle period (eleventh to sixteenth centuries), Korean was a tonal language, but is no longer. It is an agglutinative language, that is, it contains many suffixes that may be added — that agglutinate — one after the other to noun and verb stems to express conjugational and derivative forms. These suffixes are employed to convey style of speech, verbal mood and aspect of tense, to mark case, to indicate connective and prepositional, or rather post-positional, relationships and to signal honorific endings. The main verb comes always at the end of the sentence, and the preferred word order is subject–object–verb. Modifying words, phrases and clauses precede the word modified. The Korean vocabulary is rich in onomatopoeic words and has taken many loan words — estimated at over half the dictionary entries — from Chinese. One of its special characteristics is the system of honorific endings, now standing at three main ones, which form an essential part of any spoken communication.

The Korean language's crucial relationship from the point of view of vocabulary and writing has been with Chinese. Though spoken in neighbouring countries, the two languages are not related. Korean, in passing through its early stages, did not evolve a written form, but instead turned to a wholly different tradition for its written expression: Chinese characters. Although it is not clear when characters were first introduced, the acceptance of Chinese Buddhist and Confucian doctrines and texts into Korea from the fourth century onwards indicates a fairly early process of sinicisation among Korean scholars. The appropriation of characters by the educated class, with their exclusive use in the state examinations and in all documents, left a divide in Korean society between those who had the resources to master Chinese, the language of literacy, and the great mass of those who did not and who by consequence were illiterate. Scholars and officials were aware of the prestige that knowledge of Chinese gave them and were reluctant to yield it later in the face of *han'gŭl*. The unsuitability of Chinese ideographs to the written expression of Korean was, however, recognised early on.

Various systems were devised to facilitate the rendering of Korean words into characters, but these still demanded an adequate knowledge of ideographs to be successful. Only with the introduction of the *han'gŭl* alphabet did a writing system emerge that fitted the needs of the spoken tongue. It is a singular achievement of which Koreans are justly proud. The straitjacket of Chinese characters clearly had to be loosened, and the product that emerged had and retains great simplicity and elegance.

The new alphabet was promulgated around the middle of the decade 1440–1450 by King Sejong, the fourth Yi ruler. Known first as *hunmin chŏngŭm*, 'right sounds for the instruction of the people,' it was subsequently termed *han'gŭl*. The alphabet was the result of much study by a group of scholars working with the King's encouragement to devise a means of reproducing the sounds of the Korean language and thus make learning to read and write easy. What they created was an extremely scientific alphabet capable of representing most sounds simply and logically. It contained 28 letters (later reduced to 24) designed to express the phonological structure of Korean as it was then spoken, and combined together into syllabic blocks. Two principles operated in the formation of the letters. Initial and final letters, ie consonants, were grouped into five kinds, each kind based on the form of the speech organs that produced it. The medial letters — vowels — were rendered by symbols representing the three most important elements of nature: heaven, earth and man. In the actual delineation of the letters, it seems Sejong had several types of script to draw on: Chinese old seal script, Mongolian script, Sanskrit, the Japanese syllabaries.

Sejong instructed that the new script should be used to enable all to read. Acceptance was gradual in face of the entrenched position of Chinese learning. From the seventeenth century it was used extensively in literature at court and among the people, but right up to the early twentieth century it still had to contend with the exclusive use of Chinese characters in official documents, while some scholars continued well into the nineteenth century to prefer Chinese texts and characters in education. The modernisation movement at the end of last century gave considerable impetus to the spread of *han'gŭl*. The newspaper *The Independent*, launched in 1896, appeared in a wholly *han'gŭl* edition and an English edition. A new system incorporating the mixed use of Chinese characters and *han'gŭl* in official documents and communications was introduced in the early years of this century. Japanese colonial rule served to sharpen Koreans' awareness of their language. Further work on the standardisation of Korean was undertaken in the 1920s and 1930s by the Korean Language Research Society, which worked on the preparation of a dictionary and in 1933 produced a modern spelling system for the language, and in 1936 established the form of Korean spoken around Seoul as the basis for modern standard spoken Korean. Two newspapers, the *Dong-A Ilbo* and *Chosun Ilbo*, supported the Society's efforts, and the *Chosun Ilbo* designated a '*Han'gŭl* Day,' which is still observed on 9 October with a ceremony at King Sejong's tomb.

Trends since the war have at times veered away from any use of Chinese characters in the written language (North Korea has banished them from its language), but a mixed system is now accepted. The use of characters to render a person's name on a name card is widespread. Nowadays it is no longer only Chinese or Japanese words that threaten Korean. Exposure to English and other western languages has led to the infiltration of words from these sources, a process made easier by the very ability of *han'gŭl* to accommodate them. It is possible to put almost any foreign word into a native Korean guise, as a foreigner realises after labouring his way through a line of *han'gŭl* to find he is reading off an advertisement for Coca Cola. Working in the opposite direction, that is, transliterating Korean into a form of romanisation, is a more difficult matter. A number of systems have been devised, among which the McCune–Reischauer romanisation, first published in 1939, seems to have won out. This system aims to represent the pronunciation, but not the spelling, of Korean. The South Korean Ministry of Education, which in 1959 had drawn up its own model, in 1984 revised its system along the lines of the McCune–Reischauer romanisation, with some modifications; and it is largely with this form that the visitor to South Korea has to familiarise himself. Many Koreans, in romanising their own names, follow systems of their own devising.

Literature and the dramatic arts

At the outset it has to be recognised that these are difficult areas for the non-Korean speaker to attempt to penetrate. The fine arts allow the foreign spectator to make his own response on his own terms. But with the spoken or written word the immense hurdle of incomprehension is at once thrown up, to be surmounted only through translation or a non-native speaker's willingness to content himself with a partial understanding of what he is reading or listening to. For those nonetheless anxious to sample Korean works, a fairly wide range of literature and drama of differing genres and from various periods can now be tackled in translation: poetry, both traditional *sijo* and modern verse; legends and folk tales; romances and short stories; historical memoirs; ancient mask plays and modern drama. The Korean National Commission for UNESCO does much through its published titles and its periodical *Korea Journal* to bring translations from Korean literature and original essays written in English before a wider readership. In addition, several Korean writers living outside of Korea have produced works on Korean themes in western languages, mainly in English. In many ways their novels are more accessible to non-Korean readers than translated works.

Of the categories outlined above, the *sijo* is perhaps the one best known beyond Korea. Certainly it has attracted a number of translators, doubtless drawn by the challenge of rendering these short, three-line poems into something approaching the original. The *sijo* is made up of roughly 45 syllables or characters divided in strict groupings between the lines. Composition called for a skilful use of words and careful manipulation of thoughts and images into the tight frame of the poem. *Sijo* themes were commonly those of loyalty to one's king, filial piety, the passing of power and years, love, separation, drinking, and the delights of nature. Composers of *sijo* were drawn first from the upper reaches of society, but as the genre gained in popularity authorship extended to other classes, and a number of *sijo* were the work of professional female entertainers, *kisaeng*. The genre fell out of favour by the end of the nineteenth century, but has managed to survive, alone keeping its vitality out of the various styles of ancient poetry. Novels in the form of romances emerged in the seventeenth century from their origins in folktales, and short stories became popular. Other legends, some dealing with the founding of Korea, were gathered together as memorabilia of earlier eras by scholars who may have thought they were thereby writing history. Such are *Samguksagi* (twelfth century) and *Samguksusa* (thirteenth century), both of which approach the history of the

Three Kingdoms period. In keeping with Confucian interest in practical learning, records of the reign of each of the Yi kings were prepared, and didactic works appeared on a range of scientific, agricultural, medical, legal and ritual subjects from the end of the fourteenth century.

It is clear that quite a volume of work was produced in Korea, even in early times. The printing techniques developed over the course of centuries greatly facilitated the outflow of books. Woodblock printing was the earliest means of reproduction and was already in use in the eighth century for the printing of Buddhist sutras. Two enormous projects, each a preparation of the Tripitaka or entire sacred literature of Buddhism, were put in hand, one in the eleventh, the other in the thirteenth century, each time with the intention of propitiating disaster and securing the protection of Buddha. Both ventures called for the carving of many thousands of wooden printing blocks. The first set took 60 years to complete, but were destroyed in the Mongol invasions of the 1230s. Work started immediately on a second set, completed in 16 years, which ran to 81,137 blocks. These have survived and are now housed at Haein-sa temple. Of more enduring use was the movable metal type developed in the early thirteenth century, following on earlier Chinese experimentation. The art of typecasting was greatly stimulated by the demand in Yi times for a larger scale of book production, and copper type was introduced in 1403, lead type in 1436 and iron types in the later 1500s. Korean achievements in the technique of typecasting may be measured by the fact that in Europe movable metal type was only introduced in the early fifteenth century, some 200 years after its first use in Korea.

The vicissitudes of the past century have left their mark on the themes and emotions of contemporary writing. Equally important has been the impact of western thought, style and technique. In the early years of this century a mood of experimentation set in that probably expressed itself most thoroughly in literature. A foretaste came in what is termed the enlightenment movement, which in the last years of the nineteenth century and early years of the twentieth provided one response to the incursion of new ideas into Korea by reaching out to western culture and rejecting the conventions of earlier ages. By the end of the first decade of this century the first novels, plays and poetry representative of the 'new literature' were appearing. In themes, style and language they broke with the old literature, which no longer seemed adequate to express new situations. Work was written in *han'gŭl*, and the task of bringing the written and spoken language into accord, so that everyday speech could be incorporated into writing, was taken in hand. The rigid forms of older types of poetry gave way to free verse structures. In these early years of experimentation, Korean exposure to western literary models was largely through Japan. It is an irony that the country that came so soon to exert oppressive control over Korea nonetheless served as a channel for the transmission of western cultural patterns into Korea. The restrictions of Japanese colonial rule led to the concept of literature and poetry as vehicles of protest, but also as a means of conserving national identity, and a deep strain of nationalism runs through much of the writing of this time. Novelists and short story writers turned for inspiration to rural life and the hardships of the poor, or to historical themes. Poets drew on Buddhist and Confucian images as well as on the constant element of *han* or regretful longing in the Korean character. Fresh trials, but also fresh themes, awaited Korean writers and poets in the upheaval of the Korean War and partition and the unsettled politics of the years since then. Writers have sought to come to terms with the pain and horror of the war and with the effects of modernisation and urbanisation. For many, the search for a true form of democracy has been a continuing concern.

Korea did not develop a strong tradition of dramatic art alongside its literary achievements, and has nothing to set beside the Japanese theatrical forms or Chinese opera. Drama in Korea, as elsewhere, had its origins in primitive religious ceremonies centred around the cycle of the seasons and the production of crops. To these ancient religious elements were added shamanist and Buddhist associations. An early aspect was the wearing of masks to portray various recurring characters. Music, singing and dancing were also integral features. The result was a variegated form of entertainment, which in Silla and Koryŏ times was incorporated into the two great Buddhist festivals that marked the winter months. The festivals were discarded by the Yi dynasty, which did, however, keep earlier dramatic forms and develop them for court entertainment. Eventually these plays declined into folk drama and as such have been revived in recent years, along with puppet plays, as a result of renewed interest in indigenous art forms. The mask plays contain a recognisable set of characters who follow an invariable story line with much fall-about comedy. Above all they served for their early audiences as vehicles for satire, particularly of the upper classes and the Buddhist and shamanist orders. A later form of dramatic art that emerged during the Yi dynasty is *p'ansori*, in which a solo artist performs a type of dramatic song, accompanied by a drum player.

The innovative and experimental spirit of the early decades of this century also touched drama. The first theatre staging a new style of drama opened in Seoul in 1908. Again, a break was made with old themes and forms, with the spoken word taking the place of the singing, music and dancing of the old plays. Japanese and western influences were strong. In the 1920s and 1930s groups were formed among Korean students, some of whom had returned from Japan or were studying there, to examine realistic themes and to present foreign plays. In the area of drama, however, as across the whole literary field, Japanese hostility to Korean activities as well as to the use of the Korean language increased in the late 1930s and the early 1940s until cultural life was practically suspended. In the years since 1945 drama has had difficulty in re-establishing itself, partly under the onslaught of cinema and television, partly because of the absence of any well-grounded dramatic tradition in the country, and much work is of an experimental nature played before small audiences.

Korean film making has similarly had varied fortunes. After the introduction of cinema to Korea in the early years of this century, the industry went through a period of popularity in the 1920s. It was revived after 1945, and in the mid-fifties received financial support from the government that permitted it to grow again. The advent of television in the 1970s led to a decline in audiences, though official financial support was again forthcoming. The 1980s have brought a fresh revival in film making, with Korean films slowly gaining a place at international festivals. On the domestic front, film makers have had to cope with several difficulties. Government restrictions on the treatment of sex and nudity have been one, though such censorship is now easing somewhat. The preference of Korean audiences for foreign films, imported on a quota basis, is another. The content and artistic and technical quality of Korean films are improving, and the domestic product may soon be better able to hold its own with foreign imports.

Seoul: The Kyŏngbok Palace in winter.

Ulsan: Car production line at Hyundai Motors.

South Faces North: The Joint Security Area at Panmunjŏm with the military demarcation line running across the middle foreground.

Seoul: A street scene ca. 1905.

Seoul: A street scene in 1985 showing City Hall Plaza and the Anglican Cathedral.

The Republic of Korea's first President, Dr Syngman Rhee, with his Austrian-born wife.

A small Korean girl in festival dress.

Temple gates showing guardian spirits.

Seoul: Little East Gate; destroyed 1939.

Yuan Shi Kai (Chinese Resident) with, on his right, the British and
Chinese Consuls ca. 1890.

Korean soldiers ca. 1904.

Kyŏngju: Tomb guardian figure, late 8th Century.

Pusan: British war graves in the UN cemetery.

Music and dance

The beauty and singularity of Korean music and dance give a better notion than traditional drama of the subtlety and range of skills of the Korean theatre. Both have been long nurtured for their emotional and aesthetic qualities. Music draws a heartfelt response from many Koreans, who clearly find in it a congenial medium for the expression of emotions that cannot easily be fitted into words. (Koreans, though ready talkers, find it hard to convey their feelings directly. Music, singing and the elliptical form of *sijo* verse are all outlets for emotional release.) Korean choral and solo singing can be magnificent. As ever, though, a distinction has to be made between Korean and western styles of music and dance. The choral tradition is taken from the west and reflects the large role that Christian missionary hymn singing had in the introduction of western music into the country. Much of what is heard on Korean radio is local pop music, often an unhappy mixture of western and Korean styles, or western classical music. Public practising booths for that western instrument the piano can be hired by the hour. Korean music and dance have to be sought out. Neither form of art may be easy for a foreigner to comprehend at first, since both are constructed on quite different principles to western dance and music. Patience and an open eye and ear will help the non-initiated eventually to recognise some basic patterns and admire technique and interpretation.

The structure of Korean music differs from both western music and indeed Chinese and Japanese music in some fundamental respects. It follows a pentatonic or five-note scale. Pitch is very important, with far finer discrimination between pitches than is found in western music. The tuning of some, though not all, Korean instruments has no relationship to western systems, making it difficult to achieve integration of Korean and western instruments. The Korean sense of musical harmony, it will be clear, is markedly different to the western. Korean music also has very distinctive phrasing, generally built on a basic triple rhythm. Chinese music by contrast has basic duple rhythm. Korean music, furthermore, may often be punctuated by a pause rather than by a sequence of notes arranged in cadence to convey a closing mood. A westerner may find the range of instruments in a Korean orchestra unfamiliar, though he will quickly ᵘugh recognise the function of each.

Principal instruments are types of flutes and oboes, zithers of which the twelve-stringed *kayagŭm* is the best known, the two-stringed fiddle, and a variety of drums. Orchestral players sit on the floor. There are three main categories of music: court, folk and religious, each one closely, though not invariably, bound up with dance. Three times a year it is possible to attend performances in Seoul of Confucian temple and ancestral temple music and dance; otherwise little court music is performed. Folk music, which more properly might be termed popular traditional music, covers a range of instrumental and vocal music. In country areas performances of farmers' music are quite frequent in which a band made up of gongs, drums and a type of shawm provides music for spirited dancing. Religious music evolved to meet the needs of both Buddhist and shamanist ritual by heightening the intensity of the spiritual experience. Chanting is an integral part of Buddhist worship, and simple forms of it may often be heard at Buddhist temples. Special festivals are celebrated among certain Buddhist sects with temple dancing by the monks, to the accompaniment of cymbals and drums. Shamanist music, often provided by an instrumental group that includes drums and percussive instruments, supports the shaman in her ritual dance.

If Confucian teaching attributed high moral qualities to music as a means of promoting virtue, it did not favour dance. The movements that accompany Confucian temple and ancestral ritual music are hardly more than that. The tradition of dance in Korea predates the more rigorous phases of Confucianism, however, and has absorbed much from both Buddhist and shamanist beliefs. Some of the most intense and exhilarating dances in the Korean repertoire are drawn from these two sources. Such are the Buddhist monks' and nuns' dances of meditation and spiritual ecstasy, and the drum dances. These last, now often secularised and handed over to brightly-dressed young women dancers, climax in spectacular displays of drumming. The shamanist tradition shows itself in the farmers' dances, and especially in the singular dances, full of jumps and gestures, of the shamans themselves. The style of court dance, more refined, has been preserved in a few dances now performed habitually by young women. They are marked by graceful and gliding movements that nonetheless convey intensity of feeling. As with music, there are fundamental divergences of approach and technique between Korean and western dance. In Korean dance the body is used as a vehicle to express a mood or a feeling and is not allowed to become an object of attention in its own right. Its outlines are never emphasised and are often heavily clothed. Costume is an integral part of the total impression conveyed. The dancer does not set out to dominate or even to explore the space around him or her, but rather to establish a communicative relationship with it. Essential characteristics are the use of the heel for stepping and turning, the bent knee position, very light movement of the body, a straight position for the back, and pulsing of the shoulders. There are no intricate hand or neck movements. The upper arms, chest and head form a focal unit, and perhaps because of this emphasis on the dancer's face and features, the emotional and intellectual power of the dance is enhanced.

Popular art

Some of the most accessible forms of art for the visitor to Korea belong to folk or popular art. Mask dances, farmers' bands and the accompanying dances, concerts of instrumental music, and recitations of *p'ansori* can be quickly appreciated by westerners. There are good collections of folk painting and folklore museums in Seoul and the provinces. In both urban and rural areas traditional *kut*, or rituals of exorcism, are presented as cultural events and old ceremonies revived. The initiative for such activities, though, no longer comes necessarily from the people who had once used them as a means of self-expression or to meet social and spiritual needs. The revival business has taken root in South Korea as much as in other industrialised nations. People on an outing still break into spontaneous dance as a climax of the day's pleasure, but often singing, dancing and music have to be enjoyed in a formal setting. For visitors in a hurry a concert of titbits, each item beautifully performed, can be seen most evenings at Korea House in Seoul. The Folk Village south of the capital presents a careful reconstruction of old rural Korea and its arts; but such places and such performances inevitably carry an air of self-consciousness about them.

Various motives lie behind this attention to popular forms of art. One aim is to correct the imbalance between Seoul and the rest of the country. As so often, the capital dominates the nation's cultural life. Attempts are made to dilute Seoul's ascendancy by organising celebrations of provincial art that may commemorate a local hero or event or a regional form of dance or drama. Another intention is to remind a rapidly-urbanising population of its roots in an agricultural society. Revival and perpetuation of native popular art is also a strong element in the general drive to stimulate interest and pride in the nation's past. Celebrations of such art offer colour, music and movement in an immediately-satisfying combination. The government favours them, since they raise no controversial issues, and the spectacle, in which no words have to be exchanged, is ideal for showing to foreign visitors. For such reasons, and also perhaps out of a genuine desire to widen the base of cultural experience and participation in the country, popular art is coming to hold more of the stage in South Korea.

Chapter Eleven

The World of the Spirit

As the sky darkens over the suburbs of Seoul and lights come on, illuminated crosses suddenly hover in mid air. The skeletal steel structures supporting them become invisible in the night blackness and only the cross, red or gold, stands out. In daylight the church shows itself as a small white or redbrick building, unpretentious, ugly even, a kind of lego church. It and many others, scattered the length of South Korea in towns and countryside, are witnesses of one of the more assertive, but also more recent, faiths to take nourishment in the Korean soil. Others have been there longer. A glance up the hillside above the village church picks out the long ridge and curved eaves of the main hall of a Buddhist temple. The buildings may not be very old, but the site has probably been sanctified by Buddhist worship for centuries. Down in the valley again an old farmhouse is flanked by a small roofed structure standing in its own plot — the family's ancestral shrine. In remote wooded areas a tree may be tied with white or coloured rags — a shaman's tree; or a small pile of stones has clearly been carefully added to in some animist ritual. The walker may even chance upon a rough tent or shallow cave painted with a white cross, the site of some charismatic sect. In one or two towns the dome and minaret of a Moslem mosque and the ululating call to prayer may suddenly catch the eye and ear. Over 40 percent of the population admit to practising a religion. The wide range of religious activity in Korea is a result of the assimilation and internalisation of beliefs introduced from outside combined with indigenous practices. The deeply-engrained tradition of turning to the spirit world, whether for elucidation or comfort, has ensured a religious or spiritual dimension to the lives of many Koreans.

Freedom of worship is guaranteed in the constitution, which recognises no state religion. In the past doctrinal divisions have been very sharp: between Confucianists and Buddhists at the end of the fourteenth century when the imposition of the Confucianist order at the hands of the first Yi kings led to the decline of Buddhism; and between Confucianists and Christians in the eighteenth and nineteenth centuries over the issue of ancestor worship. Buddhists complain nowadays of attempts by Christian churches to discredit their teaching. In the main, though, where dissension flares up it is between differing sects within a religion, or as a result of the confrontation of strong personalities. Factionalism shows itself every so often in the breakaway establishment of a Christian church around a powerful minister, quarrels over the succession to the post of abbot in an important Buddhist temple, or the founding of a 'new religion.' In statistical terms, Christianity claims the greatest number of followers, 3,354,000, divided into 1,865,000 Catholics with the rest — 6,489,000 — members of Protestant sects. Buddhism has 8,060,000 adh rents. Confucianism is not a religion as such, rather a body of ethics. Some 483,000 still describe themselves as Confucianists and observe Confucian rituals. Adherents of Islam in Korea number about 20,000. Yet other Koreans follow one of the 'new religions,' syncretic forms of ritual that draw on other religions and are wholly indigenous to Korea, though some, notably the Unification church of the 'Moonies,' have become well-known outside of the country and engage in missionary work. Many Koreans at a point of crisis or indecision may consult a fortune teller, while others may turn for guidance to a shaman.

Shamanism

This is the least formal and at the same time the longest-established body of religious belief and practice in Korea. The term 'shaman' itself is of Russian origin and was applied to the priest serving as intermediary in the spirit worship of north Asian tribes. The Korean words for shamanism signify 'spirit religion' and its practitioners are called *mudang*, or, more politely, *mansin*. They are those who have revealed themselves capable of acting as intermediaries between the spirits of ancestors and their living descendants. They also have powers of divination and exorcism. Shamanism has no large shrines other than one in Seoul, and no formal hierarchy. Shamanist ceremonies or *kut* are often peformed out of doors, at the house of the woman hiring the services of a *mudang*, at the shaman's own dwelling, even on board river boats. Fear of official and public disapproval is partly responsible for this flexibility of arrangement. Another reason must lie in the *ad hoc* nature of shamanist ritual, which is largely called upon to deal with individual and personal problems, though some large scale ceremonies involving *mudang* are still organised annually in various parts of Korea to honour local spirits or pray for good harvests. Yet another element in the informality of shamanist organisation is the preponderance of female practitioners, who because of their inferior status as women and social isolation as *mudang*, cannot hope to find support for an elaborate system of shrines and hierarchy. *Mudang* themselves are reluctant to draw attention to their activities, while their clients, mostly middle-aged to elderly women, may also be unwilling to admit to reliance on such ceremonies. Educated or urban men in particular deride shamanism. Government attitudes have been harsh in the past, seeing shamanism as an obstacle to modernisation and progress and *mudang* themselves as harmful and exploitative people. The present official approach is more subtle, in that it seeks to separate the cultural and dramatic elements of shamanism from its religious and psychological aspects and to promote the former by supporting and reviving various shamanist *kut* or ceremonies for their cultural content, while playing down the ritualistic and emotional aspects of a *mudang's* activities.

The origins of shamanism in Korea are obscure. Some see it as deriving from primitive animist worship. It has many resemblances to Siberian shamanist ritual. Other elements are held to have come from China. In its early stages, Korean shamanism was associated with male rulers who combined secular with priestly duties. Shaman authority, however, had to endure the encroachment first of Buddhist and then of Confucianist teaching. The Yi rulers, offended by the irrationality and disorder of shamanist practice, barred shamans from Seoul, burnt their books and branded them as outcasts. Under Confucian pressure men were discouraged from participation in their ceremonies, and shamanism became closely associated with women. Nonetheless, even the Yi authorities had to come to some sort of terms with *mudang*, whose profession was included among the four occupations officially permitted to women: shamans, palace women, female physicians and professional entertainers or *kisaeng*. Despite public censure the services of *mudang* continued to be solicited, even within the court. Their uneasy relationship with authority was perpetuated under Japanese colonial rule, which tried to suppress them.

There is no doubt that their experiences and style of life set them and their families apart from the rest of society. Some of these women may have acquired their skills from their mothers or mothers-in-law, and in turn pass them on to their own daughters or daughters-in-law. To attain the condition of *mudang* they have experienced what is known as 'spirit sickness,' often categorised as a form of mental illness, when the spirits take hold of them. Their role in shaman gatherings is, through going into a trance, to enter into communication with the spirits of dead forbears who, it is thought, are troubling their living descendants. Difficulties within a family are interpreted as a sign that the ancestors have some grievance that they are venting on the living. Ancestors may receive attention in formal acts of worship, but these are rituals largely carried out by men in support of their family lineage and as demonstrations of filial piety. At a shamanist *kut*, a wider range of ancestors including some from the wife's family may be invoked, and a far freer form of communication takes place with them. As well as ancestors, local and household deities may be propitiated. The ceremony is a lengthy and colourful affair, with the *mudang* chanting and dancing to the accompaniment of musical instruments. It is an occasion for expenditure, not just of money, but of emotion too.

Many Koreans, young as well as old, consult fortune tellers at various times in their lives or at various points of the year, such as in the days around New Year. Fortune tellers, many of whom are blind, base their predictions on a study of various classical Chinese works, especially the *I Ching* or Book of Changes. For good luck, Koreans may carry a charm bearing Buddhist or animist images or Chinese characters. Geomantic influences — the concentration of mystic energies in a given spot of the earth — are carefully considered in choosing a gravesite for oneself or a departed relative, and even those who might not consult a *mudang* are ready to relocate an ancestor's grave if they feel he or she is not comfortable in their resting place. A spate of bad luck in a firm or a locality also calls for investigation and possible rites of propitiation. Several years ago the offices of a large airline company in Seoul were 'cleansed' for just such a reason, and in another part of Seoul, local residents worried by a series of traffic accidents held a public rite to pray for the ending of these misfortunes. New houses may be protected through propitiatory ceremonies; and even foreign embassies in Korea, under local pressure, and Korean embassies abroad have been known to hold such rituals.

Buddhism

Buddhism has had a chequered history in Korea. As has been related elsewhere (chapter 3), it was introduced from China into the kingdoms of Koguryŏ and Paekche in the fourth century, and from there spread to Silla in the sixth. Under the Yi rulers it suffered a long period of decline, though it was never extinguished. Only in this century has it revived. Its influence has been considerable through its status of major religion for several centuries under the Silla and Koryŏ dynasties. It played its part in nurturing the spiritual life of the nation as well as supporting royal authority and assisting in the process of state unification. Its role as a focus of learning was invaluable in the establishment of Korea's tradition of scholarship. The inspiration it provided to artistic creativity was enormous and is still appreciated in the statuary and painting that has survived. Buddhist temples give a thread of continuity to national and cultural life that is much needed in times of change.

The branch of Buddhism that has taken root in Korea is Mahayana, the 'Greater Vehicle.' This is the form adopted in north east Asia, by contrast with Hinyana or 'Lesser Vehicle' Buddhism that spread in southern and south eastern Asia. As might be expected, its flowering in Korea has been typically vigorous and far removed from the academic dryness of classical Mahayana. One particularly strong feature of Korean Buddhism is the emphasis it places on the role of Bodhisattvas, those who have reached the threshold of becoming Buddhas but who voluntarily defer their elevation so as to help others in their striving for salvation. Korean Buddhists principally follow Sŏn or Zen teaching, introduced at an early point from China, where it had developed, partly under the influence of Taoism, as a counter to the abstract and discursive tradition that was building up in the doctrinal schools of Buddhist thought there. This meditative form of Buddhism, with its striving towards sudden enlightenment, long contended in Korea with the Kyo school that emphasised scriptural authority, scholastic knowledge and the gradual attainment of enlightenment. The trend of Korean Buddhism, however, has generally been towards a non-sectarian approach, and the two doctrinal groups have generally sought cooperation rather than confrontation. Study of texts and doctrine have been taken as the necessary intellectual counterpoint to the practice of meditation. Where disputes now arise they are often over matters of administration. For centuries the Sŏn Buddhism that developed in Korea has been known as Chogye. The main Buddhist sect now active in South Korea has kept the name and regards itself as the inheritor of the earlier Sŏn teaching.

Korean Buddhism's capacity for tolerance shows itself in the way it has absorbed elements of other beliefs such as Taoism, animism and shamanism. Practical manifestation of this cooperation is seen in the arrangement of most Buddhist temples in Korea, which shelter within their grounds shrines to the Mountain Spirit, known as Sanshin, the tutelary god of the hillside on which the temple is constructed, to the Seven Stars of the Great Bear constellation, and to other such deities.

In the later half of the nineteenth century Korean Buddhism, sharing in the country's general response to the twin pressures of western penetration and Japanese ambitions, began to stir again. Its early attempts to reorganise did not make much headway and from the mid-1870s onwards were challenged by the missionary activities of Japanese Buddhist monks, anxious to revitalise what they saw as a torpid tradition. It was at Japanese insistence that the ban on the presence of Buddhist monks in Seoul was lifted in 1895. After the annexation of Korea, ordinances of the Japanese Government-General controlled the organisation of Korean temples in such a way as to obstruct the emergence of any strong administrative centre for Korean Buddhists. Attempts were made to merge Korean Buddhist sects with Japanese ones, but assimilation was resisted on doctrinal and nationalist grounds. Three Buddhists were among those signing the 1919 Declaration of Independence. The restrictions that Japanese rule imposed on all Korean institutions had the effect of encouraging self-examination and reform among Korean Buddhists. During the 1930s Korean Buddhists moved towards agreement on the unification of the two major strands, Sŏn and Kyo, into the single Chogye sect.

The years since 1945 have been marked by a slow Buddhist revival in Korea. After centuries of confinement, Buddhism has benefited from the constitution's guarantee of freedom of worship. Buddhist clergy, both male and female, are often seen on the streets in their distinctive light-grey dress. Buddhism enjoys equal status with the Christian church in that Buddha's Birthday and Christmas Day are both celebrated as public holidays. At the same time it has had to contend with the rapid spread of Christianity and the hostile attitudes of some Christian denominations. The new ideas and experiences that have welled up in recent decades within Korea and flowed in from outside have struck Buddhism as forcibly as they have other sections of society and obliged it to acknowledge new philosophies and examine past practices. It has started to build more of its temples in urban areas to meet the needs of city dwellers. The headquarters of the Chogye sect is located at Chogye-sa in the heart of Seoul. Korean Buddhists are taking up welfare and missionary activities within Korea and are expanding their educational effort in the direction of children and young people. The talents of local art college students, for instance, may be harnessed to the painting of new temple buildings. Dongguk University in Seoul, run by the Chogye sect, is the leading centre for higher Buddhist studies. These activities reflect a general desire among Korean Buddhists to raise the levels of understanding and training among Buddhist adherents and to improve standards of preparation for those entering Buddhist orders.

Buddhist followers are spread out over a number of sects. Some two-thirds of lay followers are women. Among those in Buddhist orders, the proportion is reversed, with about one-third nuns to two-thirds monks. A couple of sects are particularly favoured by women. The T'aego sect admits married monks. Its existence is the result of secession from the mainstream Chogye sect. This split was the culmination of a dispute carried on since the annexation of Korea when the practice of a married clergy was introduced by Japanese Buddhist sects. This departure from the norm of celibacy was much resented as alien to Korean Buddhist tradition, which did not recognise married monks as legitimate members of an order. Nonetheless, a number of Korean monks took the decision to marry. After 1945, these monks sought to perpetuate the practice, but soon came under challenge from those who wanted to see celibacy restored as the norm. After a long period of strife marked by legal rulings and official intervention, the problem was partly resolved in 1970 with the formation of the new sect, but the issue of how to treat married monks still surfaces from time to time.

Korean Buddhists naturally concentrate on the needs of their own religion in their own country, but they have not shut themselves off from outside contacts, and at least one temple accepts a number of foreigners as participants in its training and worship. Indeed, the spread of interest in Buddhism in western countries may well, in a diffused and indirect way, be helping the consolidation of Buddhism in South Korea.

Confucianism

Confucius — the term is a latinised version of the family name K'ung and the title Fu-tzu — was born in 552 or 551 BC in what is now the province of Shantung in China and died there in 479 BC. A scholar by training and profession, he held minor posts at various times in his native state, but also spent some ten years travelling through other states in search of office. Throughout these years, he continued to teach and to gather around him groups of students. His conversations with his followers form the basis of the *Analects*, the name by which this work is most commonly known to westerners. It is regarded as the truest source of Confucius's teaching.

There is no mystical, indeed, hardly any religious framework to this teaching; it is rooted in human relationships and the cultivation of moral refinement, though it acknowledges the existence of a Heaven set above human activity, a Supreme Being operating not so much as a spiritual force or God, but as an impersonal force or higher reality whose will must be accepted by man. Human society itself, Confucius taught, should follow the Way of Heaven, that is, the moral order it prescribed. In social terms this order depended on distinctions between the ruler and his subjects, between superiors and inferiors, and between those of refinement and scholarship and those who were ignorant or petty-minded. A person's standing and words should correspond with his actions; thus a ruler should accept the responsibilities of a ruler and act as one. Essential qualities of the superior man as Confucius conceived him were benevolence or humanity, uprightness, loyalty and altruism. In his actions he should follow the mean, that is, he should strive to maintain a proper balance and decorum.

Confucian texts and other Chinese classics had entered Korea by the fourth century AD. Korean scholars followed the evolutions in Confucianist thought in China and were familiar with the teachings of the neo-Confucian school of eleventh- and twelfth-century Sung times. It was these later interpretations and extensions of Confucius's teaching, rather than his original doctrines, which were drawn upon by the new Yi rulers when they came to look for a suitable ethical framework for their new dynasty. The neo-Confucian philosophy and precepts that they adopted brought Koreans firmly back to a humanistic ethical code, concerned with man's relationship with nature, his fellow human beings and society, rather than with his own enlightenment and salvation. As with Confucius, the greatest virtue man could pursue remained for the neo-Confucians that of benevolence. On the political plane, neo-Confucianism in Korea set great store on the role of government as a moral institution and on the significance of the king as moral leader of his people. The new Yi administrations promoted ethical norms, models of government and patterns of social and family life that impressed even the Chinese by their rigorous adherence to those principles. The effects of this teaching on the Korean people were profound and have lasted to this day, (as the discussion in chapter 8 endeavours to show).

The formal aspects of Confucian ritual are now much diminished. Confucian shrines are not so numerous as Buddhist temples — many were put to different uses during the Japanese occupation of Korea — but they and Confucian academies can still be spotted in the countryside. Like temples, they may be built beside a river and shaded by a grove of trees, or stand on a hillside above a village, but they do not hide themselves amid wooded mountain valleys. The largest and most important shrine is that at Sŏnggyun'gwan University in north east Seoul. Here twice a year ceremonies are held honouring the memory of Confucius. The university itself, the oldest in Korea, remains the country's centre for Confucian studies.

Among family rites once dictated by Confucian practice, wedding and mourning rituals may still be observed. The choice of ceremony to accompany the civil marriage, the only form recognised by the state, is now left to individual preference. Some young people continue to favour the traditional Confucian wedding rite. Honouring of the ancestors, either at home or at ancestral graves, is still much followed. The annual ritual at the Chongmyo royal ancestral shrine in Seoul to honour the Yi kings and queens is the grandest expression of this custom. In some areas the local branch of a family may hold a ceremony to commemorate the founder of their clan, whose portrait is kept in a special shrine. For other Koreans the festival of *ch'usŏk* in the late summer is a recognised time for paying respects to family ancestors. The rites of death are extremely important, combining as they do the need to safeguard the passage of the dead person's soul into the other world (a reminder of Buddhist beliefs) and to institute the deceased's status as an ancestor. Mourning is a noisy affair when loud expressions of grief and clear demonstrations of filial duty are called for. The coffin may be taken a great distance to the ancestral tomb — it is not uncommon to see one or two coaches on the highway speeding out of Seoul bearing coffin and mourners in their white hemp robes — or is carried along country roads on a brightly-decorated bier accompanied by relatives. The gravesite must be carefully chosen, and a stone tablet may be set up. Within the dead person's home a wooden or paper spirit tablet may be installed, and offerings, at first frequent, later on at more extended intervals, may be made, lasting over a period of up to two years. Such rites were once the unavoidable duty of all save the lowliest Korean families, but their observance is now voluntary.

Confucianism suffered one blow in 1894 when the state examination was abolished and another in 1910 when the demise of the Korean monarchy removed its political underpinning. Though Confucianism has lost much of its organisational force, it can still put a modest body of opposition into the field over social issues such as the present campaign to revise further the Family Law. This campaign, largely the concerted work of women's groups, aims to bring yet further equality into family relationships, and specifically to ease the ban on marriage between those of the same surname and place of family origin. Such challenges to what some still regard as cardinal points of Confucian practice have been taken up by devotees of Confucianism, in the main elderly people living in rural areas. Revision of the Family Law provides both reformers and their opponents with a ready rallying point to express differing views on the course of social developments in South Korea.

Christianity

The vigorous growth of Christianity in Korea over the past century has caused some wonder to outside observers and no small joy to missionary organisations that praise Korea as one of the few Asian countries to have accepted the Christian message. Only the Philippines, and to some extent Singapore, have embraced the Christian religion to a similar degree. The initial route by which Christianity entered Korea was again China. Emissaries from the Yi kings to the Ming court brought back the teachings of Catholicism. One of them was baptised in Peking in 1784. The early Catholic church in Korea suffered considerable persecution. (An account of its trials is carried in chapter 4.)

The second wave of Christianity started in the mid-1880s with the arrival of American Protestant missionaries. Church work continued under the Japanese annexation of Korea, though under various restrictions that amounted at times to persecution and led to a serious split over the issue of *shinto* worship. In the late 1930s and early 1940s the Japanese colonial administration put increasing pressure on both foreign and Korean Christians to participate in *shintō* ceremonies, which incorporated veneration of the emperor. Some resisted, some gave way. After the war, the question of how to deal with those who had joined in such worship gravely disrupted congregations, particularly in the Presbyterian church, which through its schools had been much affected by the Japanese demands. The active participation of Christian students in the March First movement of 1919 against the Japanese occupation, alongside members of other religious affiliations, indicated their support for national survival. After the liberation of Korea in 1945,

167

Christianity grew further in the south. In numerical terms it was augmented by an influx of Christians fleeing from the north. In secular terms, the standing of the Christian church gained from its association with the incoming US administration after liberation, and the fact that the first president of the Republic of Korea, Syngman Rhee, was a Christian (a Methodist). In spiritual terms it came to offer a sense of security and comfort to those uprooted by war and subsequently further unsettled by industrialisation and city life.

There are further reasons for the Christian churches' strong standing in South Korea. They are still in a mode of expansion, with the emphasis on evangelising and growth. Congregations can be enormous: the Full Gospel Church building in Seoul can accommodate 12,000 in its main hall, with an overspill of worshippers into every part of the church and even into the area around it outside. Other churches claim congregations of several thousands at each of their Sunday services. With such support some churches have accumulated much wealth, a development that is causing concern. The very speed of expansion also draws fears that quantity is overtaking quality as a criterion in the growth of the churches. The wideranging forms of Christianity in South Korea mean that the social and intellectual reach of the churches is considerable, and they attract followers in both rural and urban areas. There appear to be no political affiliations marking off particular denominations. The church has, however, retained a capacity for opposition to the political order. On a number of occasions during the past two decades both Catholics and Protestants have brought themselves before the public eye through their defiance or censure of government policies. Sometimes church leaders, such as Cardinal Stephen Kim, head of the Catholic church in Korea, speak out on an issue. Other church workers through their involvement in rural or urban Christian organisations encourage people to examine their living and working conditions and to defend their interests. Others again raise questions of human rights or try through political activity to bring about more democratic procedures in the political field. Christian-oriented sections of the media, such as the privately-run Christian Broadcasting System, have also added their comment on various issues. These activities do not necessarily enjoy any great volume of support among church followers, however, and the main impression is of religious, political and social conservatism, reinforced by an awareness of the communist presence in the northern half of the peninsula.

The South Korean Catholic church is in full communion with the Vatican. In 1984 Pope John Paul II visited Seoul and promulgated the canonisation of 103 martyrs — 93 Koreans and ten French missionaries — who had died in the persecutions of the nineteenth century. The Anglican church, which has a small following, has retained the High Church tone of its founders. Its cathedral stands in the centre of Seoul, a fine building in the romanesque style. Among the other Protestant denominations, numbered at around 70, the Presbyterians are the largest, though split and split again, with Methodists, Baptists and Lutherans coming behind. The ministries of the Christian churches in South Korea are now largely in the hands of native Koreans. Some foreigners still function as priests in a few denominations, but most of those involved in religious work in Korea serve as teachers, advisers or missionaries. In a reversal of roles, Korean missionaries are starting to work overseas.

The government in South Korea takes a careful line on the Christian element in the population, aware of the need to keep a proper balance between the various religious groups in the country. It does not overlook the contribution to educational and social welfare already made by the churches, which moreover claim they are putting more of their wealth into charitable ventures. It welcomes the conservative standards of many church people. At the same time the churches remain suspect since they represent centres of authority and influence outside direct state control. The government is in particular angered by the independent political and social line of some church activists and on occasion of some church leaders. The international connections of the main Christian denominations, especially with the United States, are a further complicating factor that doubtless influences to some extent official views on the Christian community.

Islam

Islam, which claims about 20,000 followers in South Korea, was established in rather unusual circumstances. A number of converts may have existed in Korea among those who had returned after the Pacific War from Manchuria (the Chinese population contains a number of Hui or Moslems). However, the religion was only formally introduced in the 1950s, when it was brought by the Moslem imams attending the Turkish contingent to the UN forces in the Korean War. Since then it has received legal status, and several mosques have been built. The central one, dedicated in Seoul in 1976, stands conspicuously above the shopping street of It'aewon. Korean workers doing stints in Middle Eastern and Gulf countries reinforce contacts with the rest of Islam.

New religions

One of the most important aspects of religious practice in South Korea today lies in the many 'new religions.' Estimates of their number range from over 240 to more than 300. The total volume of their adherents is put at between 1.6 million and 5 million. Many are breakaway movements from recognised Christian sects or the result of schisms within older-established religious groups. Buddhism, too, has seen new forms develop. Some movements have looked to wholly indigenous sources of inspiration, such as the legend of Tan'gun, the mythical founder of Korea. The first group to which the name 'new' is given, the Tonghak or eastern learning movement, emerged in 1860. Both the timing and the title of that group say much about the basic reasons for the development and popularity of the new religions.

They are an essentially Korean response to the pressures the country and its people have endured and continue to endure as they move into new ways of life and meet new influences. The Tonghak movement sought to challenge the *sohak* or western learning that had been seeping into Korea since the eighteenth century, but also to bring comfort to ordinary people suffering under the heavy taxation and corruption and inefficiency of late Yi rule. The threat of foreign intervention in Korea, culminating in the imposition of colonial status on the country in 1910, was a blow to national fortunes, but at the same time had the effect of pushing people towards an examination of means of spiritual, if not physical, relief from alien standards. The stringencies of the Pacific War, the upheaval of the Korean War, and the subsequent division of the peninsula brought further dislocation in almost every sphere of life. Some of the most powerful of the new religions, such as the Chŏndogwan or Olive Tree church and the T'ongil or Unification church, date from the post-Korean War years of turmoil. The rapid urbanisation and industrialisation of the last three decades have put considerable pressure on Korean society, challenging familial, social, and economic norms. The continuing growth of foreign influences is a further unsettling factor. The new religions with their pronounced doctrines, sometimes well-defined structures, and often emotive styles of worship, provide support to the insecure.

These groups are wholly indigenous, with their inspiration lying within Korea. They tend to identify themselves with Korean interests, according a central place to Korea in their order of things, pledging support for Korean values and rejecting foreign influences. Politically they can be relied on to take an anti-communist stance, which has won them a measure of official approval. Other points of doctrine they often share are belief in the concept of the unity of man and nature or of man and the universe, a desire to mend divisions within society and other religions and to reconcile man with God, and belief in the imminence of a paradise on earth and preparation for it. Healing and divining are often essential parts of the ministry of these groups. They are concerned with man's salvation in this world rather than with his immortal soul. In doctrine and style they are syncretic, taking elements from a range of other religions and practices, even though these may be foreign imports. Their teaching, once established, tends to be exclusive, however, and they have all borne the stamp of their founder and incorporated the interpretations flowing from his or her experience of enlightenment.

As their doctrines vary, so also does the range of their activities. Of the older groups Ch'ŏndogyo, the successor to Tonghak, follows the pattern of established churches with its body of doctrine, organised structure and emphasis on worship. Other older sects advocated withdrawal to a sacred spot in preparation for the establishment of paradise on earth. The newer groups are charismatic, even messianic, movements, dependent on the personality of a strong leader and owing something in style to the emotional appeal of shamanism and its techniques. They put much emphasis on proselytising and missionary work, on the development of business and cultural activities (the Unification church has a network of such activities, including a large conglomerate), and on the establishment of new communities. Relations between the new religions and the rest of society, and in particular official authorities, have been difficult in the past and can still cause strain. The Tonghak movement, which had started off as a religious group, in 1894 erupted in political protest. In 1919 members of the Ch'ŏndogyo sect were among the signatories of the Declaration of Independence. Such open defiance of official power has not re-occurred, but leaders of the newer sects have been charged with personal irregularities, even criminal offences, and with disruption of social order. Government attitudes towards the Unification church in particular have veered from cautious tolerance when the activities of its founder, the Reverend Mun or Moon Sŏn-myŏng, have chimed with official objectives to hostility over his involvement in tax evasion and corruption in the United States.

Minjung theology

Over the past two decades a new approach towards Christian doctrine and practice has been developing in South Korea. This is known as *minjung* theology. It cannot be regarded as a new sect or church, but is perhaps best described as a new interpretation of the Christian message, in particular of the social and political aspects of that message and their implications for Korea. The movement has support among both Catholic and Protestant groups, but does not seem to take ecumenism as a primary goal. Its two basic concepts lie in the words *minjung* and *han*. Neither is easily translated. *Minjung* signifies 'the masses,' 'people,' 'populace.' *Han* conveys both the sense of 'regret,' 'grievance over injustice,' and the acceptance of suffering. These two words have long been in Korean usage, but have now acquired a more specialised role as key expressions in the new teaching. *Minjung* theology is not easy to define; its practitioners say that it has to be assessed by its actions as much as by its doctrine. It revolves around the *minjung*, the mass of Korean people who, it is argued, have always suffered and still do suffer oppression, but refuses to give them the status of objects to be ministered to. Rather it sees them as the 'subjects of history.' The boundaries of the group of people comprising the *minjung* shift constantly with circumstances and situation, but always include those who find themselves in an oppressed condition. The social, political and historical reality of the masses is given emotional and psychological value by the burden of resentment, the *han*, they feel over their unjust treatment. The resolution of this sorrow is one of the greatest yearnings of the people, and the teaching of Christ's crucifixion and resurrection a source of powerful inspiration to them.

Apologists of *minjung* theology seek to define it in part by describing what it is not. They distance it emphatically from communist ideology, and allow no parallel between the concept of *minjung* and that of the proletariat. Putting forward people as the 'subjects of history,' it argues, cannot be equated with support for the dictatorship of the proletariat, which in fact masks the totalitarian rule of a national leader. The avoidance of Marxist reasoning and terminology is, of course, essential if the movement is to survive in South Korea. The government has already shown itself unwilling to accept the *minjung* interpretation of its teaching, and proponents of *minjung* theology such as the poet Kim Chi-ha have been charged with being pro-communist and imprisoned. (Kim even received a death sentence, later commuted, and has now been freed.) It is not, however, solely a matter of expediency. The language and inspiration of *minjung* doctrine are consciously drawn from native sources. Several events in particular are given great importance: the Tonghak rebellion of 1894, the March First uprising of 1919, liberation from Japan in 1945, and the Students' Revolution of 1960. The episode of the flight from Egypt described in the Book of Exodus, and the Gospel according to Mark are especially valued in *minjung* theology, the former for its theme of liberation from oppression, the latter for its treatment of the 'crowd' or 'gathering' of the lowly to whom Christ preached. These two strands, the one historical and specifically Korean, the other biblical and speaking to all Christians, are seen as combining to form the core of the new theology. The *minjung* movement identifies itself strongly with the interests of the Korean nation. Only in its welcome for the concept of the Maitreya, or coming Buddha — a messianic Buddha — does it appear to look beyond the Christian faith in its religious inspiration.

The elaboration of a body of doctrine followed on from a course of actions that had started in the early 1960s with the organisation of mission groups to minister to workers in Korea's rapidly-developing industries. These missions, of which the best-known was the Urban Industrial Mission, active largely in the Seoul area in the late 1960s, made the decision that their members should themselves join the labour force as workers in order to be able to understand the experiences and aspirations of those among whom they were living. This policy of participation was applied to other sections of society such as farmers and the urban poor, and is still followed by students and religious groups who endeavour to insert themselves into the daily life of the people. *Minjung* theology in some measure represents the reactions and conclusions of highly-educated church workers on their experience of witnessing at first hand the problems of the poor. Despite their commitment to establishing Korean patterns of doctrine and action, and their wariness of foreign models, the proponents of *minjung* theology have been influenced by the liberation and third world theologies that emerged in the late 1960s. An intelligent reading of their theories demands some understanding of sociological and even Marxist terminology, as well as of theological terms and also of Korean history. It is not a readily accessible teaching.

The development of *minjung* theology is part of a wider movement in South Korea to re-examine the past and in particular to identify and re-establish truly Korean patterns in thought and culture. The interest in native forms, often embedded in popular culture, has extended to art, music, dancing and literature, where it has manifested itself in revivals and scholarship. Historical studies have also started to examine the significance of mass movements and popular reaction in their assessments of the past. *Minjung* theology places especial value on two traditional forms of drama, the mask dance and *p'ansori*, as providing a means of release of feeling, of *han*, for the common people. Contemporary writers and poets in turn have been much influenced by the new theology. The basic task of what some observers term the *minjung* cultural movement is to redefine what it is to be Korean and to sift out native elements of culture from imported elements. On a wider scale the movement reflects the growing self-confidence of South Koreans. The development of national strength and pride is one of the aims of the government of the Republic of Korea. Its vision of a strong country and its understanding of the means to attain that goal differ, however, from those of *minjung* theology, and must be seen as one cause of the hostility between the movement and government. Where official policies have favoured rapid industrialisation and reliance on new technologies to achieve economic growth, and have in part accepted foreign patterns and standards, the *minjung* movement denounces what it terms the false claims of the secular messianism of technocracy. It looks first and foremost to the labour force underpinning economic advance. With its emphasis on action, the movement, by identifying itself with striking workers and evicted slum dwellers, has clashed with the interests of business and government. Political liberalisation and improvements in working conditions may blunt the demands of the movement, but in the meanwhile, *minjung* theology remains as one of the few centres of opposition to government intentions.

Section Five

The Wider World

Meeting an enemy on a single-log bridge

Chapter Twelve

Security and Foreign Affairs

The Republic of Korea's concern with the outside world seems very great. This has been particularly the case since President Chun came to power. President Park travelled in his early years in office, but not after the late 1960s. President Chun, by contrast, has set out to make an impact on other countries. This policy was put into effect soon after his inauguration, with a visit to Washington in February 1981, and continued until the end of 1986. He has visited Asia, Australia, Africa and Europe, as well as America. Even the Rangoon bombing did not stop him travelling. He was the first ROK president to make a state visit to Japan, in 1984. In addition, ROK cabinet ministers and senior officials are regular travellers. Seoul is frequently *en fête* to recieve foreign dignitaries. President Reagan has been, as have other US presidents. The Pope went in 1984. The British Prime Minister, Mrs Thatcher, made a brief visit in 1986. The 1988 Seoul Olympics are but the latest in a long line of international functions that have been held in South Korea in recent years. From Miss World to the International Monetary Fund, from Lions Conventions to the Pacific and Asia Tourist Association, Seoul has played the host city. All are well organised, attended by Korean dignitaries, and participants are lavishly wined and dined.

Ordinary diplomacy is not neglected. The ROK maintains diplomatic relations with 125 countries, and has diplomatic or consular posts in the majority of these. It has observer status at the United Nations and is an active member of many of the UN specialised agencies. The ROK's diplomats are a skilled, professional cadre of generalists, all able to speak good English and usually at least one other language. They are expected to work hard. When Lee Bum Suk, who was killed at Rangoon in 1983, was foreign minister, he issued instructions that all Korean diplomats were to study either Russian or Chinese; this had to be fitted in before the start of the working day. In addition to conventional diplomacy, ROK embassies, and various other bodies at home and abroad, conduct an extensive cultural diplomacy campaign.

Many Koreans are fascinated by the world outside Korea. Until recently it has been difficult to turn this into something more positive because of restrictions on foreign travel. These are now easing and perhaps the South Koreans will follow the Japanese as international tourists. Most of the interest in the outside world, however, especially on the part of the government, can be traced to the division of the Korean peninsula and concern about North Korea.

North–South relations: the threat from the North

There is a popular Korean proverb that says that 'a brother can be a treasure if he is good, an enemy if he is bad.' That certainly fits how the two Koreas view each other. The division of the peninsula and the experience of the Korean War has left both Korean states greatly concerned about their international legitimacy. Neither formally concedes the other's right to existence. Both claim to be the only legitimate government in the peninsula, and each claims the whole peninsula as its national territory. Until a new constitution was adopted in 1972, Seoul was still listed as the capital of the DPRK and P'yŏngyang, the actual seat of government, the 'temporary' capital. The formal refusal to acknowledge each other's existence has in fact broken down somewhat since the talks of 1971–1972, and each will now occasionally use the other's state titles, though such courtesy is rare. Generally, the ROK refers to the 'puppets' in the North, while the DPRK talks about the 'Chun Doo Hwan–Roh Tae Woo fascist clique.'

Since the end of the Korean War, the two sides have faced each other with hostility. Both maintain large armed forces; for each, the only enemy is the other. Both spend large amounts of their Gross National Product on men and weapons. South Korean sources claim that in 1984 the North Koreans spent about a quarter of a total GNP of US $14.7 billion on defence, while South Korea's expenditure was about one twentieth of US $81.1 billion GNP. Both sides have large numbers of men under arms: current estimates give about 830,000 for North Korea and 600,000 for the South, and there are large numbers of reservists on each side. Both have large quantities of military hardware, with the North ahead in strictly numerical terms. North Korean tanks are said to outnumber South Korean by a ratio of nearly three to one. Statistics vary a great deal on this issue, and numbers themselves may not mean very much. Tanks, for example, may be new or old, based on Second World War technology or the very latest product. The North Koreans appear to have a lot of aeroplanes, but not all of them are necessarily readily available for military use; shortage of fuel may reduce training time and therefore fighting capability. For the South Koreans, claimed numerical inferiority vis-á-vis the North is compensated for by better quality weapons, the presence of some 40,000 US troops, 90 US aircraft, including F-16 fighters (now also in service with the ROK air force), and, the North Koreans and their supporters claim, tactical and other nuclear weapons.

South Korean experience since the end of the Korean War makes them view North Korean intentions with great suspicion. They have watched with concern the build-up of North Korean forces, which began in the early 1960s and has continued steadily ever since. Both South Korean and US sources claim that many of these forces are now deployed in forward positions close to the Demilitarised Zone, thus reducing likely warning time in the event of an invasion. This could be an important development, given the closeness of Seoul and its satellite towns to the front line. An alternative explanation for this deployment is that it enables the North Korean forces to match more exactly the configuration of the ROK–US forces, putting them in a better position to check an invasion from the South.

Three tunnels under the Demilitarised Zone were discovered in the mid-1970s, apparently constructed by the North for infiltration purposes at a time when North–South talks were in progress. North Korean defectors have spoken of many more tunnels. There have been a number of North Korean commando raids on the South. In January 1968, one group reached the grounds of the presidential palace in Seoul before being stopped. That same year, a number of people were killed in another raid on the east coast. The South

Koreans linked North Korea with the 1974 assassination attempt on President Park (see page 83). It was claimed in 1982 that North Korean agents had tried to kill President Chun during a visit to Canada. In 1983, the Burmese government accused North Korea of responsibility for the bomb that killed seventeen high-ranking South Korean officials, including four cabinet ministers. In November 1987 a Korean Air jet disappeared on a flight from Baghdad to Seoul. A passenger who had left the flight at Abu Dhabi confessed, after being extradited to Seoul, that she was a North Korean agent and had planted a bomb on the plane. North Korean spy rings are regularly reported in the South.

Against this background, South Korean wariness of North Korean proposals about the future of the Korean peninsula is understandable. For many in South Korea, especially older people who escaped from the North between 1945 and 1950 or during the Korean War, or who lived under the North Koreans briefly from 1950 to 1951, all such initiatives arouse strong suspicions of North Korean motives. South Koreans claim that North Korean calls for dialogue have been linked to attacks on the South. They cite the June 1950 pleas for reunification on the eve of the Korean War, and more recently, the North Korean offer of tripartite talks (see below) made just before the Rangoon bombing. The creation in 1964 of a 'Revolutionary Party for Reunification,' supposedly based in Seoul, presented as the real voice of the people of the South, reinforces these suspicions, as have North Korean attempts to encourage radical movements in the South at times of political upheaval. Assassination, subversion, raids and acts of sabotage have not been conducive to a rational discussion of North Korean proposals.

Unification and talks

North Korean calls for peaceful unification date from the emergence of separate states, and began again immediately after the armistice. By the later 1950s, they had crystallised into the form that more or less prevails today. All foreign troops should leave the Korean peninsula. While North Korea and South Korea might keep their separate social structures and forms of government, they should form a federation — the 'Democratic Confederation of Koryŏ' — that should join the United Nations and conduct the external affairs and defence arrangements of the confederation. A joint commission would arrange for the conduct of a peninsula-wide election, with all truly democratic forces taking part.

In the immediate aftermath of the war and under Syngman Rhee, there was little chance of any North Korean proposals carrying much weight in the South. Rhee's concept of reunification had no place for the North Korean regime; rather it involved him marching to the Yalu with banners flying, and he spent much time complaining that he was prevented from doing this. The students in 1960 called for a new approach to the North, and the Chang government quietly dropped Rhee's bellicosity, though not the claim to represent all Korea. The military junta used the threat from the North as a justification for taking power. Park's civilian government believed that there was danger in weakness and that it was important to build up the South Korean economy before seriously considering any change in attitudes towards North Korea.

When the two sides did come to the negotiating table, in 1971, both seemed concerned at developments in East Asia and anxious to probe each other's position. The 1971 series of talks, which involved Red Cross and government representatives of the two sides, began against the background of the Sino–US rapprochement and the Vietnam negotiations. The talks continued until 1973, raised hopes for a time, but possibly also some concern on the North Korean side. The latter lost interest when it became clear that the South Koreans were not prepared to discuss reunification, but instead were seeking a North Korean acceptance of the 'present realities' — ie the existence of separate states and continued division. For the North, this was confirmed when Park announced on 23 June 1973 that the ROK would not oppose the entry of two Korean states to the United Nations. This was promptly rejected by the North. Park's increasingly authoritarian rule may also have been a factor, since it removed the immediate possibility of radical change in the ROK.

There followed several years in which each side waved olive branches, offered proposals that to the outsider differed very little in substance, but that each side vehemently denounced. Following Park's death, there was a brief moment when working-level talks recommenced, but the North broke these off after Chun came to power. Chun offered to talk with Kim Il-sung in January 1981, but this was rejected. In 1983, just before Rangoon, the North Koreans secretly proposed through the Chinese that there should be tripartite talks with the South Koreans and the US. Although this suggestion echoed an earlier ROK–US proposal, turned down by the North, the bombing removed any chance that it would be seriously considered. Severe floods in 1984 provided an opportunity for the North Koreans to offer humanitarian aid. After some hesitation the South accepted. The South Koreans then suggested a resumption of the earlier Red Cross talks, together with economic talks. Both were accepted. By the end of 1984 the two sides were again in dialogue. Parliamentary talks were added later.

The 1984–1985 talks were particularly poignant, for they led in autumn 1985 to the first direct contact between separated family members since 1953, arranged under the auspices of the two Red Cross societies. Both sides used the meetings for propaganda purposes, while the brief reunions showed how far apart North and South Korea had grown since 1953. Again the impetus faded, with the usual accusations of mutual bad faith. North Korea appeared to find little value in continued discussions, and cancelled talks scheduled for January 1986, arguing that the Team Spirit exercise, which the ROK and US forces had held annually since 1976, was not conducive to dialogue. None of the meetings have so far (January 1988) resumed, though each side has added new proposals to those already on the table. Since 1986, the only public forum in which North and South have continued to speak to each other has been under the auspices of the International Olympic Committee (IOC) in Lausanne, where the North Koreans have sought a share of the 1988 Olympics. No agreement on this issue of 'co-hosting' had been reached by the time invitations for the Olympics closed on 17 January 1988, and the North Koreans announced that they would not attend the Games.

To many South Koreans, the attempts at dialogue showed that the North only sought to talk when it believed there was immediate advantage to be gained. In 1971 the North was seen as attempting to exploit South Korean uncertainty following the Nixon dialogue with China. In 1984 the North's motives seemed to be twofold. One was a desire to undo some of the damage done to its international position by the Rangoon bombing. The other was a wish to use this improved international standing to obtain economic assistance. Both motives seemed equally cynical. Similarly, the campaign to 'co-host' the 1988 Olympic Games is seen by many in South Korea as a spoiling tactic, begun when the 1984–1985 talks were clearly not going to advance North Korea's cause. Nevertheless, the South Korean government remains publicly committed to the establishment of contacts with the North and to building up a relationship on a step-by-step basis. All candidates in the 1987 presidential election in the ROK promised new initiatives towards the North.

The North Korean view appears to be that the South is insincere in the dialogue, since it does not accept from the outset that there should be a 'confederative' state. The ROK is described as 'splittist' and composed of 'national traitors,' similar to those who 'sold out to the Japanese' from 1905 to 1910. This is blamed on 'US imperialism,' and the puppet nature of successive South Korean governments. But the government of the DPRK also remains publicly committed to continued contacts between North and South.

The foreign policy of the Republic of Korea

It is against this background that the ROK's external affairs must be seen. The 'threat from the North' has to be combatted not just with military force but also through support in the wider world. Although the United Nations is a very different body now from the one that was midwife to the ROK in 1947–1948, and that came to the country's rescue in the Korean War, successive ROK governments have attached great importance to links with the UN and its specialised agencies. The South Koreans are generally pleased that the UN flag still flies over some military installations in their country and that 'UN troops,' even if the reality is somewhat different (see below), are still in South Korea. ROK attempts to join the UN, made regularly until 1975, were always blocked by the Soviet Union and its allies. UN entry, with or without North Korea, still remains the ROK goal, though it has not been pursued in recent years.

In fact, since 1948, most of the ROK's diplomatic energies have been directed towards relations with the United States. Whatever the charges about US responsibility for the original division of Korea in 1945, the US was the guardian of the new state, and it was primarily US action that saved it in the Korean War. Among many Koreans there has long been a sentimental attachment to the United States, which even at the end of the nineteenth century was seen as more 'altruistic' in its approach to Asia than was the more frankly imperialistic Great Britain. Such attitudes have persisted, reinforced by the relatively large numbers of Koreans who have studied or lived in the United States.

Following the 1953 armistice agreement, which the US, in Syngman Rhee's eyes, had forced on the ROK, the US continued to provide the main guarantee for the ROK's survival. US troops were the largest part of the UN forces remaining in Korea, and for operational purposes, ROK forces were under US command. The ROK–US Mutual Defence Treaty, signed in October 1953 and ratified the following year, provided a more precise US guarantee of South Korean safety and remains in force today. (At the time of its signature, it also provided a means of checking Syngman Rhee's ambitions of invading the North, but this has become a progressively less important aspect as the years have passed.) Since 1978, US and ROK forces have been integrated in a Combined Forces Command, which replaced the earlier, less precise, 'UN Command' form of joint operation. The 'UN Command' still exists, but is a shadow of its former self. The US military commitment is shown today by the presence of some 40,000 US troops in the ROK, together with aircraft and support services. Some US forces in Japan are expected to play a role should there be further conflict on the Korean peninsula. Since 1976 there has been an annual joint exercise involving ROK and US forces, known as Team Spirit, designed to test the capabilities and the organisational cooperation of the two sides. At times of tension on the peninsula, such as in the wake of President Park's death, the Americans have moved quickly to warn the North Koreans against any attempt to exploit the situation. For understandable reasons, the ROK–US relationship has tended to mean a greater US commitment to the ROK than vice versa, although it was to sustain the relationship that President Park sent ROK forces to fight in Vietnam. (Where both Chun Doo Hwan and Roh Tae Woo gained combat experience.)

The ROK–US relationship has not always been an easy one. Some of the problems with Rhee have been indicated, but they were not the only ones. Clearly the presence of US forces in Korea and the nature of the joint command has caused tension from time to time.

The Americans were not happy about the 1961 coup, but refused to interfere. It was an open secret that the then Combined Forces Commander, General Wickham, disliked the 1979 coup; rumour had it that he refused to speak to Chun thereafter. During the political upheavals of 1986–1987, the US government made it very clear that it did not think a further military takeover was an appropriate reaction to political developments in the ROK.

The presence of US troops has always led to some anti-American feeling, which in recent years has occasionally been very vocal. There are some in the US who also question the presence of American troops in Korea. Usually these have been on the left, but in recent years, with trade difficulties with the ROK, there have been similar views from the right. The American government, while noting these sentiments, has said that the US forces will not leave until the Koreans ask them. So far, no South Korean government has felt able to do so. The withdrawal of some US troops in 1969 caused much concern in South Korea, as did President Carter's proposal in 1978 to withdraw all ground forces. The effort the ROK put into overturning the Carter proposal is a measure of how much importance the ROK attaches to US military support.

The issue of human rights in the ROK has caused problems on a number of occasions, especially during the Carter administration. In recent years the American government has protested over the 1980 death sentence on Kim Dae Jung, and concern was also expressed over the heavy-handed treatment of Kim and some of his American companions on his return to Korea in February 1985.

ROK economic development has brought problems, too, as has been shown in Chapter 7. It was American aid that helped the ROK to keep going during and after the Korean War and that provided much of the foundation for the ROK takeoff. But while welcoming signs of South Korean economic maturity, the Americans have been concerned both at a growing trade deficit with the ROK, and periodic evidence of what are regarded as Korean sharp trading practices. Both sides have so far managed to avoid the various strands of their relationship becoming too mixed up, but there are those in the United States who would like to see a closer link between trade and defence issues.

Despite all the difficulties, the relationship with the United States will remain the linchpin of the ROK's foreign relations for some years to come. As long as the ROK feels that it is not alone a match for the North, it will seek outside support, and only the US is now likely to provide that. Anti-American sentiment will not disappear among more radical groups, but the majority of South Koreans do not seem hostile to the United States. The enthusiasm shown in celebrating the centenary of Korea–US relations in 1982 was probably a better guide to Korean views than students' slogans in the 1987 demonstrations.

After the United States, Japan is the ROK's next main overseas interest. It was not always so. The colonial legacy left bitter memories, and under Syngman Rhee it proved impossible for the two countries to put their relations on a proper footing. After 1960, the atmosphere improved. Tough negotiations following the military takeover led in 1965 to the signing of a Basic Treaty and to the establishment of diplomatic relations. Not all the issues were solved in 1965, but the Basic Treaty and its related subordinate agreements allowed Park's government to attract Japanese money and technology, both of which played an important part in economic development.

But the relationship has never been an easy one. ROK governments have retained a considerable suspicion of Japan and have been quick to see slights. Japanese attitudes towards issues such as the status of Koreans in Japan, relations with North Korea, fishing rights and a territorial dispute — both countries claim a set of barren rocks in the East Sea — have led to official protests and street demonstrations. The 1973 kidnapping of Kim Dae Jung from Tokyo caused a major crisis, as did the 1974 assassination attempt on President Park by a Korean living in Japan. Japanese popular songs and films have been kept out of South Korea, as possible sources of cultural pollution. Yet many Koreans are very keen on Japanese popular culture. In Korean film and television circles, much effort goes into learning the latest styles in Japan. Around Pusan in the south, where it is possible to receive Japanese television, periodic campaigns have been conducted to persuade people not to engage in the unpatriotic act of watching it, without success. In other ways, too, South Korea's Japanese legacy is obvious, at least to outsiders, whether it is the conduct of railway officials or the style of business leaders, but it is not an easy thing for some Koreans to accept.

When President Chun took over in 1981, he argued that the ROK's defence expenditure protected Japan and therefore Japan should compensate the ROK for this. A figure of six billion US dollars was mentioned as an appropriate sum. Emotions were further raised in South Korea (and indeed in North Korea and China), by claims that Japanese school textbooks were watering down references to Japanese imperialism and wartime suffering, and by other signs of an alleged revival of Japanese militarism. Eventually a compromise was reached on Japanese aid, and the Koreans accepted Japanese assurances that the offending textbooks would in due course be revised. Relations were improved further when the then Japanese Prime Minister, Mr Nakasone, visited Seoul in September 1983, the first visit by a Japanese prime minister since the 1965 Treaty. He expressed regret at the past Japanese behaviour towards Korea, as did the Emperor when President Chun visited Japan in September 1984. Suspicions still linger, however, about Japanese views of Korea; the textbook question was revived in 1987, for example, and the status of Koreans in Japan is a constant irritant. The trading imbalance heavily in Japan's favour also causes difficulties.

Beyond these key relationships, ROK interest in the rest of the world has generally not been great, in spite of occasional flurries of activity. Diplomatic relations were established with many non-communist countries after independence, but little effort was put into such links. The division of the peninsula, the competing claims of the ROK and the DPRK, and the ROK's firm anti-communist stand, precluded contact with communist countries. Syngman Rhee's main focus was on the US and the UN. He was not much interested in other countries, and indeed, was very suspicious of some, such as Great Britain, which he saw as soft on communism. There was little change after Rhee. The ROK government made few attempts to cultivate newly independent nations. Unlike North Korea (see Chapter 14), it did not play up its colonial past, and felt no need of help from countries that were like itself. It thus allowed the North Koreans to establish a strong presence in the third world. The ROK's refusal to maintain or establish diplomatic relations with countries recognising North Korea further isolated it from third world links. As a result, the DPRK, which had started a long way behind the ROK in the diplomatic recognition stakes, made up a lot of leeway by the late 1960s.

About 1969 the Park government realised that it had neglected a source of useful support in the UN and elsewhere. Efforts were now made to establish contacts with the ex-colonial states of Africa, Asia and the Middle East. When the United Nations Commission on the Unification and Reconstruction of Korea (UNCURK) was wound up in 1973, the ROK accepted that the UN would no longer involve itself in the Korean question and reunification was remote. As well as dropping its objections to North Korean membership of the UN, the ROK abandoned its previous stand on diplomatic relations and began to cultivate some of North Korea's friends. These efforts paid off, and by the mid-1970s the ROK had diplomatic relations with a large number of third world countries. Some suspicions of the ROK remained, however, because of its close links with the United States, its anti-communist tradition, and the role it played in Vietnam. It has so far proved impossible for it to join the Non-Aligned Movement, though North Korea is a member. Today, 125 countries have diplomatic relations with the ROK and 101 with the DPRK; 69 have them with both. The ROK does considerable trade with the third world, and is beginning to supply aid. Some countries, such as Malaysia, have expressed interest in South Korean economic development, and the *saemaŭl* movement has attracted attention.

Since the abandonment of the rigidly anti-communist stand of the 1950s and 1960s, successive South Korean governments have tried to make contact with both the Soviet Union and the People's Republic of China. It was believed that such moves would help to restrain North Korea and thus help to increase security in East Asia. Only in recent years has real progress been made. In the case of the Soviet Union, the shooting-down of a Korean airliner in September 1983 was a setback to the development of contacts then under way. But though the incident caused much outrage in South Korea, the government stressed that some form of détente was important for security, and contacts eventually resumed. They have been confined mainly to sporting and other low-key links, together with a modest amount of trade through third countries, but they continue to grow. The South Koreans are pleased that the Soviet Union has announced its intention of attending the Olympics. There has also been a steady build-up of trade and other exchanges with eastern European countries. In January 1988, the Hungarian Chamber of Commerce agreed to open an office in Seoul.

Contacts with the PRC are even more substantial. The historical links between Korea and China have remained important to South Koreans, despite the lack of formal relations since 1949, the PRC's role in the Korean War, and its support for North Korea. Diplomatic and other relations have been maintained with the 'Republic of China' on Taiwan, but that has become an increasingly unsatisfactory substitute for the real thing. Many older Koreans were born in China or had family connections, sometimes going back several decades. For their part, the Chinese were highly critical of the ROK under both Rhee and Park and generally rebuffed all attempts at contact. After the changes in China from 1978 onwards, this policy was gradually modified in practice and some sport and trade contacts were allowed. Indirect trade has grown, and South Korean businessmen experience little difficulty in visiting the PRC. The Chinese attended the 1986 Asian Games in Seoul, and have accepted the IOC invitation to attend the Seoul Olympic Games, despite North Korean objections. One of Roh Tae Woo's election pledges was to improve links with China and eventually to establish some form of 'official relations.'

Relations with these near neighbours have an obvious security content, and it is still basic security that is the mainspring of much of the ROK's international activity. The further away the country, the less direct interest, except for the need to combat North Korean influence. The main exception to this rule is trade, which of course is of major importance to a country such as the ROK, whose development in recent years has been firmly export-led. Both the concern with North Korea and trade issues play an important part in the ROK's consideration of western Europe. Until 1973, the former was not a problem. No western European country had relations with North Korea, though there was some small-scale trade. Following the dissolution of UNCURK, however, several countries established diplomatic relations with the North, and the ROK began to pay more attention to preventing further inroads. Trade, too, has brought its problems, which are unlikely to diminish, as individual European countries and the European Community press the ROK for more market access. But Europe is remote for most Koreans and is likely to remain so. The celebration of the centenaries of diplomatic relations with a number of European countries from 1983 onwards was far removed from the razzamatazz that marked the American centenary in 1982, but it was as clear an indication as any of the ROK's priorities.

Chapter Thirteen

Koreans Overseas

Korea is not only what is contained within the peninsula, north or south. Korean communities are found throughout the world, though not all of these groups have made the same impact on the society around them or have shared the same fortunes, and they have established themselves under the impulse of differing needs. The Korean communities in countries neighbouring on the Korean peninsula, such as China, the Soviet Union and Japan, settled there through poverty or coercion. Those in North America have largely developed out of a desire to escape poverty and develop careers. Korean emigrants to South America have likewise gone to improve their fortunes. In the Middle East, on the other hand, most Koreans are unattached men on secondment for their firms. In Europe many Koreans are now there largely for reasons of work or study, and few intend to remain permanently, though a community has grown up in West Germany.

Patterns of emigration

A distinction has thus to be made between overseas Korean communities based on permanent emigration and settled family life, and those serving the needs of specific Korean interests abroad or supporting individual needs such as study and training. In a place such as the United States there is both a permanent and a transient

Korean population. Other reasons leading to Korean emigration are adoption and marriage. Administrative measures such as legislation have also had a strong effect in recent decades on the rate of emigration from South Korea. Accurate figures for the relative strengths of overseas Korean communities are not readily available, but census returns for the countries accommodating the largest concentrations of Koreans give some indication of the size of these settlements. The Chinese census of July 1982 listed 1,763,870 Koreans, while the Soviet census of 1979 recorded 388,926 Koreans. In the United States, the 1980 census gave a figure of 354,529 Koreans, though the continuing high rate of South Korean immigration into America has probably pushed that number up to over 500,000. The Korean population of Japan is estimated at between 670,000 and 697,000. Bringing the various figures together, a total emerges of some 3.3 million Koreans settled outside of the Korean peninsula, the most important groupings being in China, Japan, the United States and the Soviet Union. The absence of diplomatic links between the Republic of Korea and its communist neighbours the People's Republic of China and the Soviet Union means that the South Korean government is unable to concern itself officially with the Korean minorities in those countries. Moreover, almost all the Korean residents in China and the Soviet Union have now taken Chinese or Soviet citizenship, and where they have not, they hold North Korean citizenship. While the fortunes of these Korean communities are of concern to South Koreans, and the possible effect of North Korean advances towards overseas Korean communities a constant source of anxiety to the government of the Republic of Korea, official and popular discussion of the issues of Korean emigration and overseas Koreans focuses on Koreans living abroad in non-communist countries, in particular in Japan and the United States.

Korean emigration has followed several strands over the past 100 years. Until the 1880s emigration was forbidden, but nonetheless took place across the northern border of Korea into Manchuria and Siberia. The numbers flowing northward increased through the last years of the nineteenth century and into the first decades of the twentieth. To this northward movement was added emigration eastwards to Japan during the period of the Japanese annexation of Korea. In these years many Koreans moved to Japan, where it was easier to avoid discrimination, especially in education. With the coming of war, many Koreans were recruited for Japanese industry. The military defeat of Japan in 1945 led to a massive repatriation of Koreans from Japan, and some movement of Koreans back from Manchuria. The present destination of many emigrating Koreans, the United States, did not start to achieve its favoured position until the late 1960s, when the liberalisation of US immigration laws towards Asians in 1965 following on the South Korean Emigration Law of 1962 encouraged many South Koreans to turn towards the United States, a country that since 1945 had held a position of pre-eminence in South Korea's estimation of the world. Other Koreans had also started in the early 1960s to look towards South America. Emigration to countries in that region has followed a fluctuating course, but is still encouraged. The South Korean presence in Asia (other than Japan), the Middle East, Africa and Europe, where the intention is employment or study rather than emigration, likewise fluctuates, largely under the pressure of varying economic conditions.

Attitudes towards emigration

If the pattern of Korean emigration has changed, so have official Korean attitudes. In the last century emigration was discouraged, even prohibited, in line with a tradition that Korea had shared with both China and Japan that its subjects should not venture into the outside world. Japan during its colonial period had likewise sought to control the movement and activities of its Korean subjects. The government of the new Republic of Korea also resisted emigration, partly to discourage any flight of capital and of brain power out of the country at a time of national reconstruction, partly to prevent the loss of morale that might have occurred if too many people, particularly prominent citizens, were seen to be leaving. The Emigration Law of 1962 represented a break with such attitudes, though even after emigration became permissible, restrictions continued on the categories of people who might leave and on the amount of money they might take with them. This type of control is easing gradually with revisions to the Emigration Law, but permission to leave the country still has to be sought formally. In presenting the 1962

Emigration Law, the South Korean government pointed to the beneficial effects emigration might have in easing population growth in Korea. This was running in the 1960s at an annual rate of 2.7 percent. In 1962 the Republic of Korea launched into its first five-year plan. The rapid rate of population increase was seen as a brake on economic development. In this light, an easing of restrictions on emigration, together with the birth control campaign initiated also in 1962, would well have appeared as useful regulators in controlling the size of the population. The Korea Overseas Development Corporation was set up under government sponsorship in 1965 to assist would-be emigrants. Official views on emigration now make less play of its demographic aspects and instead emphasise the value of remittances sent back to Korea and the economic links that can be established between Korean settlers overseas and mainland Korea. In a move away from the earlier tradition of emigrant Korean farm workers, the Korean government is encouraging new emigrants to such areas as South America to invest in small- and medium-scale businesses.

While official attitudes on emigration are largely favourable, popular views are marked by ambiguity. There is satisfaction at the success of Korean settlers in such places as North America, pride in the achievements of those who have done well in their studies abroad and an acknowledgement that they are spreading Korea's good name. At the same time, though, there is anxiety that through exposure to other ways these same people may be losing the characteristics that make them peculiarly Korean. These fears are most strongly expressed over those who have settled or worked for long periods in western countries and whose Korean upbringing or ancestry has been more severely challenged. Koreans have to grapple every day with the superficial aspects of western culture introduced into Korea, but can generally accommodate them. What they fear more is the spiritual and philosophical contamination that may result from too long a stay away from Korea. With the Korean communities in China and Siberia, different emotions come into play, those of concern and longing. Towards the Chinese Koreans and those living in Sakhalin there is an especial sense of the loss of separation, heightened in recent years by occasional reunions between elderly family members. Even some younger Koreans, those from early middle-age onwards, can claim China as their place of birth. Although South Koreans have been allowed to make discreet official visits to China in recent years, none appears so far to have been permitted to make contact with the Korean communities there. Only a few people of Korean descent but holding non-ROK nationality have been allowed to make such visits. They have reported that the Korean settlements in China have retained much of their ethnic distinctiveness.

The status of the Korean community in Japan is also a subject of concern and often resentment among Koreans. Contact between overseas Koreans living in Japan and mainland Korea is easily maintained, and among overseas Korean visitors to South Korea the Japanese contingent is largest. Cultural and family links are thus not so threatened as elsewhere and are maintained against a background of certain common cultural attitudes. These factors, however, have not eased significantly the relationship between Japan and its Korean minority. The circumstances under which many Koreans first came to Japan — migration during the period of Japanese colonisation and wartime conscription into Japanese industries — are in themselves a cause of anger. Persistent Japanese reluctance to grant naturalisation to more than a few of the Koreans living in Japan leaves the majority of the community with the status of permanent alien residents. This legal disability is matched by what many Koreans see as widespread social and economic discrimination. The situation is further complicated by the tug of allegiances within the Korean community between pro-South Korean and pro-North Korean factions.

The South Korean government seems to accept that many Koreans settled abroad have, whether voluntarily or not, taken foreign nationality. More important is a continuing healthy allegiance to Korean values among Korean communities overseas. Anxiety on this score expresses itself over such issues as language, lifestyle and marriage. Plans are in hand by the Korean Ministry of Education to extend the provision of education for Korean children living abroad with the intention of keeping them familiar with their national culture. Regular summer schools aim to bring groups of young people of Korean descent living in North America or Europe to South Korea for re-orientation into Korean culture and language. Many youngsters, second or third generation settlers abroad, have little or no command of Korean. Their reception back in Korea can be harsh when it is realised they cannot respond in Korean. Their freer manners can also arouse anger. Nonetheless, many young people, even those adopted in childhood, may make the journey back to Korea, and it is still the custom to look there for a spouse.

The issue of intermarriage is a delicate one for many Koreans, among whom concepts of racial and family purity are strong. Marriage out of the group occurs nonetheless among all Korean overseas communities to a greater or lesser extent. In South Korea itself it is extremely rare to find a Korean man with a foreign wife. More frequent are unions between Korean women and foreign men. Another issue that has caused much heartsearching among Koreans is that of adoption. In the aftermath of the Korean War and in the years since, large numbers of orphans were adopted by foreign families through charitable agencies that continued their work until quite recently. During the twenty-year period of 1963 to 1983, it has been calculated, over 78,000 Koreans emigrated through adoption. Koreans have in the past been reluctant to countenance adoption of children save by a blood relative and then in the interests of preserving the family line. (An eldest son without a male heir might, for instance, adopt a son of a younger male member of the family so as to ensure the continuation of the family line.) At the same time, they have been uneasy over the post-Korean War practice of allowing Korean children to leave the country to be reared by foreigners. Now, economic prosperity and national pride have led to the feeling that abandoned children should be cared for in their own society.

The self-confidence and pride marking many of South Korea's attitudes are coupled with a longing within the country that Korean values should receive far wider recognition in the world at large. The double role of immigrant and ambassador that these aspirations imply for Koreans settling overseas, and seemingly incompatible requirements of flexibility in meeting change while retaining loyalty to former ways, cannot always ease the path for Korean immigrants as they endeavour to make a place for themselves in a new country.

Historical aspects

China and the Soviet Union

Korean settlers were moving northwards into the north east areas of China—Manchuria—and into the maritime regions of Siberia by the

1860s; and indeed had probably been doing so for some time before. Most were farmers from the northern provinces of Korea driven by famine and economic necessity. Up till 1881 their migration into China was forbidden by both the Manchu (Ch'ing) and Yi monarchies and so had to be undertaken clandestinely, but in that year the Chinese north eastern provinces were opened to them. They settled in various parts of the north east, but formed their biggest concentration in the area to the north of the Tumen river, which has long been a natural boundary at this point between China and Korea. The district where they congregated was known formerly as Chientao province and is now called the Yanbian Korean Autonomous Prefecture. In this region the Korean immigrants settled as tenant farmers, organised local self-administration and established their own schools. Their position was quickly legalised with the Chinese authorities through the granting of land deeds and the payment of land tax. The numbers of Korean settlers in Manchuria increased rapidly from an estimated 10,000 in 1881 to 78,000 in 1904 and 323,000 by 1908.

Korean emigration into the Vladivostok area and the Ussuri river valley in Siberia seems likewise to have been rapid. The traveller Mrs Bishop, visiting Siberia in the mid-1890s, noted that in 1863 thirteen families from the north east of Korea had settled near Possiet Bay. By 1866 this number had risen to 100 families, and by 1897, she wrote, the total figure of Korean immigrants into Siberia was estimated at between 16,000 and 18,000. Many of these new settlers had taken up farming on land that they had eventually been able to buy, while others were responsible for local transport of goods and fuel. The Korean communities she visited enjoyed practical autonomy, having their own police and electing their own officials. Those settled in Siberia before 1884 could, moreover, claim rights as Russian subjects.

Growing Japanese intervention in Korea's affairs, culminating in outright annexation of the country in 1910, added political pressure to the already existing economic reasons for emigration, and the flow of Koreans to both Manchuria and Siberia stepped up considerably. In turn, the political dimensions of these Korean migrant communities became more apparent and more complicated. As has been pointed out in chapter 5, both the Chinese north east and Siberia became places of refuge for Koreans seeking escape from Japanese political pressure and persecution. Up to 1931, when

Japan created the puppet state of 'Manchukuo,' Korean emigration to Manchuria had been voluntary. After that date Japan planned to promote the settlement of up to 10,000 Koreans in Manchuria as part of a scheme to consolidate its base there and to free farmland in the Korean peninsula for use by Japanese settlers. With the establishment of 'Manchukuo,' all forms of self-government among the Korean communities were ended. The strict Japanese policies of assimilation that had been practised towards the population in Korea itself were applied to Koreans living in the puppet state. Japan's plans for Manchuria were frustrated by its defeat in 1945 at the end of the Pacific War, but it had nonetheless been able to raise the Korean population of Manchuria to some 1,400,000 by 1943. On liberation, the great majority of these Koreans chose to remain in China.

The Chinese communist hold in Manchuria, at first precarious, was gradually extended as the Chinese civil war progressed. From late 1945 Koreans living in the region were recruited by the Chinese into a volunteer corps, eventually 50,000 strong, which contributed to Chinese communist victory in the north east. During this period, the Manchurian Koreans were recognised as Korean citizens and were allowed to set up schools and, where they were in the majority, practise local self-administration. In the years immediately following the Japanese defeat, movement was easy across the Chinese border into northern Korea, and North Korean influence was strong. During the Korean War, many young Koreans fought on the side of the Democratic People's Republic of Korea (DPRK), either as members of the Chinese People's Volunteers or in the North Korean army. In the early 1950s, the People's Republic of China and the DPRK reached agreement on the status of Koreans in China: in an apparent change of policy, all those living in the north east area were to be automatically recognised as Chinese citizens whereas those living elsewhere in China were to have the choice between Chinese or North Korean citizenship. Several thousand are said to have chosen the latter option. In its policies towards its national minorities, the new People's Republic of China at first showed considerable latitude over such issues as education and use of mother language. Two bad periods followed as the earlier Chinese line gave way to policies intended to strengthen the position of the Han Chinese majority. All of China's national minorities suffered as the use of minority languages became discredited and minority initiative stifled in the interests of national unity and con-struction. From 1957 to 1959 during the 'anti-rightist' rectification movement and again, after a brief respite, during the 'cultural revolution' from 1965, local Korean leaders came under attack and local practices such as the extensive use of Korean language and literature in educational institutes were severely weakened. It was not until after the death of Mao Tse-tung in 1978 and the removal of his close followers that the former discriminatory line was reversed. The Korean language is now regarded as one of the major minority languages in China, and Korean-language studies have regained ground. Newspapers and magazines are published regularly in Korean.

Contacts with South Korea understandably are limited, but are now openly tolerated by both sides. Since 1974 people living in South Korea have been able to correspond with relatives in China, visits by Chinese Koreans to South Korea to meet their families have been permitted since 1978, and in 1984 the Chinese government indicated it would allow South Korean citizens to visit their relatives in China, though it is not known how many such reunions may have taken place. South Korean newspapers are available in China, and Radio Seoul can be heard.

Much less is known about those Koreans who remained in the Soviet Union. By the end of the Pacific War the greater part of them had Soviet nationality, some of them having acquired it by virtue of already possessing citizenship in pre-revolutionary Russia. In the mid-1930s the number of Koreans living in the Soviet Far East was estimated at between 300,000 and 500,000, with a heavy concentra-tion around Possiet Bay (the area where Mrs Bishop had found them 40 years earlier). In 1938, however, the Soviet Korean com-munity was dispersed from the Soviet Far East into parts of central Asia, notably Uzbekistan and Kazakhstan. This move was imposed as a security measure, perhaps out of fear that the Korean com-munities in Siberia might harbour Japanese agents. After the end-ing of hostilities in 1945 a number of Koreans were detained in Soviet prisoner-of-war camps as elements of captured Japanese troops or as civilians charged with collaboration or anti-communist activities. Some 45,000 Koreans whom the Japanese had brought to work in coal mines on South Sakhalin island also found themselves in Soviet hands. Despite Soviet–Allied agreements on the return of Japanese prisoners-of-war and civilians, including Koreans (whose national status had previously been that of citizens of the Japanese empire), not all the Koreans who had passed under Soviet control at the end of the war were in fact repatriated. There seems to have been no question of return to the southern half of Korea. The Soviet Union entered into close relations with the new DPRK, maintaining influence through a number of Soviet Koreans holding dual Soviet–North Korean citizenship who were returned to North Korea to occupy key positions in the political, government, social and military apparatus there. This group of men, together with those who had left Manchuria in the early years of the Pacific war to continue fighting against the Japanese, often in the Soviet army, formed the nucleus of power in North Korea and succeeded in ousting all other political groups as well as the 'Yenan Koreans' who had been trained by the Chinese communists. The dual status of the Soviet Koreans ended in 1957 with the adoption of a nationality treaty between North Korea and the Soviet Union that permitted only Soviet or North Korean citizenship for Koreans.

The Soviet census of 1979 recorded a Korean population of 388,926, over two-thirds of whom lived in three main areas: Sakhalin (34,978); Uzbek Soviet Socialist Republic (163,062); and Kazakh Soviet Socialist Republic (91,984). The 1979 census reported that 55 percent of the Korean minority counted Korean as their mother tongue. It is not known if the Soviet Korean communities support any schools, but the Korean language is studied at institutes of higher learning. Non-Soviet estimates of 40,000 to 50,000 Koreans living in Sakhalin conflict with the lower Soviet figure. The greater majority of these Koreans have taken Soviet or North Korean citizenship, but about 3000 are said to have refused to accept either nationality and are stateless. In 1987 a few of the Korean residents of Sakhalin, together with a handful in China, were reported to have sent letters to a clearing organisation seeking contact with relatives living in South Korea.

Japan

Korean immigration into Japan followed a different pattern to the northwards movement of Koreans into farming settlements in China and Siberia. In a sense it started in the first years of the Christian era, with the arrival of settlers from Korea who included some of Chinese origin. These immigrants were mostly craftsmen and farmers who introduced their skills into Japan. They seem to have prospered to the extent that by the end of the seventh century AD a Japanese peerage showed that over one-third of Japanese noble families claimed Korean or Chinese descent. Much later an enforced immigration took place when Korean craftsmen, including potters and weavers, were taken to Japan in the wake of General Toyotomi Hideyoshi's campaigns in Korea at the very end of the sixteenth century. The modern period of immigration did not start until the first decades of this century and did not assume significance until around 1920, when 40,755 Korean immigrants were recorded. This figure rose to 419,009 by 1930, and ten years later stood at 1,241,315 and went on increasing during the Pacific War. The defeat of Japan led to extensive repatriation of Koreans, and by 1950 the Korean population of Japan had been reduced to 544,903. It is now estimated at between 670,000 and 697,000, three-quarters of whom have been born and reared in Japan.

Up to the mid-1930s, many Koreans coming to Japan were farmers reduced to poverty by Japanese policies of landownership in Korea. Most came from the south of the country. In Japan they were mainly taken into the unskilled labour force. Not all of them settled, and there was considerable coming and going between Korea and Japan. From the early 1930s, the Korean immigrant labour force was seen as important in the development of Japanese war industries, which after 1936 drew in large numbers of Korean workers. From 1940 Koreans were virtually conscripted as contract labourers into Japanese war work, releasing Japanese workers for war service. Their wages and living conditions compared poorly with those of Japanese workers. They were mainly concentrated in urban industrial areas and mining districts. Today they are found in various parts of Japan but still live chiefly in the heavily-populated urban regions. Another, much smaller group of Koreans were university students who by 1930 numbered nearly 8000. Some came to espouse left wing sympathies and mingled in Japanese communist circles.

The collapse of Japanese power in 1945 and subsequent ending of Koreans' former status as citizens of the Japanese empire led to a position of legal ambiguity for those who remained in Japan, an ambiguity not yet satisfactorily resolved. In November 1946 the occupying powers classed them as Japanese nationals for 'purposes of treatment'; but the following year Koreans were obliged to register under the new Alien Registration Law. With the ratification of the San Francisco peace treaty in 1952, Koreans acquired the status of foreigners. In 1959 the Red Cross societies of Japan and North Korea negotiated an agreement on repatriation that led to the return of about 100,000 Japanese Koreans to North Korea over the next eight years. Only in 1965, when Japan and the Republic of Korea concluded a basic treaty normalising relations, was agreement reached on the legal standing of at least some of the Korean minority in Japan. The greater number were allowed to apply for permanent resident status and the social benefits that such status conferred, though eligibility was restricted to those who had lived in Japan from before the Pacific War and their families. By the deadline of January 1971, 351,955 Koreans had applied. In the event, such status has been granted only to those willing to take citizenship of the Republic of Korea (Japan has diplomatic relations only with the ROK).

The Korean community in Japan is in fact divided along political lines into the Mindan group that supports the ROK, and the Ch'ongnyon group that supports the DPRK. Even before 1948, when both the ROK and the DPRK were established, Korean sentiment had swung partly towards the communist north. The League of Koreans Residing in Japan, active from 1945 to 1949, was a left wing organisation closely aligned with the Japanese communists. The Ch'ongnyon faction, active since 1955, is alone recognised by North Korea as representing the Korean community in Japan. It is used by the Japanese authorities as an unofficial means of communication with the DPRK. Like its predecessor, the League, it is a well-organised group running its own educational institutions where Korean is used in teaching. In recent years it has, through investment in the DPRK, played a major role in the North's attempts at economic advance. The flow is two-way, because Ch'ongnyon has also on occasion received financial assistance from North Korea. The Mindan group was formed in 1946 in a breakaway from a forerunner of the present Ch'ongnyon group. After 1965 it received some financial support from South Korea. It is generally regarded as less effective than its rival in furthering its members' interests. The South Korean government, constantly alert to possibilities of North Korean infiltration into its territory through the Korean community in Japan, has taken the initiative in recent years to organise 'homecoming' tours of the South for Ch'ongnyon members. Contact between the members of the two contending factions in Japan is restricted.

The present status of the majority of Japanese Koreans as resident aliens is a cause of dissatisfaction both to the Korean community in Japan and to South Korea itself. In recent years this resentment has expressed itself in anger over the Japanese requirement that all aliens submit to finger-printing, and some Korean residents have refused to comply. What the Korean community in Japan objects to is not so much the policy of finger-printing as its application to them. They argue that many Koreans living in Japan are there as a result of forcible immigration during the war and that the circumstances of their arrival and the contribution they made to the Japanese war effort should be recognised through more favourable treatment. As it is, their lack of Japanese citizenship — only a minority of them have become naturalised Japanese — bars them from many government posts including teaching in Japanese schools, while more pervasive discrimination tends to keep them in the margins of the economy and leads to general under-achievement.

United States

Korean fortunes, by contrast, have prospered in the United States, particularly since 1965 when the Immigration and Naturalisation Act eased Asian immigration by abolishing national quota systems that had previously favoured applicants from north west Europe. Korean settlers are regarded as among the best educated and most industrious of the immigrant groups. Their professional skills and experience of urban living and a capitalist style of economy enable them to adapt well to their new environment, even if at first they may suffer a downward turn financially in that they often have to take less skilled work. They have been more prepared than other Asian immigrants to disperse to different parts of their new country, though they have still tended to congregate, notably in California, New York and Illinois. Their rate of intermarriage with other Asian immigrant groups (and indeed with non-Asians) is high. Above all, their reasons for immigration to the United States are positive: to join family members already there, to seek a good education for their children, and to improve their own careers. The rate of Korean immigration into the United States in recent years is put at around 30,000 people a year, making the Korean community one of the fastest-growing immigrant groups. The 1980 US census recorded 354,529 Koreans, which figure, given the annual rate of immigration, may now stand at around 500,000. A number of immigrants seek naturalisation each year. During the period 1950 to 1980, it has been estimated, naturalisation was granted to over 100,000 Korean applicants.

Until 1965 the pattern of Korean immigration to the United States had been very different. In the early years of this century a small number of Koreans and their families — somewhat over 7000 — were permitted to settle in Hawaii as sugar cane workers. After 1905 all Korean immigration to Hawaii stopped, largely under Japanese pressure, but the early settlers moved on to the US mainland or into non-agricultural jobs in Hawaii. With the Japanese annexation of Korea in 1910, Korean movement to the United States was reduced to women immigrating for marriage, and a small band, about 900 strong, of those leaving for political exile or study. The Korean community in America supported the March First independence movement financially and through diplomatic approaches to the great powers. Between 1924, when the United States introduced an immigrant quota system aimed against East European and Asian immigration, and 1945, Korean entry into the United States dried up. In 1950 the Korean community numbered around 7000. Between 1950 and 1965, however, its size more than doubled as the rate of Korean immigration was allowed to rise. The effects of the 1965 liberalisation did not show themselves immediately, and in the 1970 US census the number of Koreans was recorded at 70,598. The years since then have shown a remarkable increase. Many of the new immigrants have entered as US servicemen's wives. The presence of a large number of US forces in South Korea for the past three and a half decades has led to a sustained outflow of such women, estimated in late 1984 at upwards of 60,000. They, and Korean children arriving on adoption, constitute two distinct subgroups in Korean immigration into the United States.

An important element is the large group of young Koreans enrolling for higher studies at American universities, without necessarily intending to stay permanently. Indeed, the preponderance of US-trained scholars and the strength of US-inspired practices in South Korean universities are among the most marked features of academic life in the Republic of Korea. Where up to the mid-1950s higher academic posts were largely filled by graduates of Japanese universities, they have since tended to go to US-educated applicants.

Many Korean immigrants are Christians, and Korean churches flourished from the first days of Korean immigration into the United States as cultural, educational and social as much as religious centres. One characteristic of the US Korean community is the fairly high proportion of people originating from the northern part of Korea who had later moved to the southern half. Christianity was especially strong among the northerners, and their religious persuasion, together with their earlier experience of migration, may have encouraged them to make a second move to the United States. For new immigrants lack of English may be a handicap in seeking employment and in social contacts, while, in a familiar enough pattern, it may lead to problems in family relationships as the second generation grows up in a largely non-Korean environment. The pull between values centred on the mother country and those of the new society is felt within the Korean community as much as in any other. Relations between the Korean minority and other ethnic and racial minorities in the United States can also be difficult. These obstacles, however, clearly do not outweigh the attractions of a new life, and Korean immigration to the United States seems set to continue.

Chapter Fourteen

North Korea since 1945

In North Korean accounts since the late 1950s, there is a continuity between the struggle against imperialism in the nineteenth century, the events of 1919, the guerrilla war waged from Manchuria, and the liberation in 1945. This link is provided by Kim Il-sung, whose family have led the revolutionary struggle of the Korean people since the American 'warship,' the 'General Sherman' was attacked and destroyed in the Taedong river in 1866. In this version, the Korean communists, under the leadership of Kim Il-sung, liberated Korea from the Japanese in August 1945 and eventually established the Democratic People's Republic of Korea (DPRK) in 1948. Having won power by their own efforts, this argument goes, the communists and the DPRK are the only legitimate government on the Korean peninsula, and the legitimate heirs to the old empire of Korea.

In reality, the communists were one group among many in 1945, and those led by Kim Il-sung, while known to the Japanese, were by no means the most important. Indeed, in August 1945, Kim Il-sung and his followers were almost certainly in the Soviet Union, not Korea. As we have seen, it was the defeat of Japan that led to Korea's liberation. Soviet forces moved into the northern half of the penin- sula to take the surrender of the Japanese troops. They stopped at the 38th parallel, as agreed among the allies. This allowed a number of Korean resistance groups, including some from the Soviet Union, to move back into Korea. Even then these groups, some communist, some not, were only part of the story, for as many political organ- isations appeared north of the 38th parallel as did south of it. The role of the Soviet forces is not entirely ignored in North Korea today, but it does not feature prominently in historical accounts, and is normally only mentioned around the 15 August anniversary.

There is nothing to indicate that the Russians had any more advanced plans for postwar Korea than the other allies. The Russians had experience, derived from the central Asian republics, which could be put to some use, but there is no clear evidence of a Soviet blueprint for takeover. Like the Americans, the Russians' first instinct seems to have been to treat Korea much as though it were a defeated enemy. The Japanese were disarmed and the Russians began to strip factories of machinery and other movable things. There was also some private looting and widespread rape by the Soviet soldiers, until firm military discipline was restored. In general the Russians did not make the American mistake of using Japanese to continue the administration in the north, but they did use those who were Japanese-trained for this purpose and a few hundred Japanese technicians were used to run factories and give professional advice at least until 1948. It is difficult to see how the Russians could have done otherwise. Japanese policies meant that there was no readily-available pool of Korean talent on which to draw and, in the meantime, the country had to be kept going. While large numbers of Soviet troops were in Korea by early September, they had other tasks to perform apart from running the economy or organising town halls. The Russians were better off in one way because they brought a number of Soviet Koreans with them to act as interpreters, but numbers were limited. Japanese-trained Koreans could be used to make the colonial apparatus work. There seems little doubt that the Russians found that highly-centralised machine familiar and they had no difficulty using it.

The Russians faced the same political turmoil as confronted the Americans. The end of the war awakened hopes on all sides. People's committees were formed in many places, and there were widespread demands for economic, political and social reform. In the north, the strongest group in August 1945 were the Nationalists, led by a well-known conservative, Cho Man-sik. In early September 1945, on hearing of the declaration of the Korean People's Republic in Seoul, Cho and his followers placed themselves under its authority. When it failed to get recognition, however, they abandoned it, and organised their own 'North Korean Five Province Administrative Bureau,' with Cho as chairman. This proved to be weak and had little control over the people's committees, nominally subordinate to it. There was a small group of domestic communists, organised as the North Korean Bureau of the Korean Communist Party, but now gradually cut off from the party leadership in Seoul. Koreans from China began to return too. Many of these were communists, but not all. Generally known as the 'Independence League,' they were to organise themselves as the 'New People's Party' during 1946. At first the Soviet forces worked with whatever was available, but gradually they began to favour the people's committees and by early 1946 these were the main political organisation in North Korea. By then much had changed from the early days of the Soviet occupation. In September or October 1945 — both dates are found — there returned to Korea a man known as Kim Il-sung; his original name was Kim Sŏng-ju. He was largely unknown to his fellow-countrymen, although he had led one of the anti-Japanese guerilla bands active in Manchuria in the late 1930s. He now returned, in some accounts, in the uniform of a major in the Soviet armed forces. There followed a series of moves that brought Kim to supreme power.

As we have seen, in December 1945 the four allied powers decided in Moscow that Korea should undergo a five-year period of trusteeship, and this led to violent opposition throughout Korea. At first the communists supported this opposition, but then they changed their stand and in North Korea this provided the opportunity for Kim and his followers to deal with their opponents. Kim himself became head of the northern branch of the Korean Communist Party in December 1945. The Nationalists, who had been most vehement in their opposition to the Moscow agreement, were pushed to one side; by January 1946, Cho Man-sik was under house arrest. The domestic communists, who were equally opposed to the Moscow agreement, were also dealt with. By early 1946 Kim Il-sung was clearly a major force in the north, even though he still held only subordinate party positions. When the North Korean Workers' Party was formed in July 1946, Kim Tu-bong, a veteran communist from China, was the chairman and Kim Il-sung was only the vice chairman. But the younger Kim was increasingly the man who called the tune. From February 1946 he was the chairman of the newly-formed North Korean Provisional People's Committee, which, under the Russians, was now the government of North Korea.

These developments were taking place against the backdrop of the failure of negotiations on the future of Korea described in Chapter Six, and of a steady move towards the establishment of separate regimes in the peninsula. In North Korea this process was aided by the measures already under way to transform society. There is little doubt that a major revolution took place north of the 38th parallel from the autumn of 1945 onwards. By the end of 1946, all land had been distributed to those who actually worked it. Although the northern half of the peninsula had been the main area of industrial development under the Japanese, agriculture still played a major role. At the end of the war, some 75 percent of the population in the north were engaged in work on the land, yet just under 7 percent of farmers held 54 percent of the cultivated land, while over half of the total cultivated less than 6 percent of the entire land. (These are North Korean figures, and may be exaggerated, but only slightly.) This task of redistribution was made easier with the departure of the Japanese, which freed large areas of government and private land. Among the 2 million people from the north who are believed to have left for the south between 1945 and 1948 were many landlords, who feared either their tenants or the Russians. These departures simplified the takeover of land and the cancellation of farmers' debts. As a consequence, land reform was effected with little bloodshed and much rejoicing.

In other ways, too, the circumstances at the end of the war made radical changes easy. Most industry had also been Japanese owned, and its nationalisation presented few difficulties. Similarly, banks, insurance companies, and other financial institutions could easily be taken over for the same reasons, as could the transport and communications systems. The departure of many people to the south, often those most likely to be conservative in their thinking, the general sense of change and movement caused by the sudden end of the war, and the youth of many of those who now found themselves in positions of authority, meant that there was a climate of change, a desire for a new system. Hence it was not difficult to introduce fundamental changes in fields such as health, the equality of the sexes and education. New laws covering all these areas were introduced in 1946, under the auspices of the Provisional People's Committee. Even the decision to stop using Chinese characters in favour of the *han'gŭl* alphabet could be presented as a break from the old ways, especially since Japanese, like Korean, used a mixture of characters and native script. (It was paralleled by a similar decision in the south, somewhat later, which was eventually abandoned. In fact, knowledge of characters has by no means died out in North Korea, official publicity to the contrary notwithstanding.)

Undoubtedly many suffered because of the changes. Those who had worked with the Japanese found life hard, as did anybody whose class background was deemed to be wrong. Despite the need for skilled technicians and administrators, there was widespread suspicion of those who appeared to be educated. Religious believers, especially those linked with Christianity and western missionaries, were harassed and land belonging to various religious organisations was confiscated in the land reform process. As we have seen, large numbers fled south. But for many people the changes were welcome and overdue. Later many would have cause for grievance, but before 1950 life for those who stayed in North Korea and who did not come from the old ruling circles generally improved. Incomes were high and living conditions were steadily getting better.

The changes were not necessarily imposed by the Russians. There was Soviet aid and assistance, just as in the south there was American aid and assistance, but there is no real evidence to substantiate earlier claims that the Russians sought to turn North Korea into another Soviet republic. The measures now implemented met a desire, strongly expressed both north and south, for major reforms. They reflected the departure of the country's rulers without time to leave an alternative government in place. They also reflected disillusionment with the old ruling class of Korea and its *mores*. The people who made up that class were seen as having failed to resist the Japanese takeover 40 years previously, and as having then cooperated with these alien rulers. None of this was displeasing to the Russians, perhaps, who were naturally disposed towards the type and scale of changes being made and who clearly provided assistance and technical advice — they had little choice if they did not want the North Korean economy to collapse — but the main impetus for it seems to have come from the Koreans.

The next two years saw a consolidation of these policies. They also saw the first heavy demands placed on the peasants, in the form of extra rice quotas and a demand for extra work either in factories or on other projects. There were also developments on the political

front. Kim Il-sung steadily improved his position as the chief communist leader in the north. When the southern communists fled to
the north in 1948, their leader, Pak Hŏn-yŏng, who had confidently
expected to take over the party leadership, found that he was
expected to be number two to Kim. He accepted, but grudgingly.
The flight of the southern communists was a symptom of the way
north and south were dividing. By February 1948, a draft constitution for the whole of Korea was before the North Korean Supreme
People's Assembly.

At the same time, efforts were made publicly at least to prevent
the split. In April 1948 two of the leading nationalists in South
Korea, Kim Ku and Kim Kyu-sik, defied Syngman Rhee and
attended a conference on unification in the north. It was perhaps the
last chance, but nothing came of the first meeting and Kim Kyu-sik
declined to return for a second. In May 1948 the North Koreans
refused to allow UN-supervised elections in the north, and when
elections went ahead in the south, the North attacked them. Instead,
elections were held in the north in August 1948 for a Supreme
People's Assembly that supposedly represented all Korea. This
body, acting as a constituent assembly, accepted a constitution for
the Democratic People's Republic of Korea that was ratified on 8
September 1948, and the DPRK was proclaimed on 9 September.
Kim Il-sung was the premier, with Pak Hŏn-yŏng the vice premier
and foreign minister of the new state. The new constitution was
modelled on that of the Soviet Union, and contained the same heavy
centralisation of power. Yet it was also possible to see the tradition of
the former colonial administration at work in this and other features
of the new state. Some of the centralisation may have also come from
the need for a system of regular checks on not very skilled workers,
whether in factories or offices.

In December 1948 the Soviet Union announced the complete
withdrawal of its troops. Advisers remained with most military units
of the Korean People's Army, organised from old guerilla units and
new recruits, but there was a clear reduction of obvious Soviet involvement in North Korea. In June 1949 the North Korean Workers'
Party formally absorbed what was left of the South Korean Workers'
Party, and renamed itself the Korean Workers' Party (KWP). This
was a further sign of Kim Il-sung's dominance. It also showed that
as far as the North Korean communists were concerned, the centre
of revolutionary activity had shifted to P'yŏngyang.

The establishment of separate governments and the eventual withdrawal of the occupation forces left two increasingly hostile regimes facing each other, each equally determined that the division of the peninsula was intolerable and each unwilling to compromise. Continued political turmoil in South Korea during 1948 and 1949 seemed to offer hope that unification could be achieved on the North Korean terms. The North also brought pressure in other ways. In mid-May 1948, supplies of electricity to the South ceased. Guerilla raids across the 38th parallel increased in number and intensity. South Korean forces replied in kind, and no doubt also initiated raids. To the North Koreans, it must have seemed sensible to settle the issue before the odds against them grew longer. South Korean armed forces, although in 1950 still much smaller than those of the (North) Korean People's Army, were nevertheless expanding, training under American advisers, and acquiring new equipment. Since the United States apparently did not see South Korea as part of its own defence perimeter, there should be no trouble from that quarter. Stalin may have been encouraging and certainly supplied much of the advanced weaponry possessed by the North Koreans, but there were good reasons why the latter should have decided to go to war when they did.

Whatever the reasons for the gamble, it failed disastrously. Long before the armistice was signed in July 1953, North Korea was in ruins, with much of the progress recorded after 1945 wiped out. UN bombing raids had largely ended early on in the war, since there were no more targets to hit. Much of the industry inherited from the Japanese was destroyed. The loss of life and the economic and social disruption were enormous. If the Russians had sanctioned the gamble, they had played the game very low key. It was the Chinese who had saved North Korea, at huge cost to themselves. Korean unification was even further away than it had been in 1950.

The war was not all catastrophic, at least for Kim Il-sung and his group. One gain was political. Kim used the events of the war to further consolidate his position. The southern communists were broken during and after the war, denounced as spies and traitors and shot. A few years later, in 1956, he confronted those who were opposed to his influence and defeated them. This marked the end of the Yenan faction who had returned from China. From 1956 onwards, Kim's position as North Korea's leader appears to have been maintained virtually unchallenged. Gradually, a cult of personality has been built up around him and selected members of his family that has little to equal it elsewhere. Not a factory functions, nor a collective farm harvests, without some form of 'on the spot guidance' from the 'Great Leader.' Much of the recent history of Korea is presented in terms of the achievements of Kim and his ancestors. The revised North Korean constitution of 1972 put Kim at the head of the state, paralleling his already dominant position in the KWP. Since 1972 his eldest son by his first marriage, Kim Jong-il, has been marked out as his successor, thus continuing the revolutionary dynasty, and adding, incidentally, yet another category of guidance, from the 'Dear Leader.' South Korean accounts tend to attribute actions such as the Rangoon bombing and other extremist acts to the younger Kim, though the evidence is not always convincing.

Those who have had contact with North Korea report no whisper of opposition from the relatively small circle of people who deal with foreigners. Yet it is hard to believe that there is not some substance to the constant reports of opposition to the Kim cult, even if such stories often emerge in Seoul. It is reported that the build-up of Kim Jong-il as the chosen successor did not go unopposed in the early 1970s, not least among the leader's own domestic circle. North Korean defectors tell tales of a spoilt young man — he is now officially 46 — given to fast cars and pleasure, not likely to endear himself to older leaders. In the early 1980s, there were rumours of generals fleeing to China, allegedly because they opposed the rise of the younger Kim. Senior figures do disappear from the leadership line-up in North Korea, but some at least eventually reappear. In 1986 it was rumoured, not for the first time, that Kim Il-sung himself was dead, possibly as a result of factional fighting. He appeared, clearly as well as ever, two days later.

Against this political background, postwar reconstruction proceeded rapidly in the north. Much was done with aid from China, the Soviet Union and Eastern Europe. This aid is now little acknowledged, but both China and the Soviet Union occasionally draw attention to it. Sometimes it came in the form of heavy plant, sometimes in actual labour, provided by Chinese troops who remained in North Korea until 1958. Some of this reconstruction work, such as the repair of the Yalu river dams, was also of direct advantage to China. In addition to aid, the Chinese annulled wartime debts and provided reconstruction funds. During and after the war, many orphans and other children from North Korea were sent to live and be educated in the Soviet Union and Eastern Europe. But much of the reconstruction was carried out by the North Koreans themselves. Here, too, the war and its effects had advantages. The wartime system of exhortation and temporary sacrifice was now firmly carried into peacetime.

The industrial base of the country needed to be rebuilt. As in the Soviet Union and China, agriculture was to provide the funds for a massive investment in heavy industry. It was unlikely that the farmers who had received land in 1946 would have been able or willing to make the sacrifices required to produce the surplus value needed. Inevitably, the war had led to a considerable loss of productivity in agriculture, but it had also provided the means of effecting changes to the arrangements of 1946 without too much disruption. Many farmers were dead and others had become refugees. In any case, the regime was inclined to see in the peasants a tendency towards capitalist practices, and it welcomed the opportunity to end these. Ideology and reality came together neatly and the result was a second major land reform. This took the form of agricultural cooperatives, first introduced in August 1953. Five years later it was claimed that this process was complete, and there were 13,309 cooperatives, with an average of 80 households in each. At that stage, in imitation of the Chinese 'Great Leap Forward,' the authorities decided on a further stage of collectivisation. The cooperatives were amalgamated into larger units, with an average of 300 households in each. As well as working for the cooperative, the North Korean media made clear that those living in such an organisation were expected to take part in a whole range of extra activities, most of which involved additional production.

By the end of the 1950s this policy appeared to have paid off. Levels of production in agriculture and industry had reached or surpassed pre-Korean war levels. *Per capita* income, and probably the general standard of living, was well in advance of the South. The balance between those engaged in agriculture and those in industry had swung firmly in favour of the latter. By 1960 over 50 percent of national income came from industry; in 1946 it had been under 17 percent. Increasingly the government and party stressed that all this was done through self-reliance. The role of outside assistance was played down and the contribution of the Koreans themselves, correctly led by Kim Il-sung, was emphasised. This *juche* (self-reliance) doctrine began to be heard about 1955. It was followed in 1958 by the *chollima* (flying horse) campaign, which again made much of Koreans doing things themselves. Both were useful in the striving for production, but both also had origins in the breakup of communist unity that followed Stalin's death in 1953, and even more, Khruschev's de-Stalinisation speech of 1956. In an uncertain world, the North Koreans could only rely on themselves.

The impressive advances of the reconstruction years appear not to have been maintained into the 1960s. There was a series of five-year plans from 1956, but it proved increasingly difficult to meet targets. It may well have been difficult to keep up the momentum of the immediate postwar years, and it was certainly hard to go on recording invariably high levels of success year after year, even if the official line demanded it. The burden of maintaining large armed forces was a heavy one, both in terms of current costs and the loss of productive capacity. Outside assistance probably fell off, both because those supplying it felt that the immediate need had passed, and, in the case of China, because domestic economic difficulties made the provision of such assistance difficult. The development of the Sino–Soviet dispute meant that the Chinese, after 1960 deprived of Soviet economic aid, needed themselves what they had once been able to make available to North Korea. The thawing of the cold war made the Russians less willing to provide military aid. One sign of economic difficulties was the failure of North Korea to publish hard economic data. These stopped about 1962 and have so far not resumed. Yet in spite of such problems, most outside observers agree that North Korea maintained its economic edge over South Korea until the late 1960s.

The realisation that their advantage over the south was beginning to slip did not escape some at least in the North Korean leadership. In interviews with Japanese newsmen in the 1970s, Kim Il-sung appeared well-aware of developments in the rest of the world, including South Korea. He and some of his planners could study South Korea's economic advance, which by about 1971 was beginning to outstrip the north. They were also aware that much of the Soviet and Chinese industrial plant supplied in the 1950s or early 1960s was now out of date and inefficient. Any doubts on these matters must have been dispelled by the visit of North Korean negotiators to Seoul in 1972. What they found then seems to have convinced a number of them that the north was well behind the south in economic development. As one of the North Korean team members reportedly said to a southern counterpart, after a tour of Seoul: 'You boys have got it made.'

Whatever the reason, the early seventies saw both a determined stress on the concept of *juche*, coupled with a search for modern technology. Some have linked this to the rise of Kim Jong-il, who is sometimes portrayed as fascinated by computers and other contemporary technology. Using its commodity production as a source of funds, North Korea began to make extensive purchases of the most up-to-date industrial equipment. Then came the oil crisis of 1973, which hit North Korea in two ways. Oil became more expensive and the bottom dropped out of the commodity market. Rather than practising self-reliance North Korea found itself suddenly a debtor nation, with no means of paying. Western banks, which had provided much of the money required for the purchase of new equipment, began to demand repayment, as did the Japanese and other companies that had often supplied. North Korea has not yet paid its debts but has avoided formal bankruptcy so far, although coming close to it in 1987.

These economic difficulties have been one factor in the attempt in recent years to engage in a dialogue with the South, and they have also been an important impetus behind the policy, introduced in 1984, of trying to attract joint ventures to North Korea. So far this has not achieved much, with most joint ventures concluded with companies organised by pro-North Koreans in Japan. These have long provided support for North Korea but do not have access to the new technology now wanted. China, the Soviet Union, and Eastern Europe, while all important trading partners, have their own debt problems with North Korea, and in any case appear reluctant or unable to supply what the North Koreans want in the way of modern technology.

In foreign affairs North Korea for some years turned most of its attention to other communist countries, since few others would have much to do with it, and most energies were concentrated on reconstruction at home and opposition to the South. As former colonies became independent North Korea was able to widen its diplomatic links both because it could point to its own colonial experience, to its current 'anti-imperialist' stand and to its experience of development, which, it was argued, provided a good model for poor countries to follow. The Sino–Soviet dispute was a major concern to the North Koreans, given the role these two countries had played in the past, and the existence of friendship treaties with both of them since 1961. North Korea tried to steer a neutral course, but eventually sided more with China, because of opposition to Soviet attempts to dominate the international communist movement and to the 'Brezhnev doctrine' that claimed the right of interference in 'socialist' countries.

Since the ending of the United Nations Commission for the Unification and Rehabilitation of Korea in 1973, North Korea has had observer status at the UN, and has joined a number of international organisations. North Korea refuses to apply to join the UN itself, arguing that this would perpetuate the division of Korea. Since 1973 North Korea has established diplomatic relations with a number of western European countries, but its main diplomatic effort has been directed at the third world. It provides some aid, including military aid, to the third world, and is active in the Non-Aligned Movement.

Despite much anti-US propaganda, there have been frequent signs in recent years that the North Koreans would like to establish a dialogue with the United States, but little has come of the overtures made. In January 1988, following the airline bomb incident in which North Korea was allegedly involved, the US government added North Korea to its list of states engaged in 'state-sponsored terrorism.' A number of other governments, including those of Britain and Japan, also condemned the incident. The Korean community in Japan is an important source of trade and other contacts with the western world, but there are no formal links between Japan and the DPRK.

Section Six

The Future

Though heaven may fall, there will be a way of escape

Chapter Fifteen

Whither Korea?

In a sense the future begins for South Korea the day after the Olympic flags are folded away. The Games have been used as a focus for unity and effort ever since Seoul was chosen in September 1981 as the next host after Los Angeles. An 'Olympic image' has been promoted that has emphasised naturally enough the nation's strengths and its fitness to receive the world. This has been a controlled image, admitting of no blemishes and allowing no alternative. The events of 1987, however, have obtruded on to the picture. There will be a determined push to keep dissension out of the way during the Games, but thereafter international and political uncertainties will again have to be faced.

The Games themselves will almost certainly be a major triumph. Careful planning and much expenditure, together with Korean exuberance, will ensure a smooth staging, while the high acceptance rate from countries of all political shades including the Soviet Union and the People's Republic of China augurs well for their success. Many Koreans hope that the Games will mark as significant an advance for their country as the 1964 Olympics did for postwar Japan. The ROK enters its fortieth year in August 1988, and the Games are a fitting celebration. There are shadows, however, as there have been for all of South Korea's history since the ending of the Pacific war. The North Korean threat remains, brought dramatically to life, yet again, at the end of 1987 with the loss of a South Korean civilian aircraft, apparently at North Korean hands. Within the country the search for responsive political institutions goes on, sharpened by the feeling that old patterns of autocracy and control should be modified. The economy remains in good shape, though disputes with trading partners are looming. The government has announced its intention of leaving business to manage more of its own affairs. If it does indeed slacken its involvement in one sphere of activity, there may be pressure on it to intervene less in others.

For the ordinary people of the Republic of Korea these wider issues resolve down into problems of housing, employment, education and the general tone of their lives. Perhaps, they increasingly argue, if less could be spent on security, more could be made available for improving living standards. A change in political leadership might make the bureaucracy listen more to their needs and curtail the probing activities of the various security agencies. Changes in trading practices might mean more goods from abroad and improvements in the quality and availability of domestic products. It is only just that more of those producing the country's wealth should have a share in the fruits of economic development, be it a new car or a pension. Roh Tae Woo made many election promises that people will hope to see redeemed.

Social changes already under way are bound to influence these expectations. Fewer children are prepared to support elderly parents. This has not yet become the problem it is in the west or in Japan, but it is growing and has all sorts of implications. Korean women are unlikely to continue for ever to accept the discrimination that keeps them in low-paid jobs with little future. The spread of television and the relaxation of censorship will affect the way people think, not only about politics but also about moral and social questions. The urge to conform to a vaguely-defined 'Confucian' norm will remain strong, but will come under increasingly steady challenge. South Korean society in the twenty-first century, saving some major upheaval, will be more open and less certain of itself than it has been up until now.

Looking to the more distant future, the most important issue is that of unification. Few South Koreans, even those with family in the north, realistically expect reunification of the two halves of the peninsula in this generation. The 1984–1985 exchanges and the brief family reunions they led to, showed the scale of the problem. The hope that one day there will again be a united Korea will not disappear, but people will behave as though it is not going to happen. Instead, most hope that the changes which must come in North Korea when power passes from Kim Il-sung will lead, not to renewed danger, though they accept this is possible, but to an acceptance by North Korea that the division of the peninsula is a fact and that two states exist. Perhaps contact can then begin as between the two Germanies, or between China and Taiwan, and a new relationship be built.

Over the past 40 years and more, the people of South Korea have had their share of trials and suffering; but also of achievement and pride. For most of them, as they gather round their television sets to watch the opening ceremony of the Olympic Games, the mood will be one of celebration. They know there are dangers and uncertainties lurking inside and outside their country, but the signs are that they will be equal to them. Invasion, war and famine have not defeated the Koreans. They will survive.

Further Reading

The dog that chased the chicken now sits looking at the roof

The first western visitors to Korea in the nineteenth century noted a lack of books on Korea and even as late as the Japanese annexation in 1910, it would have been possible for a person of modest means to possess every book in western languages about the country. Twenty years or so later, when Horace H. Underwood compiled his guide to writings on Korea in English in 1931 for the Korea Branch of the Royal Asiatic Society, he noted some 2800 items. Since then the published material on Korea has grown at a phenomenal rate. What is listed below is only a small part of the whole, and is confined to books and periodicals chosen because they are both useful and comparatively easily available. Those requiring additional information will find more comprehensive bibliographies in many of the books described below. It should be noted that some of the categories overlap.

General

Kim, Han-kyo (ed.), *Studies on Korea: A Scholar's Guide*, Honolulu, Korean National Commission for UNESCO and University Press of Hawaii, 1980. A valuable collection of bibliographical essays on most aspects of Korea North and South, with detailed comments on current scholarship.
Korean Overseas Information Service (publisher), *A Handbook of Korea*, Sixth edition, Seoul, 1987. An ROK government official publication, well-produced and illustrated.

Kwangmyong Publishing Company, *Korea Past and Present*, Seoul, 1972. Produced for the ROK government.

Reischauer, E. O., Fairbank, J. K. and Craig, A. M., *East Asia: Tradition and Transformation*, Boston, Houghton Mifflin, 1973.

Vreeland, N. (ed.), *South Korea: A Country Study*, Washington, DC, Department of Army, US Government, 1982. One in the series of well-known country studies, produced for the United States' Department of Defence.

Yonhap News Agency (publisher) *Korea Annual*, Seoul, 1981 to date. Before 1981, this was produced by the Hapdong News Agency. Useful annual publication, reflecting official views. Contains a partial ROK 'Who's Who', which can be equally important for deciding who is not who, in any given year!

Journals

Regular articles on current affairs in both North and South Korea appear in the *Far Eastern Economic Review*, published in Hong Kong, and in *Asiaweek*, published in Singapore. The *Far Eastern Economic Review*'s annual survey of Asia is also useful. The semi-official weekly *Korea Newsreview* and the monthly *Business Korea* provide day-to-day accounts of current news stories. For North Korea, both the weekly *Pyongyang Times* and the monthly *Korea Today* are heavy on propaganda and light on information.

More scholarly articles appear from time to time in the *Journal of Asian Studies* (formerly the *Far Eastern Quarterly*), which publishes an annual bibliography, *Asian Survey*, and *Pacific Affairs*.

The following are some current periodicals specifically devoted to Korea. The year shown is that in which publication began. All are produced in Seoul, unless otherwise stated:

Koreana, 1987. Quarterly.

Korea and World Affairs, 1977. Quarterly.

Korea Journal, 1961. Monthly, published by the Korean National Commission for UNESCO. Covers all subjects.

Korea Observer, 1968. Quarterly.

Korean Culture, Los Angeles, 1979, Quarterly.

Korean Studies, Honolulu, 1977. Annual.

North Korea Quarterly, Hamburg, 1974. Quarterly.

Transactions of the Korea Branch Royal Asiatic Society, 1900–1940, 1948 onwards. Annual. The oldest established journal in Korean studies.

Guidebooks

Note: Korea National Tourist Corporation produces various short, free guides, including one for Seoul. They are well worth collecting.

Adams, E. B., *Korea Guide*, Seoul, Seoul International Tourist Publishing Co., 1976. Well-illustrated, but now of limited use.

Adams, E. B., *Through Gates of Seoul: Trails and Treasures of Chosŏn Dynasty*, Two vols., Seoul, Taewon Publishing Co., 1978. Again dated, but many good stories and illustrations.

Adams, E. B., *Palaces of Seoul*, Seoul, Taewon Publishing Co., 1972, reprinted 1982. A useful pocket-sized guide to the Royal Palaces, based on *Through Gates of Seoul.*

Adams, E. B., *Kyongju Guide: Cultural Spirit of Shilla in Korea*, Seoul, Seoul International Tourist Publishing Co., latest reprint 1983.

Adams E. B., *Seoul: 1988 Olympic Site*, Seoul, Seoul International Publishing House, 1984. Already dated.

Clark, A. D. and Clark, D. N., *Seoul Past and Present: A Guide to Yi T'aejo's Capital*, Seoul, Royal Asiatic Society, Hollym Corporation, 1969. Although not a great deal of use on the ground, since so much of Seoul has changed, this has still a good collection of stories about Seoul and the surrounding countryside.

Clark, D. N. and Grayson, J. H., *Discovering Seoul*, Seoul, Royal Asiatic Society, Seoul Computer Press, 1986. Clear maps.

Crowther, G., *Korea and Taiwan: A Travel Survival Kit*, South Yarra, Lonely Planet Publications, 1982. For the cheap place to go.

Grayson, J. H., Jacobson, L. T. and Olson, L. *Taegu Guide*, Taegu, Royal Asiatic Society, Keimyung University Press, 1980. That rare thing, a guide to another Korean city apart from Seoul and Kyŏngju.

Hoefer, H. J. (director), *Insight Guide: The Republic of Korea*, Hong Kong, Apa Productions (H.K.) Ltd, 1986. Originally published in 1981. Beautifully illustrated, though perhaps for reading in the hotel, rather than carrying about.

Honam Oil Company, (publisher) *Inside Seoul: The Honam Oil Guide to Seoul*, Seoul, 1985. Aimed at the (usually American) resident foreigner.

Kim, Jong-ki, *Seoul: Host City of the '88 Olympics*, Seoul, KBS Enterprises, 1983.

Popham, P., *The Insider's Guide to Korea*, London, Merehurst Press, 1987. Similar to the *Insight Guides*, but not so comprehensive.

Steenson, G. P., *Coping with Korea*, Oxford, Basil Blackwell Ltd, 1987. Good, straightforward account.

Geography

Bartz, P. M., *South Korea*, Oxford, Clarendon Press, 1972.

Dept. of Mines and Technical Surveys, Geographical Branch, Government of Canada, *Korea: A Geographical Appreciation*, Ottawa, 1951.

McCune, S., *Korea's Heritage: A Regional and Social Geography*, Rutland, VT., and Tokyo, Tuttle, 1956. Full of useful insights. Well illustrated.

History

Beasley, W. G., *Japanese Imperialism, 1894–1945*, Oxford, Clarendon Press, 1987.

Bishop, I. L. B., *Korea and Her Neighbours: A Narrative of Travel with an account of the Recent Vicissitudes and Present Condition*, 2 Vols, London, John Murray, 1897, reprinted in one volume, Seoul, Yonsei University Press, 1970; London, KPI, 1985. A classic work, by one of the great Victorian lady travellers.

Choe, Ching Young, *The Rule of the Taewŏn'gun, 1864–1873: Restoration in Yi Korea*, Cambridge, Mass., East Asian Research Center, Harvard University, 1972.

Choe-Wall, Yang-hi (ed.), *Memoirs of a Korean Queen*, London, KPI, 1985.

Conroy, H., *The Japanese Seizure of Korea, 1868–1910: A Study of Realism and Idealism in International Relations*, Philadelphia, University of Pennsylvania Press, 1960. A book much disliked by many Korean historians, who saw in it an attempt to justify the Japanese takeover of Korea.

Deuchler, M., *Confucian Gentlemen and Barbarian Envoys: The Opening of Korea, 1875–1885*, Seattle, Royal Asiatic Society, University of Washington Press, 1977.

Grajdanzev, A., *Modern Korea*, New York, Institute of Pacific Relations, 1946; reprinted Seoul, Royal Asiatic Society, Kyung-In Publishing Co., 1975.

Han Woo-keun, *The History of Korea*, Seoul, Eul-Yoo Publishing Co. Ltd, 1970.

Hoare, J. E., *The British Embassy Compound Seoul, 1884–1984*, Seoul, Korean–British Society, 1984. Contains a brief essay on Korean–British relations.

Joe, Wanne J., *Traditional Korea: A Cultural History*, Seoul, Chung'ang University Press, 1972.

Kim, C. I. Eugene, and Kim, Han-kyo, *Korea and the Politics of Imperialism, 1876–1910*, Berkeley, University of California Press, 1967.

Ku, Dae-yeol, *Korea under Colonialism: The March First Movement and Anglo–Japanese Relations*, Seoul, Seoul Computer Press, 1985.

Lee Ki-baik, *A New History of Korea*, London and Cambridge, Mass., Harvard University Press, 1984. The most up-to-date general history. Contains an extensive bibliography.

Ledyard, G., *The Dutch come to Korea*, Seoul, Royal Asiatic Society, Taewon Publishing Co., 1971. The first European contact with Korea.

Lensen, G. A., *Balance of Intrigue: International Rivalry in Korea and Manchuria, 1884–1889*, Two vols., Tallahassee, University Presses of Florida, 1982. Contains an exhaustive bibliography.

Myers, R. H., and Peattie, M. R., *The Japanese Colonial Empire, 1895–1945*, Princeton, Princeton University Press, 1984. A valuable collection of papers.

Nahm, A. C. (ed.), *Korea under Japanese Colonial Rule: Studies of the Policies and Technique of Japanese Colonialism*, Kalamazoo, Center for Korean Studies, Western Michigan University, 1973.

Nish, I. H., *The Anglo–Japanese Alliance: A Study of Two Island Empires*, London, The Athlone Press, 1966.

Nish, I. H., *The Origins of the Russo–Japanese War*, London and New York, Longman, 1985.

Rutt, R., *A Biography of James Scarth Gale and a new edition of his History of the Korean People*, Seoul, Royal Asiatic Society, Taewon Publishing Co., 1972. The *History*, originally written in the 1920s, is now dated, but the biography is interesting.

Weems, B., *Reform, Rebellion and the Heavenly Way*, Tucson, University of Arizona, 1966. The Tonghaks and what became of them.

Korea since 1945

A. War and Politics

Baldwin, F., *Without Parallel: The Korean–American Relationship since 1945*, New York, Pantheon Books, 1974. An interesting collection of 're-visionist' essays.

Boettcher, R. with Freedman, G. L., *Gifts of Deceit: Sun Myung Moon, Tongsun Park and the Korean Scandal*, New York, Holt, Rinehart and Winston, 1980.

Bridges, B., *Korea and the West*, London, Routledge and Kegan Paul, 1986.

Cumings, B., *The Origins of the Korean War: Liberation and the Emergence of Separate Regimes 1945–1947*, Princeton, Princeton University Press, 1981. Full of new insights.

Cumings, B. (ed.), *Child of Conflict: The Korean–American Relationship, 1943–1953*. London and Seattle, University of Washington Press, 1983.

Foot, R., *The Wrong War: American Policy and the Dimensions of the Korean Conflict, 1950–1953*, Ithaca and London, Cornell University Press, 1985. Shows how some American military leaders were prepared to go much further than limited war in Korea.

Han, Sungjoo, *The Failure of Democracy in South Korea*, Berkeley, University of California Press, 1974. The short 1960–1961 Second Republic.

Han, Sung-joo (ed.), *After One Hundred Years: Continuity and Change in Korean–American Relations*, Seoul, Asiatic Research Center, Korea University, 1982.

Hastings, M., *The Korean War*, London, Michael Joseph, 1987.

Henderson, G., *Korea: The Politics of the Vortex*, Cambridge, Mass., Harvard University Press, 1968. A stimulating attempt to explain the Korean political system.

Keon, M., *Korean Phoenix: A Nation from the Ashes*, Englewood Cliffs, N. J., Prentice-Hall International, 1977.

Koo, Youngnok, and Suh, Dae-sook (eds), *Korea and the United States: A Century of Co-operation*, Honolulu, University of Hawaii Press, 1984.

Koo, Youngnok, and Han, Sung-joo (eds.), *The Foreign Policy of the Republic of Korea*, New York, Columbia University Press, 1985.

Lowe, P., *The Origins of the Korean War*, London and New York, Longman, 1985. Concentrates on the international dimensions.

MacDonald, C. A., *Korea: The War Before Vietnam*, London, Macmillan, 1986.

Matry, J. I., *The Reluctant Crusade: American Foreign Policy in Korea, 1941–1950*, Honolulu, University of Hawaii Press, 1985.

Oliver, R. T., *Syngman Rhee and American Involvement in Korea, 1942–1960*, Seoul, Panmun Book Co., 1978.

O'Neill, R., *Australia in the Korean War, 1950–1953*, Two Vols., Australian War Memorial, Australian Government Publishing Service, Canberra, 1981. The official Australian history.

Rees, D., *Korea: The Limited War*, London, Macmillan, 1964. Still the best one-volume account.

Reeve, W. D., *The Republic of Korea: A Political and Economic Study*, London, Oxford University Press, 1963. The author served as an adviser to the ROK government.

Sandusky, M. C., *America's Parallel*, Alexandria, Va., Old Dominion Press, 1983. How the 38th parallel was chosen to divide Korea.

Stone, I. F., *The Hidden History of the Korean War*, New York and London, Monthly Review Press, 1952. The original 'revisionist' work on why war came in 1950.

Sullivan, J. and Foss, R. (eds.), *Two Koreas — One Future?*, Lanham, Md., University Press of America and American Friends Service Committee, 1987.

Wright, E. R. (ed.) *Korean Politics in Transition*, Seattle and London, Royal Asiatic Society, University of Washington Press, 1975.

B. Economic Development

Jacobs, N., *The Korean Road to Modernization and Development*, Urbana and Chicago, University of Illinois Press, 1985.

Jones, L. and Sakong, Il, *Government, Business and Entrepreneurship in Economic Development: The Korean Case*, Cambridge, Mass., and London, Council on East Asian Studies, Harvard University, 1980.

Lau, L. J. (ed.), *Models of Development: A Comparative Study of Economic Growth in South Korea and Taiwan*, San Francisco, ICS Press, 1986.

Lee, Changsoo, *Modernization of Korea and the Impact of the West*, Los Angeles, University of Southern California, 1981.

McGinn, N. F., et al., *Education and Development in Korea*, Cambridge, Mass., and London, Council on East Asian Studies, Harvard University, 1980.

Woronoff, J. *Korea's Economy: Man-Made Miracle*, Seoul and Arch Cape, Oregon, Si-sa-yong-o-sa Publishers, Seoul, and Pace International Research Inc., 1983.

Korean Values — Social, Cultural, Education and Religion

Batchelor, S., *The Way of Korean Zen*, New York, Weatherill, 1986.

Clark, A., *Religions of Old Korea*, New York 1932, reprinted Seoul, Christian Literature Society of Korea, 1961.

Clark, A., *A History of the Church in Korea*, Seoul, Christian Literature Society of Korea, 1971.

Chun, Kyong-soo, *Reciprocity and Korean Society: An Ethnography of Hasami*, Seoul, Seoul National University, 1984.

Chung, Chong-wha, *Love in Mid-Winter Night: Korean Sijo Poetry*, London, KPI, 1985.

Commission on Theological Concerns of the Christian Conferences of Asia, (eds.), *Minjung Theology: People as the Subjects of History*, London, Zed Press; New York, Orbis Books, and Singapore, Christian Conference of Asia, 1981.

Crane, P. S., *Korean Patterns*, Seoul, Royal Asiatic Society, Kwangjin, 1967, reprinted 1986.

Goepper, R. (introduction), Whitfield, R. (ed.), *Treasures from Korea: Art Through 5000 Years*, London, British Museum Publications, 1984.

Gompertz, G. St G. M., *Korean Celadon*, London, Faber and Faber, 1963.

Grant, B., *Korean Proverbs: Dragon Head, Snake tail and a Frog in a Well*, Salt Lake City, Moth House and Seoul, Wu Ah Dang, 1982.

Hahm, Pyong-Choon, *The Korean Political Tradition and the Law: Essays in Korean Law and Legal History*, Seoul, Royal Asiatic Society, Seoul Computer Press, 1967.

Harvey, Youngsook Kim, *Six Korea Women: The Socialisation of Shamans*, St Paul, West Publishing Company, 1979.

Jayasuriya, J. E., *Education in Korea: A Third World Success Story*, Seoul, Korean National Commission for UNESCO, 1983.

Kendall, L. and Peterson, M. (eds.), *Korean Women: View from the Inner Room*, Newhaven, Conn., East Rock Press, 1983.

Lee, P. H. (compiler), *Anthology of Korean Literature from Early Times to the Nineteenth Century*, Honolulu, University of Hawaii Press, 1981.

Kim, Richard, *The Innocent*, Seoul, Si-sa-yong-o-sa Publishers, 1968.

Kim, Richard. *The Martyred*, Seoul, Si-sa-yong-o-sa Publishers, 1969.

Kim, Richard, *Lost Names*, Seoul, Si-sa-yong-o-sa Publishers, 1970.

Kim, Yung-Chung (editor and translator), *Women of Korea: A History from Ancient Times to 1945*, Seoul, Ewha Women's University Press, 1979.

Mattieli, S. (ed.), *Virtues in Conflict: Tradition and the Korean Woman Today*, Seoul, Royal Asiatic Society, Samhwa Publishing Co., 1977.

Moffet, S. H., *The Christians of Korea*, New York, Friendship Press, 1962.

Morse, R. (ed.), *Wild Asters: Explorations in Korean Thought, Culture and Society*, Washington, DC, Asia Program, Woodrow Wilson International Center for Scholars, 1986.

O'Rourke, K. (translator), *A Washed-out Dream*, New York, Royal Asiatic Society, 1980.

Pares, S., *Crosscurrents: Korean–Western Culture in Contrast*, Seoul, International Publishing House, 1985.

Rutt, R., *Korean Works and Days: Notes from the Diary of a Country Priest*, Seoul, Royal Asiatic Society, 1964.

Rutt. R., *The Bamboo Grove: An Introduction to Sijo*, Berkeley, University of California Press, 1971.

Rutt. R., and Kim Chong-un, (translators), *Virtuous Women: Three Masterpieces of Traditional Korean Fiction*, Seoul, 1974.

Sym, Myungo-Ho, *The Making of Modern Korean Poetry: Foreign Influence and Native Creativity*, Seoul, Korean National Commission for UNESCO, 1982.

Zŏng, In-sŏb, *Folk Tales from Korea*, Seoul, Hollym Corporation, 1970.

North Korea and Korean Communism

Bunge, F. M., *North Korea: A Country Study*, Washington, D. C., Department of Army, US Government, 1981.

Inoue, Shuhachi, *Modern Korea and Kim Jong Il*, Tokyo, Yuzankaku Publishers, 1984. A hagiographic account.

Park, Jae-Ky, and Kim, Jung-Gun (eds.), *The Politics of North Korea*, Seoul, Institute for Far Eastern Studies, Kyungnam University, 1979.

Kim, Ilpyong J., *Communist Politics in North Korea*, New York, Praeger Special Studies, 1976.

Scalapino, R. A. (ed.), *North Korea Today*, New York, Praeger, 1963.

Scalapino, R. A., and Kim, Jun-yop (eds.), *North Korea Today: Strategic Issues*, Berkeley, Institute of East Asian Studies, University of California, 1983.

Scalapino, R. A., and Lee, Chong-sik, *Communism in Korea*, Two vols., Berkeley, University of California Press, 1972.

Simmons, R. R., *The Strained Alliance: Peking, Pyongyang and Moscow and the Politics of the Korean Civil War*, New York and London, Free Press, 1975.

Suh, Dae-sook, *The Korean Communist Movement: 1918–1948*, Princeton, Princeton University Press, 1967.

Index